BIG IDEAS MATH®
Modeling Real Life

Grade 1
Volume 1

Ron Larson
Laurie Boswell

Big Ideas Learning™

Erie, Pennsylvania
BigIdeasLearning.com

Big Ideas Learning, LLC
1762 Norcross Road
Erie, PA 16510-3838
USA

For product information and customer support, contact Big Ideas Learning at **1-877-552-7766** or visit us at *BigIdeasLearning.com*.

Cover Image:
Valdis Torms, bgblue/DigitalVision Vectors/Getty Images

Copyright © 2022 by Big Ideas Learning, LLC. All rights reserved.

No part of this work may be reproduced or transmitted in any form or by any means, electronic or mechanical, including, but not limited to, photocopying and recording, or by any information storage or retrieval system, without prior written permission of Big Ideas Learning, LLC, unless such copying is expressly permitted by copyright law. Address inquiries to Permissions, Big Ideas Learning, LLC, 1762 Norcross Road, Erie, PA 16510.

Big Ideas Learning and *Big Ideas Math* are registered trademarks of Larson Texts, Inc.

Printed in the U.S.A.

ISBN 13: 978-1-64727-927-1

3 4 5 6 7 8 9 10—25 24 23

One Voice from Kindergarten Through Algebra 2

Written by renowned authors, Dr. Ron Larson and Dr. Laurie Boswell, *Big Ideas Math* offers a seamless math pedagogy from elementary through high school. Together, Ron and Laurie provide a consistent voice that encourages students to make connections through cohesive progressions and clear instruction. Since 1992, Ron and Laurie have authored over 50 mathematics programs.

" Each time Laurie and I start working on a new program, we spend time putting ourselves in the position of the reader. How old is the reader? What is the reader's experience with mathematics? The answers to these questions become our writing guides. Our goal is to make the learning targets understandable and to develop these targets in a clear path that leads to student success. "

Ron Larson

Ron Larson, Ph.D., is well known as lead author of a comprehensive and widely used mathematics program that ranges from elementary school through college. He holds the distinction of Professor Emeritus from Penn State Erie, The Behrend College, where he taught for nearly 40 years. He received his Ph.D. in mathematics from the University of Colorado. Dr. Larson engages in the latest research and advancements in mathematics education and consistently incorporates key pedagogical elements to ensure focus, coherence, rigor, and student self-reflection.

" My passion and goal in writing is to provide an essential resource for exploring and making sense of mathematics. Our program is guided by research around the learning and teaching of mathematics in the hopes of improving the achievement of all students. May this be a successful year for you! "

Laurie Boswell

Laurie Boswell, Ed.D., is the former Head of School at Riverside School in Lyndonville, Vermont. In addition to authoring textbooks, she provides mathematics consulting and embedded coaching sessions. Dr. Boswell received her Ed.D. from the University of Vermont in 2010. She is a recipient of the Presidential Award for Excellence in Mathematics Teaching and later served as president of CPAM. Laurie has taught math to students at all levels, elementary through college. In addition, Laurie has served on the NCTM Board of Directors and as a Regional Director for NCSM. Along with Ron, Laurie has co-authored numerous math programs and has become a popular national speaker.

Contributors, Reviewers, and Research

Big Ideas Learning would like to express our gratitude to the mathematics education and instruction experts who served as our advisory panel, contributing specialists, and reviewers during the writing of *Big Ideas Math: Modeling Real Life*. Their input was an invaluable asset during the development of this program.

Contributing Specialists and Reviewers

- **Sophie Murphy**, Ph.D. Candidate, Melbourne School of Education, Melbourne, Australia
  Learning Targets and Success Criteria Specialist and Visible Learning Reviewer
- **Linda Hall**, Mathematics Educational Consultant, Edmond, OK
  Advisory Panel
- **Michael McDowell**, Ed.D., Superintendent, Ross, CA
  Project-Based Learning Specialist
- **Kelly Byrne**, Math Supervisor and Coordinator of Data Analysis, Downingtown, PA
  Advisory Panel
- **Jean Carwin**, Math Specialist/TOSA, Snohomish, WA
  Advisory Panel
- **Nancy Siddens**, Independent Language Teaching Consultant, Las Cruces, NM
  English Language Learner Specialist
- **Kristen Karbon**, Curriculum and Assessment Coordinator, Troy, MI
  Advisory Panel
- **Kery Obradovich**, K–8 Math/Science Coordinator, Northbrook, IL
  Advisory Panel
- **Jennifer Rollins**, Math Curriculum Content Specialist, Golden, CO
  Advisory Panel
- **Becky Walker**, Ph.D., School Improvement Services Director, Green Bay, WI
  Advisory Panel and Content Reviewer
- **Deborah Donovan**, Mathematics Consultant, Lexington, SC
  Content Reviewer
- **Tom Muchlinski**, Ph.D., Mathematics Consultant, Plymouth, MN
  Content Reviewer and Teaching Edition Contributor
- **Mary Goetz**, Elementary School Teacher, Troy, MI
  Content Reviewer
- **Nanci N. Smith**, Ph.D., International Curriculum and Instruction Consultant, Peoria, AZ
  Teaching Edition Contributor
- **Robyn Seifert-Decker**, Mathematics Consultant, Grand Haven, MI
  Teaching Edition Contributor
- **Bonnie Spence**, Mathematics Education Specialist, Missoula, MT
  Teaching Edition Contributor
- **Suzy Gagnon**, Adjunct Instructor, University of New Hampshire, Portsmouth, NH
  Teaching Edition Contributor
- **Art Johnson**, Ed.D., Professor of Mathematics Education, Warwick, RI
  Teaching Edition Contributor
- **Anthony Smith**, Ph.D., Associate Professor, Associate Dean, University of Washington Bothell, Seattle, WA
  Reading and Writing Reviewer
- **Brianna Raygor**, Music Teacher, Fridley, MN
  Music Reviewer
- **Nicole Dimich Vagle**, Educator, Author, and Consultant, Hopkins, MN
  Assessment Reviewer
- **Janet Graham**, District Math Specialist, Manassas, VA
  Response to Intervention and Differentiated Instruction Reviewer
- **Sharon Huber**, Director of Elementary Mathematics, Chesapeake, VA
  Universal Design for Learning Reviewer

Student Reviewers

- T.J. Morin
- Alayna Morin
- Ethan Bauer
- Emery Bauer
- Emma Gaeta
- Ryan Gaeta
- Benjamin SanFrotello
- Bailey SanFrotello
- Samantha Grygier
- Robert Grygier IV
- Jacob Grygier
- Jessica Urso
- Ike Patton
- Jake Lobaugh
- Adam Fried
- Caroline Naser
- Charlotte Naser

Research

Ron Larson and Laurie Boswell used the latest in educational research, along with the body of knowledge collected from expert mathematics instructors, to develop the *Modeling Real Life* series. The pedagogical approach used in this program follows the best practices outlined in the most prominent and widely accepted educational research, including:

- *Visible Learning*, John Hattie © 2009
- *Visible Learning for Teachers*
  John Hattie © 2012
- *Visible Learning for Mathematics*
  John Hattie © 2017
- *Principles to Actions: Ensuring Mathematical Success for All*
  NCTM © 2014
- *Adding It Up: Helping Children Learn Mathematics*
  National Research Council © 2001
- *Mathematical Mindsets: Unleashing Students' Potential through Creative Math, Inspiring Messages and Innovative Teaching*
  Jo Boaler © 2015
- *What Works in Schools: Translating Research into Action*
  Robert Marzano © 2003
- *Classroom Instruction That Works: Research-Based Strategies for Increasing Student Achievement*
  Marzano, Pickering, and Pollock © 2001
- *Principles and Standards for School Mathematics*
  NCTM © 2000
- *Rigorous PBL by Design: Three Shifts for Developing Confident and Competent Learners*
  Michael McDowell © 2017
- *Universal Design for Learning Guidelines*
  CAST © 2011
- *Rigor/Relevance Framework®*
  International Center for Leadership in Education
- *Understanding by Design*
  Grant Wiggins and Jay McTighe © 2005
- Achieve, ACT, and The College Board
- *Elementary and Middle School Mathematics: Teaching Developmentally*
  John A. Van de Walle and Karen S. Karp © 2015
- *Evaluating the Quality of Learning: The SOLO Taxonomy*
  John B. Biggs & Kevin F. Collis © 1982
- *Unlocking Formative Assessment: Practical Strategies for Enhancing Students' Learning in the Primary and Intermediate Classroom*
  Shirley Clarke, Helen Timperley, and John Hattie © 2004
- *Formative Assessment in the Secondary Classroom*
  Shirley Clarke © 2005
- *Improving Student Achievement: A Practical Guide to Assessment for Learning*
  Toni Glasson © 2009

Focus and Coherence from

Instructional Design

A single authorship team from Kindergarten through Algebra 2 results in a logical progression of focused topics with meaningful coherence from course to course.

FOCUS
A focused program dedicates lessons, activities, and assessments to grade-level standards while simultaneously supporting and engaging you in the major work of the course.

The **Learning Target** in your book and the **Success Criteria** in the Teaching Edition focus the learning for each lesson into manageable chunks, with clear teaching text and examples.

Learning Target: Write related addition and subtraction equations to complete a fact family.

Laurie's Notes

Preparing to Teach

Students have heard about time and the language of time. Most students do not understand time or know how to tell time on an analog clock. In this lesson, students are introduced to telling time to the hour. They learn about the hour hand and telling time as o'clock.

Laurie's Notes, located in the Teaching Edition, prepare your teacher for the math concepts in each chapter and lesson and make connections to the threads of major topics for the course.

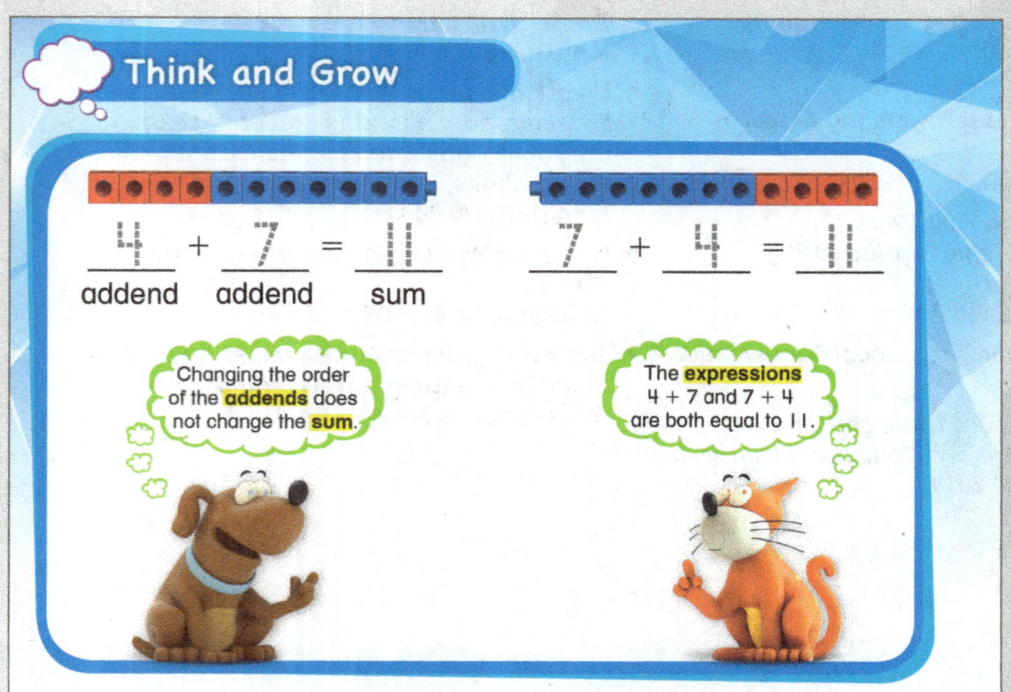

Think and Grow

$\underline{4} + \underline{7} = \underline{11}$ $\underline{7} + \underline{4} = \underline{11}$

addend   addend   sum

Changing the order of the **addends** does not change the **sum**.

The **expressions** 4 + 7 and 7 + 4 are both equal to 11.

vi

a Single Authorship Team

COHERENCE

A single authorship team built a coherent program that has intentional progression of content within each grade and between grade levels. You will build new understanding on foundations from prior grades and connect concepts throughout the course.

The authors developed content that progresses from prior chapters and grades to future ones. In addition to charts like this one, Laurie's Notes gives your teacher insights about where you have come from and where you are going in your learning progression.

Through the Grades

Kindergarten	Grade 1	Grade 2
• Represent addition and subtraction with various models and strategies. • Solve addition and subtraction word problems within 10. • Fluently add and subtract within 5.	• Solve addition and subtraction word problems within 20. • Fluently add and subtract within 10. • Determine the unknown number to complete addition and subtraction equations.	• Solve addition and subtraction word problems within 100. • Solve word problems involving length and money. • Solve one- and two-step word problems. • Fluently add and subtract within 20.

One author team thoughtfully wrote each course, creating a seamless progression of content from Kindergarten to Algebra 2.

	Grade K	Grade 1	Grade 2	Grade 3	Grade 4	Grade 5	Grade 6	
Number and Quantity	**Number and Operations – Base Ten**				**Number and Operations – Base Ten**		**The Number System**	
	Work with numbers 11–19 to gain foundations for place value. *Chapter 9*	Extend the counting sequence. Use place value and properties of operations to add and subtract. *Chapters 6–9*	Use place value and properties of operations to add and subtract. *Chapters 2–10, 14*	Use place value and properties of operations to perform multi-digit arithmetic. *Chapters 7–9, 12*	Generalize place value understanding for multi-digit whole numbers. Use place value and properties of operations to perform multi-digit arithmetic. *Chapters 1–5*	Understand the place value system. Perform operations with multi-digit whole numbers and with decimals to hundredths. *Chapters 1, 3–7*	Perform operations with multi-digit numbers and find common factors and multiples. *Chapter 1* Divide fractions by fractions. *Chapter 2* Extend understanding of numbers to the rational number system. *Chapter 8*	Perfor ration Chapt
				Num. and Oper. – Fractions	**Number and Operations – Fractions**		**Ratios and Proportional Relations**	
				Understand fractions as numbers. *Chapters 10, 11, 14*	Extend understanding of fraction equivalence and ordering. Build fractions from unit fractions.	Add, subtract, multiply, and divide fractions. *Chapters 6, 8–11*	Use ratios to solve problems. *Chapters 3, 4*	Use pr to solv Chapte

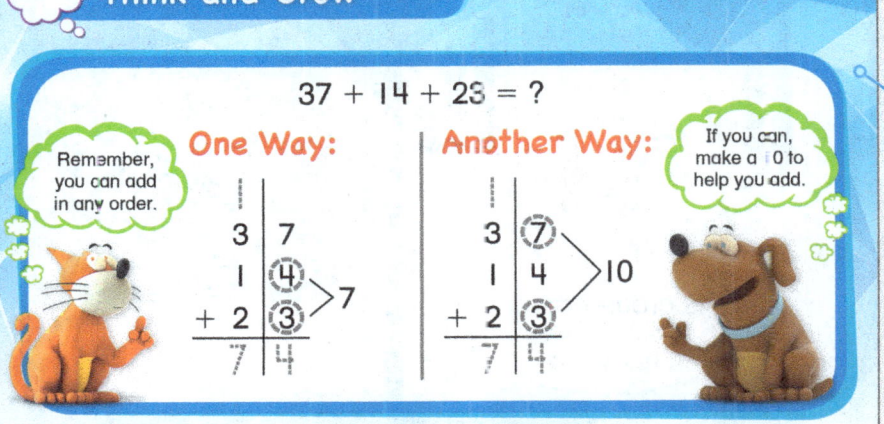

Throughout each course, lessons build on prior learning as new concepts are introduced. Here you are reminded of rules and strategies that you already know to help solve the addition problem.

vii

Rigor in Math: A Balanced Approach

Instructional Design
The authors wrote each chapter and every lesson to provide a meaningful balance of rigorous instruction.

RIGOR
A rigorous program provides a balance of three important building blocks.
- **Conceptual Understanding** Discovering why
- **Procedural Fluency** Learning how
- **Application** Knowing when to apply

Conceptual Understanding
You have the opportunity to develop foundational concepts central to the *Learning Target* in each *Explore and Grow* by experimenting with new concepts, talking with peers, and asking questions.

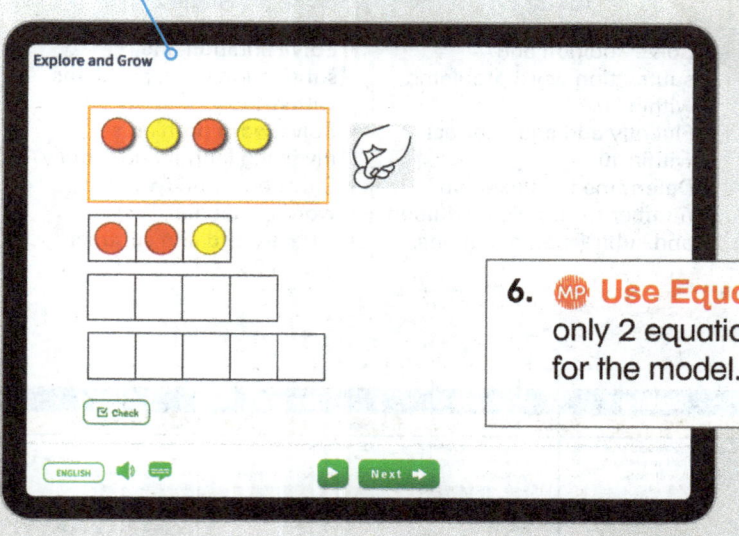

Conceptual Thinking
Conceptual questions ask you to think deeply.

6. **Use Equations** Your friend uses only 2 equations to write the fact family for the model. Is this reasonable?

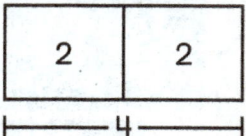

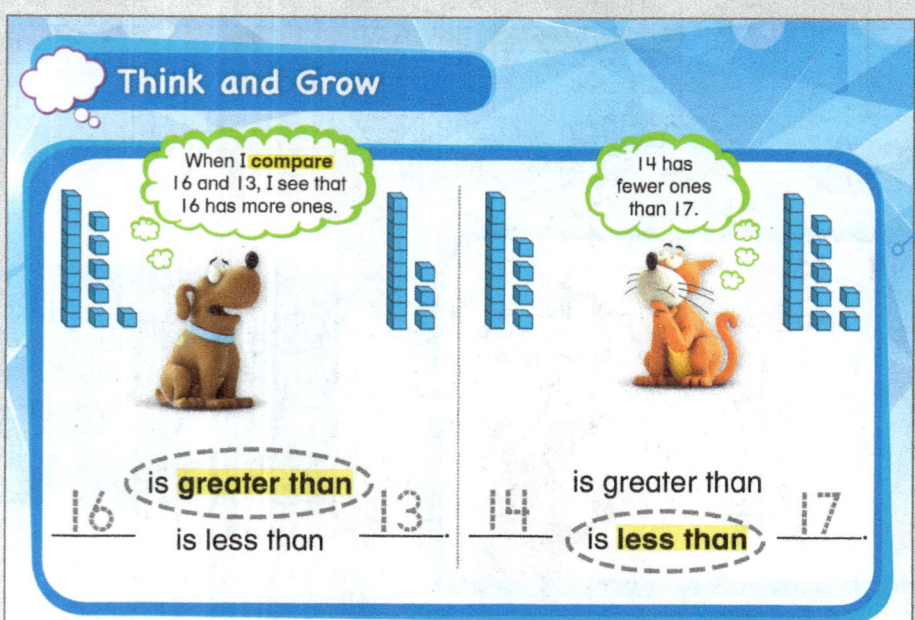

Procedural Fluency
Solidify learning with clear, stepped-out teaching in *Think and Grow* examples.

Then shift conceptual understanding into procedural fluency with *Show and Grow*, *Apply and Grow*, *Practice*, and *Review & Refresh*.

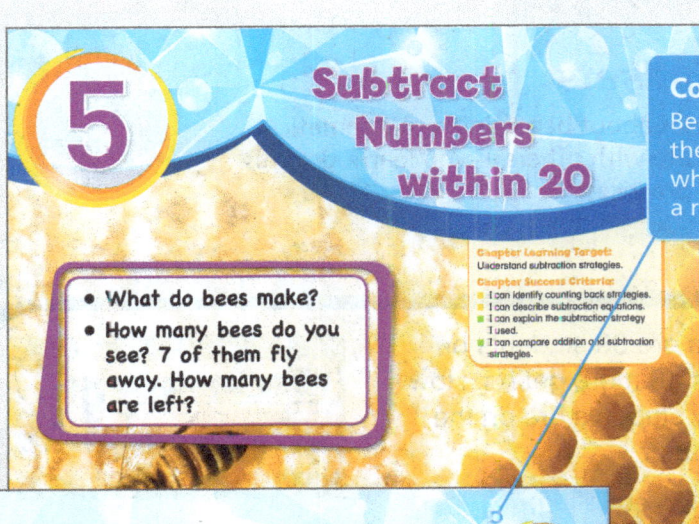

Connecting to Real Life
Begin every chapter thinking about the world around you. Then apply what you learn in the chapter with a related *Performance Task*.

Daily Application Practice
Modeling Real Life, *Dig Deeper*, and other non-routine problems help you apply surface-level skills to gain a deeper understanding. These problems lead to independent problem-solving.

15. **Modeling Real Life** Your magic book has 163 tricks. Your friend's magic book has 100 more tricks than yours. How many tricks does your friend's magic book have?

_____ tricks

16. **DIG DEEPER!** You have 624 songs. Newton has 100 fewer than you. Descartes has 10 more than Newton. How many songs does Descartes have?

_____ songs

THE PROBLEM-SOLVING PLAN

1. **Understand the Problem**
   Think about what the problem is asking. Circle what you know and underline what you need to find.

2. **Make a Plan**
   Plan your solution pathway before jumping in to solve. Identify any relationships and decide on a problem-solving strategy.

3. **Solve and Check**
   As you solve the problem, be sure to evaluate your progress and check your answers. Throughout the problem-solving process, you must continually ask, "Does this make sense?" and be willing to change course if necessary.

Problem-Solving Plan
Walk through the Problem-Solving Plan, featured in many *Think and Grow* examples, to help you make sense of problems with confidence.

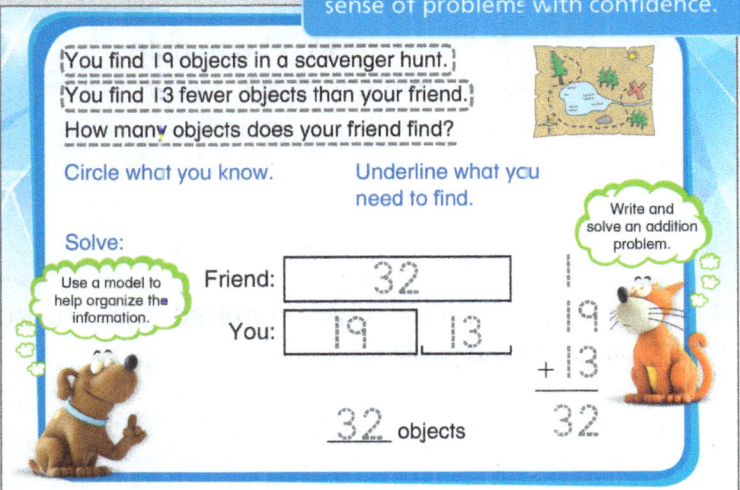

Embedded Mathematical Practices

Encouraging Mathematical Mindsets

Developing proficiency in the **Mathematical Practices** is about becoming a mathematical thinker. Learn to ask why, and reason and communicate with others as you learn. Use this guide to develop proficiency with the mathematical practices.

1

One way to **Make Sense of Problems and Persevere in Solving Them** is to use the Problem-Solving Plan. Take time to analyze the given information and what the problem is asking to help you plan a solution pathway.

Look for labels such as:
- Find Entry Points
- Analyze a Problem
- Interpret a Solution
- Make a Plan
- Use a Similar Problem
- Check Your Work

There are 33 students on a bus. 10 more get on. How many students are on the bus now?

Addition equation:

_____ students

Check Your Work When adding 10, should the digit in the tens place or the ones place change?

5. **Analyze a Problem** Use the numbers shown to write two addition equations.

8   10   2

___ + ___ = ___
___ + ___ = ___

7. **Reasoning** The minute hand points to the 7. What number will it point to in 10 minutes?

Reason Abstractly when you explore an example using numbers and models to represent the problem. Other times, **Reason Quantitatively** when you see relationships in numbers or models and draw conclusions about the problem.

2

Look for labels such as:
- Reasoning
- Number Sense
- Use Equations
- Use Expressions

3. **Number Sense** Which numbers can you subtract from 55 without regrouping?

15   49   33   24

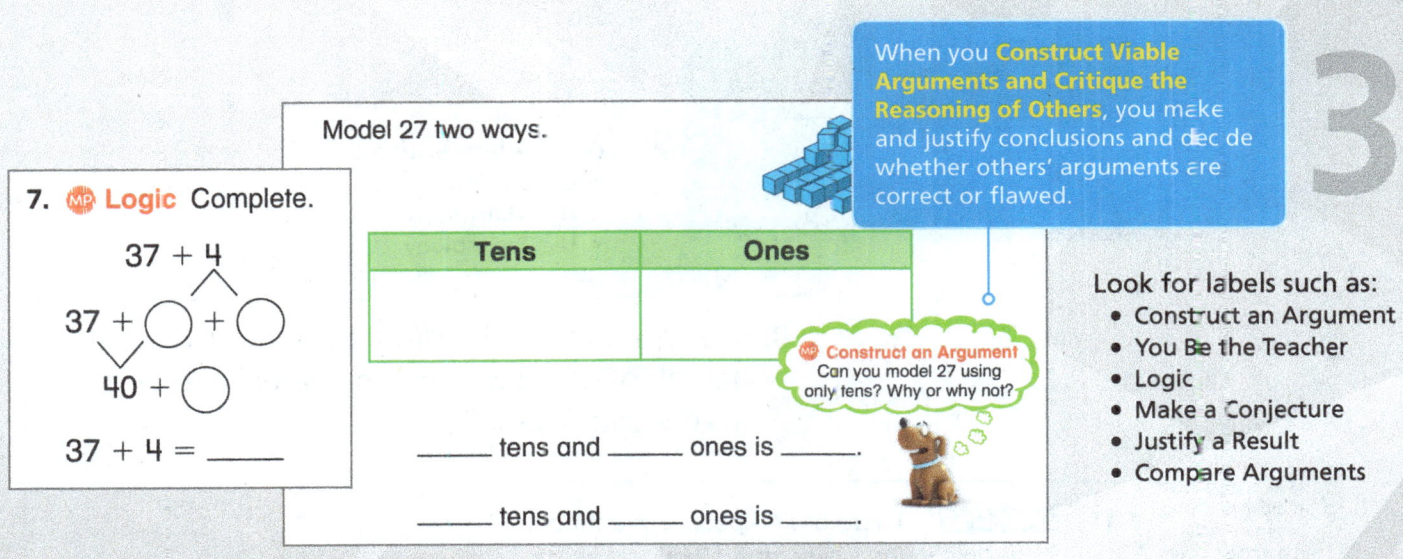

7. Logic Complete.

37 + 4
37 + ◯ + ◯
40 + ◯
37 + 4 = _____

Model 27 two ways.

Tens	Ones

_____ tens and _____ ones is _____.

_____ tens and _____ ones is _____.

Construct an Argument
Can you model 27 using only tens? Why or why not?

3

When you **Construct Viable Arguments and Critique the Reasoning of Others**, you make and justify conclusions and decide whether others' arguments are correct or flawed.

Look for labels such as:
- Construct an Argument
- You Be the Teacher
- Logic
- Make a Conjecture
- Justify a Result
- Compare Arguments

7. Graph Data Complete the weather chart to show an equal number of sunny days and rainy days. Write an equation to show how many sunny days and rainy days there are in all.

SUN	MON	TUE	WED	THU	FRI	SAT

___ + ___ = ___

Think and Grow: Modeling Real Life

Will the scissors fit inside a pencil case that is 7 color tiles long?

Circle: Yes   No

Tell how you know:

Does It Make Sense?
To fit inside, should the scissors be shorter or longer than the case?

4

To **Model with Mathematics**, apply the math you learned to a real-life problem and interpret mathematical results in the context of the situation.

Look for labels such as:
- Modeling Real Life
- Graph Data
- Analyze a Relationship
- Does It Make Sense?

BUILDING TO FULL UNDERSTANDING

Throughout each course, you have opportunities to demonstrate specific aspects of the mathematical practices. Labels throughout the book indicate gateways to those aspects. Collectively, these opportunities will lead to a full understanding of each mathematical practice. Developing these mindsets and habits will give meaning to the mathematics you learn.

Embedded Mathematical Practices (continued)

5 To **Use Appropriate Tools Strategically**, you need to know what tools are available and think about how each tool might help you solve a mathematical problem. When you choose a tool to use, remember that it may have limitations.

Look for labels such as:
- Choose Tools
- Use Math Tools
- Use Technology

8. **Choose Tools** Would you measure the length of a bus with a centimeter ruler or a meter stick? Why?

Use Math Tools How can you use a drawing to help organize the information given?

11. **DIG DEEPER!** There are 63 people in a theater, 21 people in the lobby, and 10 people in the parking lot. How many more people are in the theater than in both the lobby and the parking lot?

_____ more people

6 When you **Attend to Precision**, you are developing a habit of being careful in how you talk about concepts, label work, and write answers.

7. **DIG DEEPER!** Complete the model and the equation to match.

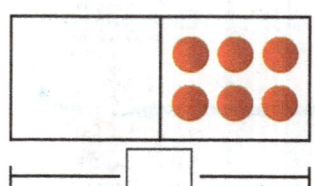

___ + ___ = 8

Communicate Clearly In the model, what shows the addends? the sum?

Look for labels such as:
- Precision
- Communicate Clearly
- Maintain Accuracy

5. **Precision** Which picture shows the correct way to measure the straw?

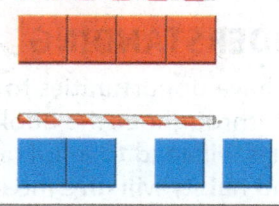

6. **Patterns** Find the sums. Think: What do you notice?

    4 + 5 = ___

    4 + 4 = ___

    5 + 5 = ___

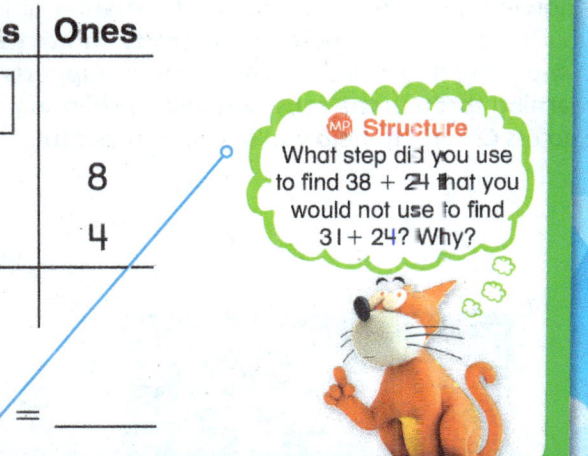

Look For and Make Use of Structure by looking closely to see structure within a mathematical statement, or stepping back for an overview to see how individual parts make one single object.

Look for labels such as:
- Structure
- Patterns

8. **Repeated Reasoning** What other shape has the same number of surfaces, vertices, and edges as a rectangular prism? How is that shape different from a rectangular prism?

When you **Look For and Express Regularity in Repeated Reasoning**, you can notice patterns and make generalizations. Remember to keep in mind the goal of a problem, which will help you evaluate reasonableness of answers along the way.

Look for labels such as:
- Repeated Reasoning
- Find a Rule

Visible Learning Through Learning Targets,

Making Learning Visible

Knowing the learning intention of a chapter or lesson helps you focus on the purpose of an activity, rather than simply completing it in isolation. This program supports visible learning through the consistent use of Learning Targets and Success Criteria to help you become successful.

> Every chapter shows a **Learning Target** and four related **Success Criteria**. These are incorporated throughout the chapter content to help guide you in your learning.

> Every lesson shows a **Learning Target** that is purposefully integrated into each carefully written lesson.

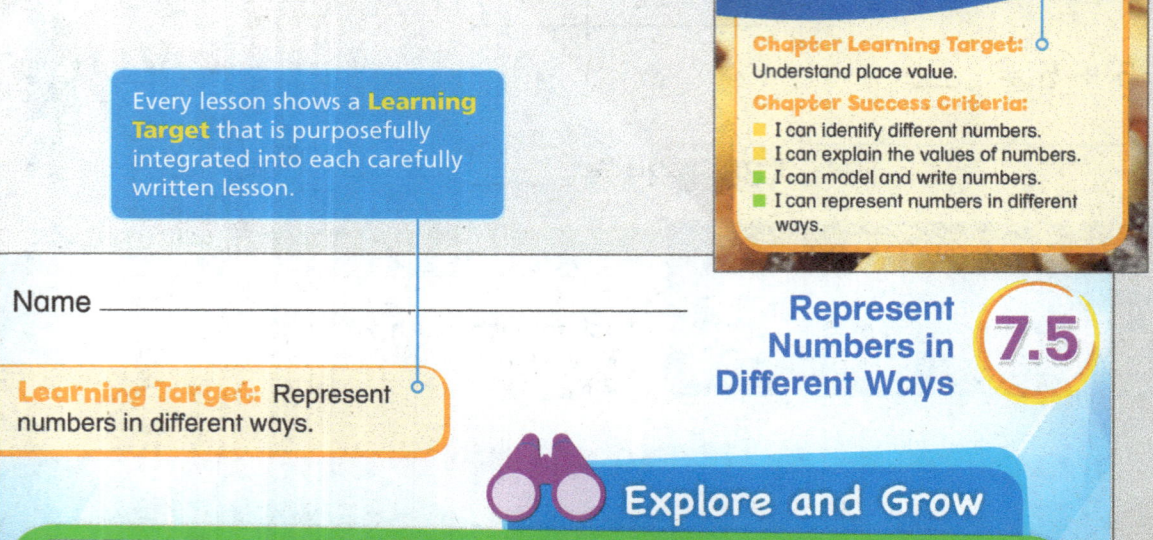

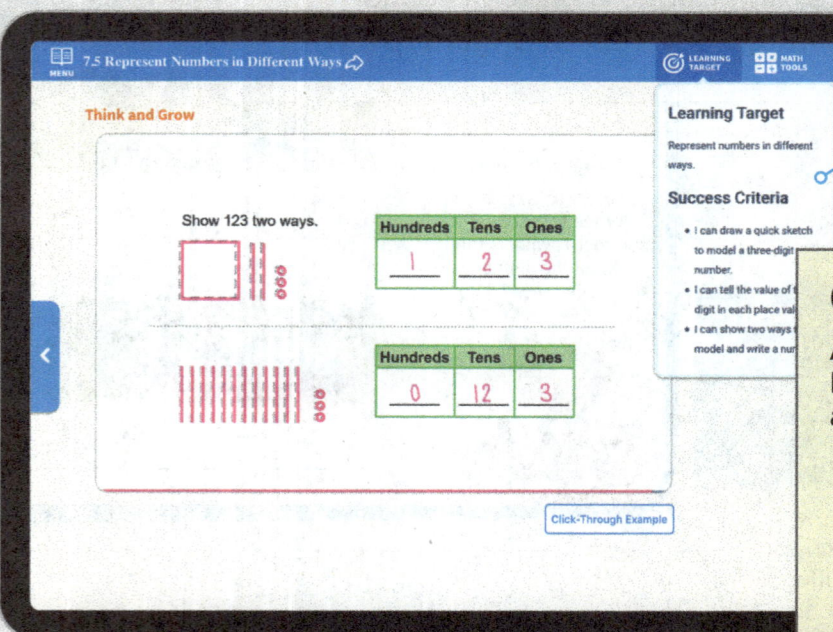

> Access the **Learning Target** and **Success Criteria** on every page of the Dynamic Student Edition.

QUESTIONS FOR LEARNING

As you progress through a lesson, you should be able to answer the following questions.

- What am I learning?
- Why am I learning this?
- Where am I in my learning?
- How will I know when I have learned it?
- Where am I going next?

Success Criteria, and Self-Assessment

> Have students indicate with their thumb signals how well they can find the sum in a word problem and write an addition equation. Have students turn and talk with a partner to explain all of the math vocabulary in an addition equation.

Use your thumb signals to rate your understanding of each success criterion. Your teacher will prompt you to self-assess throughout each lesson, and you can keep track of your learning online.

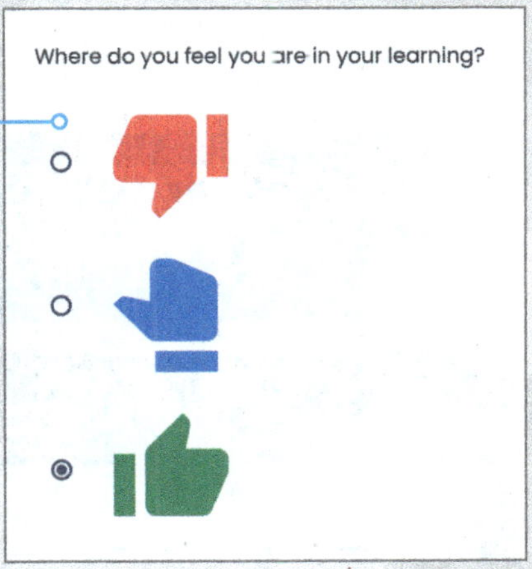

Where do you feel you are in your learning?

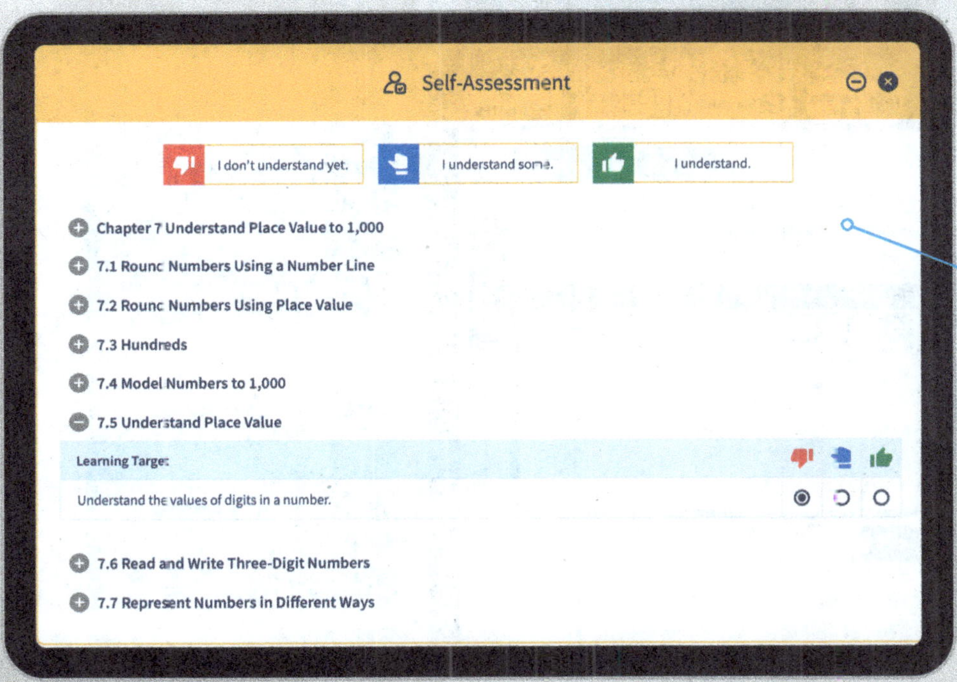

Self-Assessment

- I don't understand yet.
- I understand some.
- I understand.

- Chapter 7 Understand Place Value to 1,000
- 7.1 Round Numbers Using a Number Line
- 7.2 Round Numbers Using Place Value
- 7.3 Hundreds
- 7.4 Model Numbers to 1,000
- 7.5 Understand Place Value
  - Learning Target:
  - Understand the values of digits in a number.
- 7.6 Read and Write Three-Digit Numbers
- 7.7 Represent Numbers in Different Ways

Self-Assessments are included throughout every lesson, and in the **Chapter Review**, to help you take ownership of your learning and think about where to go next

Ensuring Positive Outcomes

John Hattie's *Visible Learning* research consistently shows that using Learning Targets and Success Criteria can result in two years' growth in one year, ensuring positive outcomes for your learning and achievement.

Sophie Murphy, M.Ed., wrote the chapter-level Learning Targets and Success Criteria for this program. Sophie is currently completing her Ph.D. at the University of Melbourne in Australia with Professor John Hattie as her leading supervisor. Sophie completed her Master's thesis with Professor John Hattie in 2015. Sophie has over 20 years of experience as a teacher and school leader in private and public school settings in Australia.

Strategic Support for Online Learning

Get the Support You Need, When You Need It

There will be times throughout this course when you may need help. Whether you missed a lesson, did not understand the content, or just want to review, take advantage of the resources provided in the *Dynamic Student Edition*.

Use the **Self-Assessment** tool to keep track of your understanding of the lesson's Learning Target and Success Criteria.

Choose **Math Tools** to engage with pattern blocks, digital number lines, linking cubes, and other tools to explore and understand math concepts.

Check your answers to selected exercises as you work through the lesson. Use the **Help** option to view the Digital Example videos.

Use the available **tools**, such as the calculator or sketchpad, to help clearly show your work and demonstrate your math knowledge.

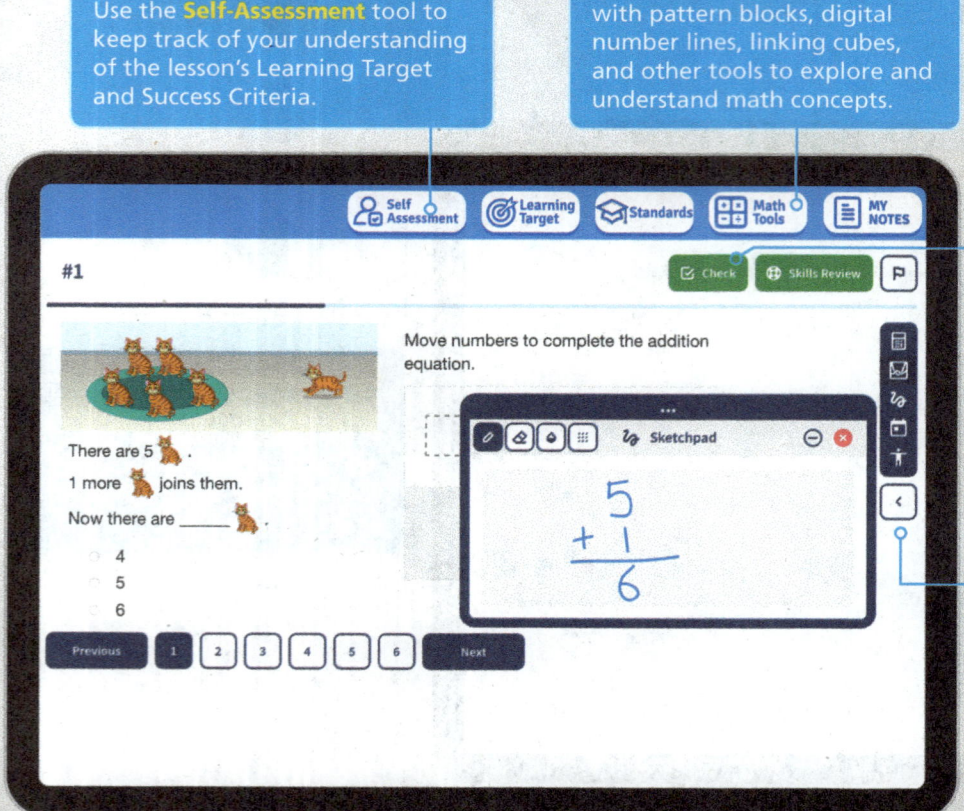

USE THESE QR CODES TO EXPLORE ADDITIONAL RESOURCES

Multi-Language Glossary
View definitions and examples of vocabulary words

Skills Trainer
Practice previously learned skills

Interactive Tools
Visualize mathematical concepts

Skills Review Handbook
A collection of review topics

Learning with Newton and Descartes

Who are Newton and Descartes?

Newton and Descartes are helpful math assistants who appear throughout your math book! They encourage you to think deeply about concepts and develop strong mathematical mindsets with Mathematical Practice questions.

MP Check Your Work
How can you use the addition facts to check that the differences are correct?

MP Precision
Which unit of measure did you use in your answer? Why?

Newton & Descartes's Math Musicals

Math Musicals offer an engaging connection between math, literature, and music! Newton and Descartes team up in these educational stories and songs to bring mathematics to life!

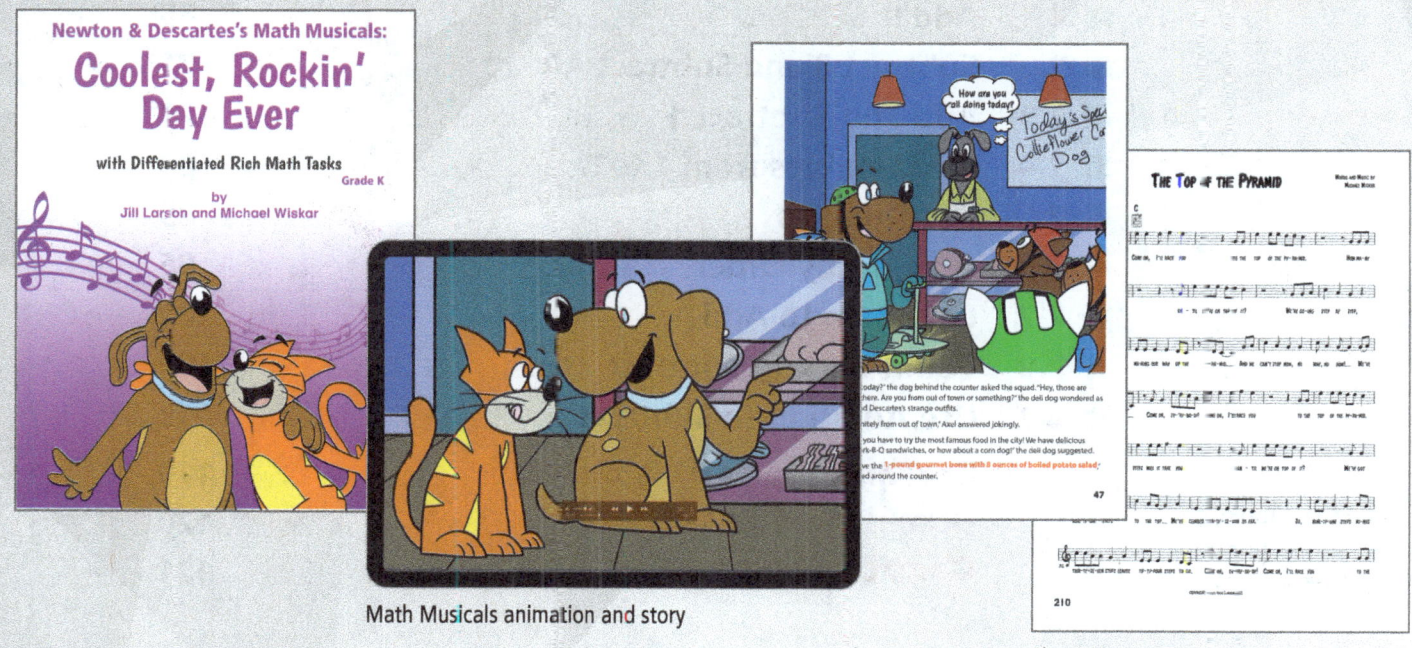

Math Musicals animation and story

Sheet Music

xvii

1 Addition and Subtraction Situations

Vocabulary 2
- 1.1 Addition: *Add To* 3
- 1.2 Solve *Add To* Problems 9
- 1.3 Solve *Put Together* Problems 15
- 1.4 Solve *Put Together* Problems with Both Addends Unknown 21
- 1.5 Solve *Take From* Problems 27
- 1.6 Solve *Compare* Problems: More 33
- 1.7 Solve *Compare* Problems: Fewer 39
- 1.8 Solve *Add To* Problems with Change Unknown 45
- 1.9 Connect *Put Together* and *Take Apart* Problems 51

Performance Task: Birds 57
Game: Three in a Row 58
Chapter Practice 59

2 Fluency and Strategies within 10

Vocabulary 64
- 2.1 Add 0 65
- 2.2 Subtract 0 and Subtract All 71
- 2.3 Add and Subtract 1 77
- 2.4 Add Doubles from 1 to 5 83
- 2.5 Use Doubles 89
- 2.6 Add in Any Order 95
- 2.7 Count On to Add 101
- 2.8 Count Back to Subtract 107
- 2.9 Use Addition to Subtract 113

Performance Task: Flowers 119
Game: Add or Subtract 120
Chapter Practice 121

■ Major Topic
■ Supporting Topic
■ Additional Topic

3 More Addition and Subtraction Situations

	Vocabulary	126
■ 3.1	Solve *Add To* Problems with Start Unknown	127
■ 3.2	Solve *Take From* Problems with Change Unknown	133
■ 3.3	Solve *Take From* Problems with Start Unknown	139
■ 3.4	*Compare* Problems: Bigger Unknown	145
■ 3.5	*Compare* Problems: Smaller Unknown	151
■ 3.6	True or False Equations	157
■ 3.7	Find Numbers That Make 10	163
■ 3.8	Fact Families	169
	Performance Task: Baking	175
	Game: Number Land	176
	Chapter Practice	177
	Cumulative Practice	181

Number Land

To Play: Put the Addition and Subtraction Cards in a pile. Start at Newton. Take turns drawing a card and moving your piece to the missing number in the equation. Repeat this process until a player gets back to Newton.

Add Numbers within 20

	Vocabulary	186
■	4.1 Add Doubles from 6 to 10	187
■	4.2 Use Doubles within 20	193
■	4.3 Count On to Add within 20	199
■	4.4 Add Three Numbers	205
■	4.5 Add Three Numbers by Making a 10	211
■	4.6 Add 9	217
■	4.7 Make a 10 to Add	223
■	4.8 Problem Solving: Addition within 20	229
	Performance Task: Weather	235
	Game: Roll and Cover	236
	Chapter Practice	237

Subtract Numbers within 20

	Vocabulary	242
■	5.1 Count Back to Subtract within 20	243
■	5.2 Use Addition to Subtract within 20	249
■	5.3 Subtract 9	255
■	5.4 Get to 10 to Subtract	261
■	5.5 More True or False Equations	267
■	5.6 Make True Equations	273
■	5.7 Problem Solving: Subtraction within 20	279
	Performance Task: Bees	285
	Game: Three in a Row: Subtraction	286
	Chapter Practice	287

■ Major Topic
■ Supporting Topic
■ Additional Topic

Count and Write Numbers to 120

	Vocabulary	292
6.1	Count to 120 by Ones	293
6.2	Count to 120 by Tens	299
6.3	Compose Numbers 11 to 19	305
6.4	Tens	311
6.5	Tens and Ones	317
6.6	Make Quick Sketches	323
6.7	Understand Place Value	329
6.8	Write Numbers in Different Ways	335
6.9	Count and Write Numbers to 120	341
	Performance Task: Fundraiser	347
	Game: Drop and Build	348
	Chapter Practice	349

Compare Two-Digit Numbers

	Vocabulary	354
7.1	Compare Numbers 11 to 19	355
7.2	Compare Numbers	361
7.3	Compare Numbers Using Place Value	367
7.4	Compare Numbers Using Symbols	373
7.5	Compare Numbers Using a Number Line	379
7.6	1 More, 1 Less; 10 More, 10 Less	385
	Performance Task: Toy Drive	391
	Game: Number Boss	392
	Chapter Practice	393
	Cumulative Practice	397

Let's learn how to compare two-digit numbers!

Add and Subtract Tens

	Vocabulary	402
8.1	Mental Math: 10 More	403
8.2	Mental Math: 10 Less	409
8.3	Add Tens	415
8.4	Add Tens Using a Number Line	421
8.5	Subtract Tens	427
8.6	Subtract Tens Using a Number Line	433
8.7	Use Addition to Subtract Tens	439
8.8	Add Tens to a Number	445
	Performance Task: Motion	451
	Game: 10 More or 10 Less	452
	Chapter Practice	453

Add Two-Digit Numbers

	Vocabulary	458
9.1	Add Tens and Ones	459
9.2	Add Tens and Ones Using a Number Line	465
9.3	Make a 10 to Add	471
9.4	Add Two-Digit Numbers	477
9.5	Practice Addition Strategies	483
9.6	Problem Solving: Addition	489
	Performance Task: Games	495
	Game: Race for 100	496
	Chapter Practice	497

■ Major Topic
■ Supporting Topic
■ Additional Topic

10 Measure and Compare Lengths

Vocabulary 502
- 10.1 Order Objects by Length 503
- 10.2 Compare Lengths Indirectly 509
- 10.3 Measure Lengths 515
- 10.4 Measure More Lengths 521
- 10.5 Solve *Compare* Problems Involving Length 527

Performance Task: Maps 533
Game: Fish Measurement 534
Chapter Practice 535

Think and Grow

Use color tiles to **measure** lengths of objects.

Do not leave gaps or overlap the tiles.

length unit

about __4__ color tiles

Represent and Interpret Data

	Vocabulary	540
■ 11.1	Sort and Organize Data	541
■ 11.2	Read and Interpret Picture Graphs	547
■ 11.3	Read and Interpret Bar Graphs	553
■ 11.4	Represent Data	559
■ 11.5	Solve Problems Involving Data	565
	Performance Task: Eye Color	571
	Game: Spin and Graph	572
	Chapter Practice	573
	Cumulative Practice	577

Tell Time

	Vocabulary	582
■ 12.1	Tell Time to the Hour	583
■ 12.2	Tell Time to the Half Hour	589
■ 12.3	Tell Time to the Hour and Half Hour	595
■ 12.4	Tell Time Using Analog and Digital Clocks	601
	Performance Task: Field Trip	607
	Game: Time Flip and Find	608
	Chapter Practice	609

■ Major Topic
■ Supporting Topic
■ Additional Topic

13 Two- and Three-Dimensional Shapes

	Vocabulary	612
13.1	Sort Two-Dimensional Shapes	613
13.2	Describe Two-Dimensional Shapes	619
13.3	Combine Two-Dimensional Shapes	625
13.4	Create More Shapes	631
13.5	Take Apart Two-Dimensional Shapes	637
13.6	Sort Three-Dimensional Shapes	643
13.7	Describe Three-Dimensional Shapes	649
13.8	Combine Three-Dimensional Shapes	655
13.9	Take Apart Three-Dimensional Shapes	661
	Performance Task: Sandcastles	667
	Game: Shape Roll and Build	668
	Chapter Practice	669

14 Equal Shares

	Vocabulary	674
14.1	Equal Shares	675
14.2	Partition Shapes into Halves	681
14.3	Partition Shapes into Fourths	687
	Performance Task: Picnic	693
	Game: Three in a Row: Equal Shares	694
	Chapter Practice	695
	Cumulative Practice	697

Glossary	A1
Index	A11
Reference Sheet	A25

Let's learn about equal shares!

Addition and Subtraction Situations

Chapter Learning Target:
Understand addition.

Chapter Success Criteria:
- I can identify a group of objects.
- I can describe numbers as a group.
- I can write an addition equation and a subtraction equation.
- I can model addition and subtraction.

- How many birds do you see? How many are flying away?
- How many birds are left on the wire?

one 1

Name _____

Vocabulary

Organize It

Review Words
equal sign
minus sign
plus sign

Use the review words to complete the graphic organizer.

☐ ⟶ $2 + 3 = 5$

☐ ⟶ $5 - 3 = 2$

☐ (pointing to both)

Define It

Use your vocabulary cards to match.

1. more $9 - 5 = 4$

2. fewer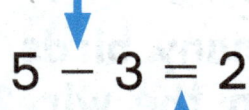

3. addition equation $4 + 5 = 9$

4. subtraction equation

2   two

Chapter 1 Vocabulary Cards

add	addend
addition equation	difference
equals	fewer
minus	more

$4 + 3 = 7$	🔴🔴 + 🟡🟡🟡 = 🔴🔴🟡🟡🟡 🔴🔴 🟡 🔴🔴🟡 $2 + 4 = 6$
$8 - 3 = 5$	$4 + 5 = 9$
(cubes image: row of 8 blue cubes, row of 4 red cubes circled)	$8 + 2 = 10$ 8 plus 2 equals 10
(cubes image: row of 9 blue cubes circled, row of 4 red cubes)	$3 - 1$ 3 minus 1

Chapter 1 Vocabulary Cards

part	part-part-whole model
plus	subtract
subtraction equation	sum
whole	

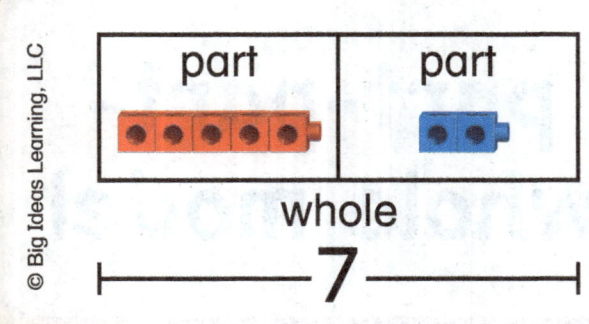

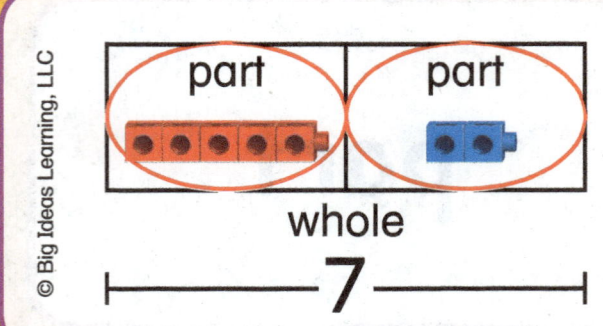

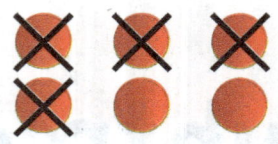

6 − 4 = 2

2 + 1
2 plus 1

5 + 3 = 8

9 − 5 = 4

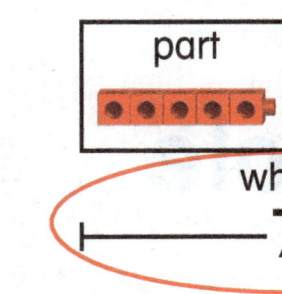

Name _____

Learning Target: Add to a group of objects and write an addition equation.

Addition: Add To

1.1

Explore and Grow

Use linking cubes to model the story.

There are 4 🐻. 2 more 🐻 join them.
How many 🐻 are there now?

_____ 🐻

Chapter 1 | Lesson 1

three 3

 **Think and Grow**

There are 3 🐕.

2 more 🐕 join them.

Now there are __5__ 🐕.

An addition sentence is also called an addition equation.

addition equation

__3__ + __2__ = __5__

Show and Grow I can do it!

1.

There are 5 🐱.

1 more 🐱 joins them.

Now there are ____ 🐱.

Addition equation: ____ + ____ = ____

 **Use Math Tools** How can you use 🧊 to help?

4 four

Name _____

 **Apply and Grow: Practice**

2.

There are 3 🦀.

6 more 🦀 join them.

Now there are ____ 🦀.   ____ + ____ = ____

3.

There are 8 🐖.

2 more 🐖 join them.

Now there are ____ 🐖.   ____ + ____ = ____

4. **DIG DEEPER!** Complete the picture and the story.

There are ____ 🦉.

3 more 🦉 join them.

Now there are ____ 🦉.   ____ + ____ = ____

Chapter 1 | Lesson 1   five 5

Think and Grow: Modeling Real Life

There are 5 🐟. 3 more 🐟 join them. How many 🐟 are there now?

Draw a picture:

Addition equation:

_____ 🐟

Show and Grow — I can think deeper!

5. There are 2 🐢. 7 more 🐢 join them. How many 🐢 are there now?

Draw a picture:

Addition equation:

_____ 🐢

Name _____

Practice

Learning Target: Add to a group of objects and write an addition equation.

There are 2 🐑.

5 more 🐑 join them.

Now there are __7__ 🐑.

Addition equation:

__2__ + __5__ = __7__

1.

There are 6 🦊.

1 more 🦊 joins them.

Now there are ____ 🦊.

____ + ____ = ____

2.

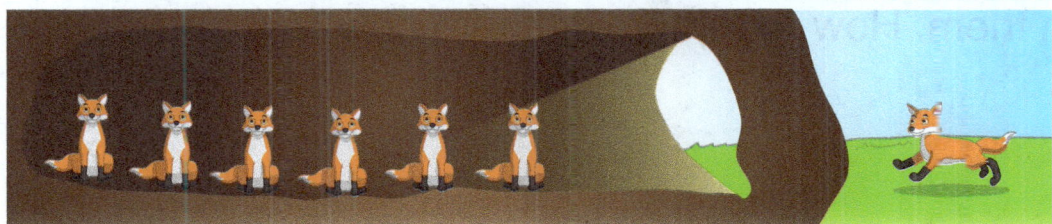

There are 7 🐞.

3 more 🐞 join them.

Now there are ____ 🐞.

____ + ____ = ____

Chapter 1 | Lesson 1

seven 7

3. **DIG DEEPER!** Complete the picture and the story.

There are ____ 🦜.

2 more 🦜 join them.

Now there are ____ 🦜.

____ + ____ = ____

4. **Modeling Real Life** There are 2 🦆. 7 more 🦆 join them. How many 🦆 are there now?

Review & Refresh

Write the number of objects.

5.

____

6.

____

8 eight

Name _____

Learning Target: Solve *add to* word problems.

Solve *Add To* Problems 1.2

Use linking cubes to model the story.

There are 5 🎩.

You add 2 more 🎩.

How many 🎩 are there now?

____

Chapter 1 | **Lesson 2**

nine 9

Think and Grow

You have 3 🟥.

You **add** 4 more 🟥.

How many 🟥 do you have now?

$$\underset{\text{addend}}{3} \;+\; \underset{\text{addend}}{4} \;=\; \underset{\text{sum}}{7}$$
$$\text{plus} \qquad\quad \text{equals}$$

____7____ 🟥

Show and Grow — I can do it!

1. You have 4 🟣.

   You find 2 more 🟣.

   How many 🟣 do you have now?

   Addition equation:

   ___ + ___ = ___

   ___

2. There are 4 🐰.

   4 more 🐰 join them.

   How many 🐰 are there now?

   Addition equation:

   ___ + ___ = ___

   ___

**Apply and Grow: Practice**

3. You have 2 .

   You buy 2 more .

   How many  do you have now?

   ___ + ___ = ___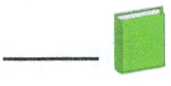

4. There are 3 .

   5 more  join them.

   How many  are there now?

   ___ + ___ = ___

5. You eat 9 .

   You eat 1 more .

   How many  do you eat?

   ___ + ___ = ___

6. **DIG DEEPER!** Complete the picture and the story.

   There are 4 🐌.

   3 more 🐌 join them.

   Now there are ___ 🐌.

   ___ + ___ = ___

Chapter 1 | Lesson 2   eleven 11

Think and Grow: Modeling Real Life

You have 3 🍎. You buy 7 🍎.

How many 🍎 do you have now?

Draw a picture:

Addition equation:

Communicate Clearly
Which numbers are the addends? Which number is the sum?

_____ 🍎

Show and Grow — I can think deeper!

7. You have 6 🧊. Your friend gives you 3 🧊. How many 🧊 do you have now?

Draw a picture:

Addition equation:

_____ 🧊

Name _____

Practice **1.2**

Learning Target: Solve *add to* word problems.

You have 1 🟥.

You add 4 more 🟥.

How many 🟥 do you have now?

$\underline{1} + \underline{4} = \underline{5}$

$\underline{5}$ 🟥

1. You have 2 ✏.

   You buy 3 more ✏.

   How many ✏ do you have now?

   ___ + ___ = ___

   ___ ✏

2. There are 6 🌸.

   You add 4 more 🌸.

   How many 🌸 are there now?

   ___ + ___ = ___

   ___ 🌸

3. There are 5 🦋.

   4 more 🦋 join them.

   How many 🦋 are there now?

   ___ + ___ = ___

   ___ 🦋

Chapter 1 | Lesson 2

thirteen **13**

4. **DIG DEEPER!** Complete the picture and the story.

There are 7 🐸.

3 more 🐸 join them.

Now there are ____ 🐸.

____ + ____ = ____

5. **Modeling Real Life** You have 2 ⚽. You buy 4 ⚽. How many ⚽ do you have now?

____ ⚽

Review & Refresh

6. Use the picture to complete the number bond.

Name _____

Learning Target: Solve *put together* word problems.

Solve *Put Together* Problems **1.3**

Explore and Grow

Use counters to model the story.

You have 7  and 2 . How many toys do you have in all?

____ toys

Communicate Clearly
Why do you think this is called a *put together* problem?

Chapter 1 | Lesson 3

fifteen **15**

Think and Grow

You have 5 🖍 and 2 🖍. How many crayons do you have in all?

I can use a part-part-whole model to show the parts and the whole.

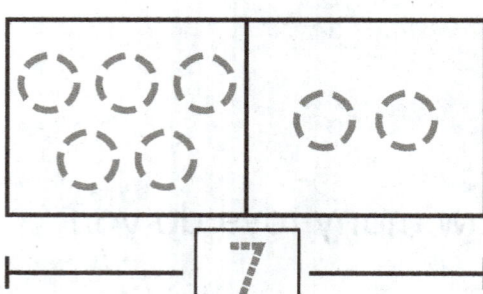

$\underline{5} + \underline{2} = \underline{7}$
part part whole

part-part-whole model

$\underline{7}$ crayons

Show and Grow — I can do it!

1. You have 3 🏀 and 1 ⚽. How many balls do you have in all?

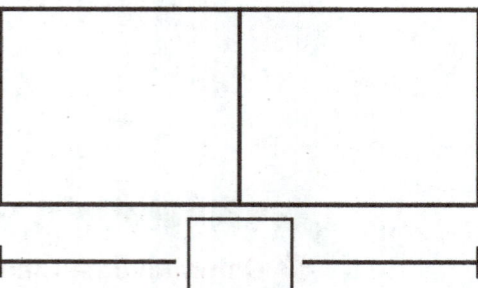

___ + ___ = ___

___ balls

2. There are 2 🐟 and 6 🐟. How many fish are there in all?

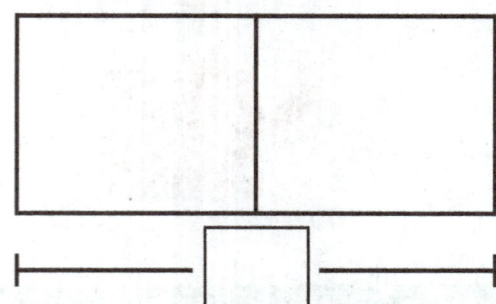

___ + ___ = ___

___ fish

16   sixteen

Apply and Grow: Practice

3. You have 1  and 5 🐱. How many pets do you have in all?

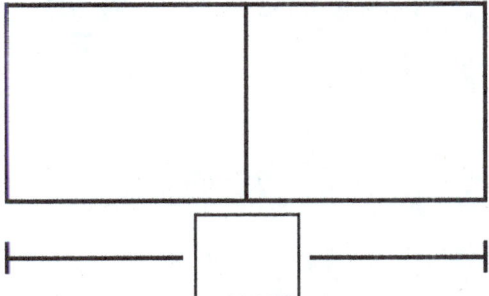

___ + ___ = ___

___ pets

4. There are 4 🐴 and 6 🐔. How many animals are there in all?

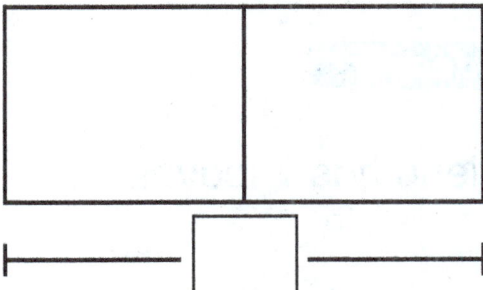

___ + ___ = ___

___ animals

5. **Number Sense** Circle two groups of bugs to match the addition problem. Then find the sum.

3 + 5 = ___

Chapter 1 | Lesson 3   seventeen   17

Think and Grow: Modeling Real Life

You have 3 🌷 and 4 🌷. Your friend has 8 flowers. Who has more flowers?

Model:

Addition equation: _____

Who has more flowers?   You   Friend

Show and Grow — I can think deeper!

6. You have 4 🍂 and 5 🍃. Your friend has 7 leaves. Who has more leaves?

Model:

Addition equation: _____

Who has more leaves?   You   Friend

Name _____

Practice 1.3

Learning Target: Solve *put together* word problems.

You have 4 🟧 and 1 🟦. How many linking cubes do you have in all?

$\underline{4} + \underline{1} = \underline{5}$

$\underline{5}$ cubes

1. You buy 1 🍍 and 7 🍌. How many pieces of fruit do you buy in all?

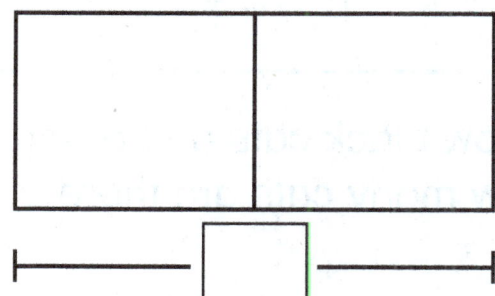

___ + ___ = ___

___ pieces of fruit

2. There are 5 🐦 and 5 🐦. How many birds are there in all?

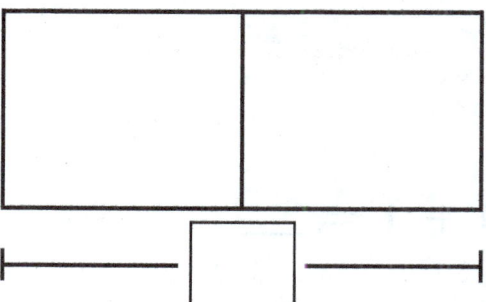

___ + ___ = ___

___ birds

Chapter 1 | Lesson 3

nineteen 19

3. **Number Sense** Circle two groups of hats to match the addition problem. Then find the sum.

6 + 1 = ___

4. **Modeling Real Life** You have 4 🚙 and 5 🚗. Your friend has 8 cars. Who has more cars?

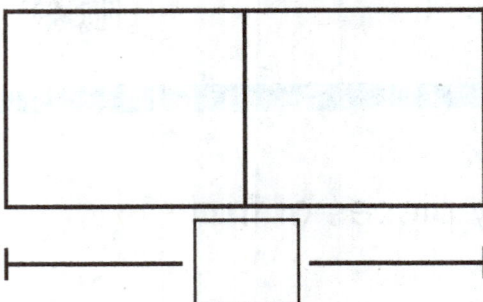

Who has more cars?

You   Friend

5. **DIG DEEPER!** Write a picture story. Show black cats and orange cats. Write an addition equation. How many cats are there in all?

___ ◯ ___ ◯ ___ cats

Review & Refresh

Find the sum.

6. 5 + 1 = ___   7. 9 + 1 = ___

20   twenty

Name _____

Learning Target: Find addends for a given sum.

Solve *Put Together* Problems with Both Addends Unknown — 1.4

Explore and Grow

Use linking cubes to model the story.

There are 10 . Some are on the court and some are on the rack.

Construct an Argument
Is it okay to have different answers? How do you know?

____ on the court

____ on the rack

Chapter 1 | Lesson 4

Think and Grow

There are 6 🦋. Some are inside a jar. Some more are outside the jar. Draw the 🦋.

Addition equation: $\underline{6} = \underline{2} + \underline{4}$

Show and Grow   I can do it!

1. There are 7 🍒. Some are on a tree. Some more are on the ground. Draw the 🍒.

Addition equation: ___ = ___ + ___

Name _____

✓ Apply and Grow: Practice

2. There are 5 🐕. Some are on a couch. Some more are on a rug. Draw the 🐕.

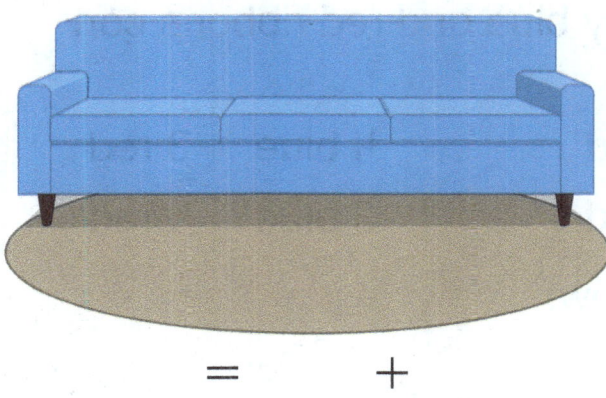

___ = ___ + ___

3. **Use Equations** There are 8 🐍. Some are in a pond. Some more are in the grass. Draw two different pictures to show the 🐍.

___ = ___ + ___   ___ = ___ + ___

4. **DIG DEEPER!** Newton has 4 toy trucks. Some are red. The rest are blue. Write two different addition equations to describe his trucks.

___ = ___ + ___   ___ = ___ + ___

Chapter 1 | Lesson 4   twenty-three 23

Think and Grow: Modeling Real Life

You have 7 ribbons. Some are blue. The rest are red. You have more blue ribbons than red ribbons. How many blue and red ribbons can you have?

    2 blue   5 red   4 blue   3 red
    6 blue   1 red   3 blue   4 red

Show how you know:

Show and Grow — I can think deeper!

5. There are 10 kites. Some are green. The rest are yellow. There are more yellow kites than green kites. How many green and yellow kites can there be?

    4 green   6 yellow   6 green   4 yellow
    5 green   5 yellow   3 green   7 yellow

Show how you know:

Name _____

Practice 1.4

Learning Target: Find addends for a given sum.

There are 4 🐻. Some are inside a box. Some more are outside the box. Draw the 🐻.

Addition equation: 4 = 1 + 3

1. There are 6 🐜. Some are on a hill. Some more are in the grass. Draw the 🐜.

___ = ___ + ___

2. There are 8 🐸. Some are in the water. Some more are on the dirt. Draw the 🐸.

___ = ___ + ___

Chapter 1 | Lesson 4

3. **Use Equations** There are 5 ⚽. Some are inside a bin. Some more are outside the bin. Draw two different pictures to show the ⚽.

___ = ___ + ___   ___ = ___ + ___

4. **Modeling Real Life** You have 9 hats. Some are blue. The rest are red. You have more red hats than blue hats. How many red and blue hats can you have?

    4 red   5 blue   6 red   3 blue

    3 red   6 blue   7 red   2 blue

Show how you know:

Review & Refresh

Use the picture to write a subtraction sentence.

5.
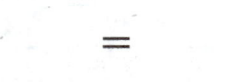

  ___ − ___ = ___

6.

  ___ − ___ = ___

Name _____

Learning Target: Solve *take from* word problems.

Solve Take From Problems

Explore and Grow

Use linking cubes to model the story.

There are 6 🐰. 3 🐰 hop away.

How many 🐰 are left?

_____

Chapter 1 | Lesson 5   twenty-seven 27

Think and Grow

You have 4 ▪.

You take away 1 ▪.

How many ▪ do you have left?

subtraction equation

4 − 1 = 3

minus   difference

3 ▪

Subtract to find the *difference*.

Show and Grow   I can do it!

1. There are 6 🐵.

   2 🐵 jump away.

   How many 🐵 are left?

   Subtraction equation:

   ___ − ___ = ___

   ___

2. There are 8 🍌.

   A monkey eats 5 🍌.

   How many 🍌 are left?

   Subtraction equation:

   ___ − ___ = ___

   ___

Name _____

 Apply and Grow: Practice

3. There are 7 🐜.

   3 🐜 walk away.

   How many 🐜 are left?

   ___ − ___ = ___

   ___ 🐜

4. There are 8 🐦.

   6 🐦 fly away.

   How many 🐦 are left?

   ___ − ___ = ___

   ___ 🐦

5. 10 🐱 play.

   5 🐱 run away.

   How many 🐱 are left?

   ___ − ___ = ___

   ___ 🐱

6. **Check Your Work** Find the difference. Draw a picture to match.

   7 − 4 = ___

Chapter 1 | Lesson 5

Think and Grow: Modeling Real Life

7 students play tag. 2 of them leave. How many students are left?

Which equation matches the story?

$9 - 7 = 2$ $7 - 2 = 5$ $7 - 5 = 2$

Show how you know:

_____ students are left.

Show and Grow   I can think deeper!

7. You have 9 coins. You give 3 coins away. How many coins are left?

Which equation matches the story?

$9 - 3 = 6$ $6 - 3 = 3$ $9 - 6 = 3$

Show how you know:

_____ coins are left.

Name _____

Practice 1.5

Learning Target: Solve *take from* word problems.

You have 6 🟦.

You take away 4 🟦.

How many 🟦 do you have left?

Subtraction equation:

$\underline{6} - \underline{4} = \underline{2}$

$\underline{2}$ 🟦

1. There are 5 🐅.

   3 🐅 leave.

   How many 🐅 are left?

   ___ − ___ = ___

   ___ 🐅

2. There are 7 🐟.

   A cat eats 5 🐟.

   How many 🐟 are left?

   ___ − ___ = ___

   ___ 🐟

3. You have 10 🎾.

   You give away 10 🎾.

   How many 🎾 do you have left?

   ___ − ___ = ___

   ___ 🎾

Chapter 1 | Lesson 5

4. **Check Your Work** Find the difference. Draw a picture to match.

    8 − 2 = ____

5. **Modeling Real Life** 6 students play soccer. 4 of them leave. How many students are left?

    Which equation matches the story?

    6 − 2 = 4   8 − 6 = 2   6 − 4 = 2

    Show how you know:

    ____ students are left.

6. **DIG DEEPER!** You have 7 crackers. You give 2 to your friend. Then you eat 3. How many crackers do you have left?

    ____ crackers

Review & Refresh

7. Write the numbers of dogs and bones. Circle the number that is greater than the other number.

____

____

Name _____

Learning Target: Solve *compare* word problems by finding how many more.

Solve *Compare* Problems: More

1.6

Explore and Grow

Use counters to model the story.

Newton has 4 apples. Descartes has 6 apples. Who has more apples? How many more?

 has ____ more apples.

(Circle one.)

Chapter 1 | **Lesson 6**

thirty-three 33

Think and Grow

Newton has 5 balloons. Descartes has 3 balloons. How many **more** balloons does Newton have?

Subtraction equation: 5 − 3 = 2

__2__ more balloons

Show and Grow   I can do it!

1. You have 7 books. Your friend has 3 books. How many more books do you have?

Repeated Reasoning
How does the picture help you answer the question?

Subtraction equation: ___ − ___ = ___

____ more books

Name _____

✓ Apply and Grow: Practice

2. Your friend has 6 crayons. You have 3 crayons. How many more crayons does your friend have?

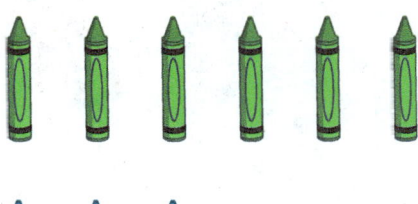

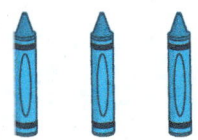

____ − ____ = ____

____ more crayons

3. There are 9 purple flowers and 5 yellow flowers. Draw the missing flowers. How many more purple flowers are there?

____ − ____ = ____

____ more purple flowers

4. You have 2 yellow buckets. Your friend has 6 blue buckets. Draw the missing buckets. How many more buckets does your friend have?

____ − ____ = ____

____ more buckets

Chapter 1 | Lesson 6

Think and Grow: Modeling Real Life

You have 2 dog puppets. You have more cat puppets than dog puppets. How many more cat puppets do you have?

Draw a picture:

Subtraction equation:

_____ more cat puppets

Show and Grow — I can think deeper!

5. You have 9 toy cars. You have more cars than trucks. How many more cars do you have?

Draw a picture:

Subtraction equation:

_____ more toy cars

Name _____

Practice 1.6

Learning Target: Solve *compare* word problems by finding how many more.

> You have 8 marbles. Your friend has 5 marbles. How many more marbles do you have?
>
>
>
>
>
> Subtraction equation: __8__ − __5__ = __3__
>
> __3__ more marbles
>
>

1. There are 4 blue scarves and 3 green scarves. How many more blue scarves are there?

___ − ___ = ___

___ more blue scarf

2. You have 6 strawberries and 2 blueberries. Draw the missing fruit. How many more strawberries do you have?

___ − ___ = ___

___ more strawberries

3. You have 2 blue towels. Your friend has 7 red towels. Draw the missing towels. How many more towels does your friend have?

____ − ____ = ____

____ more towels

4. **Modeling Real Life** You have 3 toy bears. You have more yo-yos than toy bears. How many more yo-yos do you have?

____ more yo-yos

Review & Refresh

5. Write the number of each type of sea creature. Draw a line through the number that is less than the other number.

      ____

     ____

Name _____

Learning Target: Solve *compare* word problems by finding how many fewer.

Solve *Compare* Problems: Fewer 1.7

Explore and Grow

Use counters to model the story.

Newton has 7 games. Descartes has 5 games. Who has fewer games? How many fewer?

 _____ has _____ fewer games.

(circle one)

Chapter 1 | Lesson 7 thirty-nine 39

Think and Grow

Newton has 4 balls. Descartes has 7 balls. How many **fewer** balls does Newton have?

Subtraction equation: __7__ − __4__ = __3__

__3__ fewer balls

Show and Grow   I can do it!

1. There are 2 green pinwheels and 8 yellow pinwheels. How many fewer green pinwheels are there?

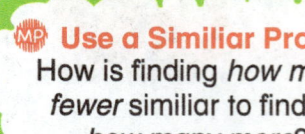
Use a Similiar Problem
How is finding *how many fewer* similiar to finding *how many more*?

Subtraction equation: ___ − ___ = ___

___ fewer green pinwheels

40   forty

Name _____

✓ Apply and Grow: Practice

2. You have 3 key chains. Your friend has 7 key chains. How many fewer key chains do you have?

____ – ____ = ____

____ fewer key chains

3. There are 6 brown horses and 10 gray horses. Draw the missing horses. How many fewer brown horses are there?

____ – ____ = ____

____ fewer brown horses

4. You have 8 red trains. Your friend has 5 orange trains. Draw the missing trains. How many fewer trains does your friend have?

____ – ____ = ____

____ fewer trains

Chapter 1 | Lesson 7

Think and Grow: Modeling Real Life

There are 10 hens. There are fewer chicks than hens. How many fewer chicks are there?

Draw a picture:

Subtraction equation:

_____ fewer chicks

Show and Grow   I can think deeper!

5. There are 4 pigs. There are fewer pigs than piglets. How many fewer pigs are there?

Draw a picture:

Subtraction equation:

_____ fewer pigs

42   forty-two

Name _____

Practice 1.7

Learning Target: Solve *compare* word problems by finding how many fewer.

Descartes has 2 blocks. Newton has 5 blocks. How many fewer blocks does Descartes have?

Subtraction equation: __5__ − __2__ = __3__

__3__ fewer blocks

1. There are 7 black bears and 8 brown bears. How many fewer black bears are there?

___ − ___ = ___

____ fewer black bear

2. You have 4 purple blocks. Your friend has 9 yellow blocks. Draw the missing blocks. How many fewer blocks do you have?

___ − ___ = ___

____ fewer blocks

Chapter 1 | Lesson 7

3. There are 7 orange kittens and 2 black kittens. Draw the missing kittens. How many fewer black kittens are there?

___ − ___ = ___

___ fewer black kittens

4. **Modeling Real Life** There are 9 lions. There are fewer cubs than lions. How many fewer cubs are there?

___ fewer cubs

5. **DIG DEEPER!** Write a different answer for Exercise 4.

___ fewer cubs

Review & Refresh

6. Draw more counters to show how many in all. Use the ten frame to complete the addition equation.

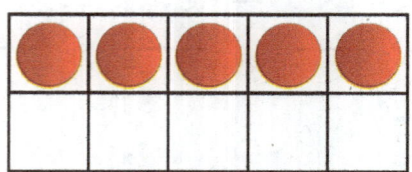

5 + ___ = 7

Name _____

Learning Target: Solve *add to* word problems that involve a missing addend.

Solve Add To Problems with Change Unknown 1.8

 Explore and Grow

Use counters to model the story.

5 people are on a subway. Some more people get on at the subway stop. Now there are 8 people on the subway. How many people got on at the subway stop?

_____ people

Chapter 1 | **Lesson 8**

forty-five 45

Think and Grow

You have 6 pennies. Your friend gives you some more. Now you have 8. How many pennies did your friend give you?

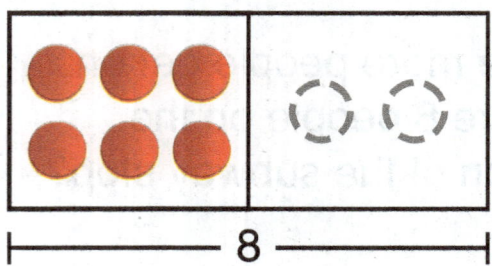

Addition equation: $\underline{6} + \underline{2} = \underline{8}$

$\underline{2}$ pennies

6 plus what is equal to 8?

Show and Grow — I can do it!

1. You have 3 oranges. You buy some more. Now you have 6. How many oranges did you buy?

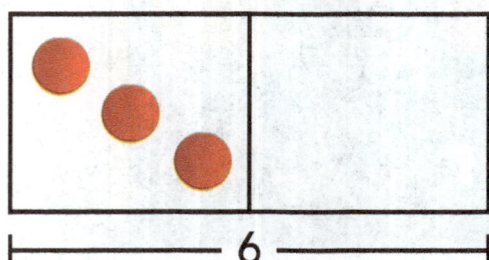

Addition equation: ___ + ___ = ___

___ oranges

Name _____

 **Apply and Grow: Practice**

2. 5 kids are in a pool. Some more jump in. Now there are 7 kids. How many kids jumped in the pool?

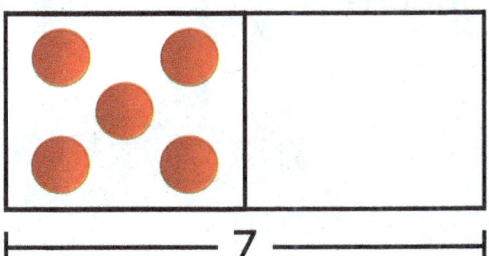

___ + ___ = ___

___ kids

3. You hop 6 times. You hop some more times. You hop 10 times in all. How many more times did you hop?

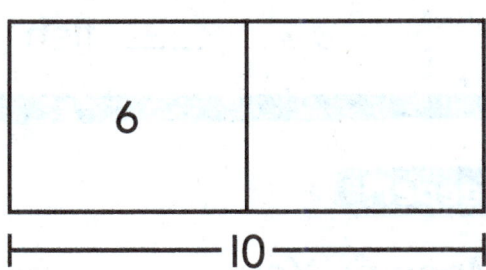

___ + ___ = ___

___ times

4. 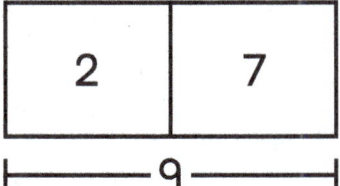 **Structure** Circle the model that shows the missing number.

2 + ___ = 7

2	7
9	

2	5
7	

3	4
7	

Chapter 1 | Lesson 8

forty-seven 47

Think and Grow: Modeling Real Life

You catch 2 fish before lunch. You catch some more after lunch. You catch 10 in all. How many fish did you catch after lunch?

Model:

Addition equation:

_____ fish

Show and Grow — I can think deeper!

5. You read 7 books. You read 4 on Monday. You read the rest on Tuesday. How many books do you read on Tuesday?

Model:

Addition equation:

_____ books

Name _____   **Practice** 1.8

Learning Target: Solve *add to* word problems that involve a missing addend.

You have 7 stickers. You earn some more. Now you have 9. How many stickers did you earn?

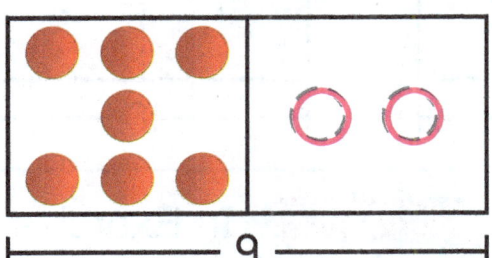

$\underline{7} + \underline{2} = \underline{9}$

$\underline{2}$ stickers

1. 2 kids ride bikes to the park. Some more kids walk to the park. Now there are 6 kids at the park. How many kids walked to the park?

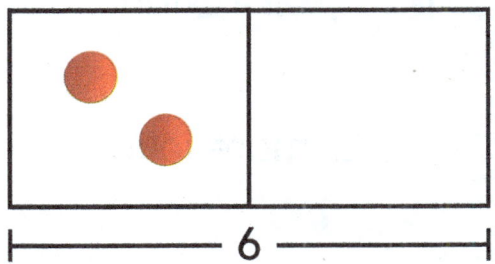

___ + ___ = ___

___ kids

2. You have 5 stamps. You buy some more. Now you have 8. How many stamps did you buy?

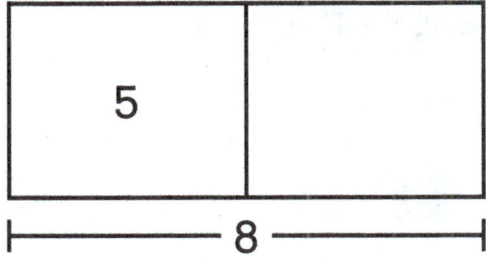

___ + ___ = ___

___ stamps

Chapter 1 | Lesson 8   forty-nine 49

3. **Structure** Circle the model that shows the missing number.

$$4 + \underline{} = 10$$

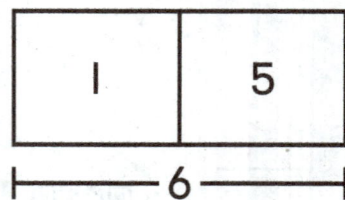

4. **Modeling Real Life** You tell 7 jokes. You tell some more jokes. You tell 10 jokes in all. How many more jokes did you tell?

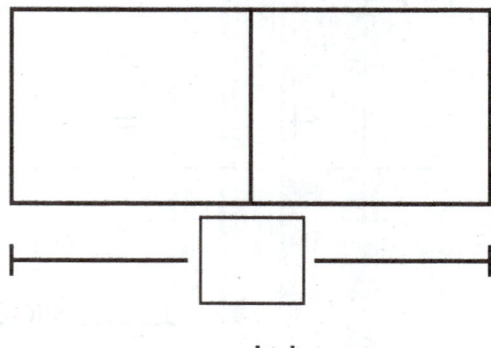

_____ jokes

5. **DIG DEEPER!** In Exercise 4, Newton tells 8 jokes. Who tells more jokes? How many more?

You   Newton

_____ more jokes

Review & Refresh

6. Write the numbers of bears and honey pots. Are the numbers equal? Circle the thumbs up for *yes* or the thumbs down for *no*.

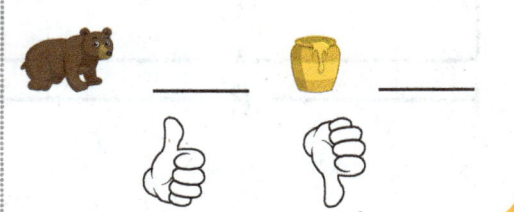

Name _____

Connect *Put Together* and *Take Apart* Problems

1.9

Learning Target: Solve word problems that involve putting together and taking apart.

 **Explore and Grow**

Use counters to model the story.

There are 9 geese. 4 are flying. The rest are on the ground. How many geese are on the ground?

_____ geese

Chapter 1 | Lesson 9

fifty-one   51

 Think and Grow

You have 6 buttons. 4 are green. The rest are black. How many black buttons do you have?

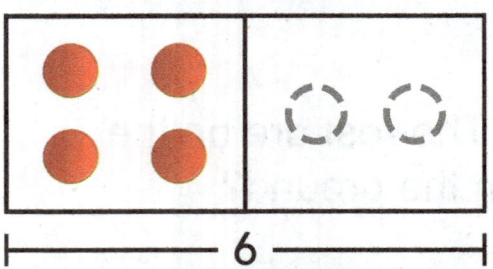

$4 + 2 = 6$

$6 - 4 = 2$

You can add *or* subtract to find the missing part!

__2__ black buttons

Show and Grow   I can do it!

1. You have 8 beads. 5 are pink. The rest are orange. How many orange beads do you have?

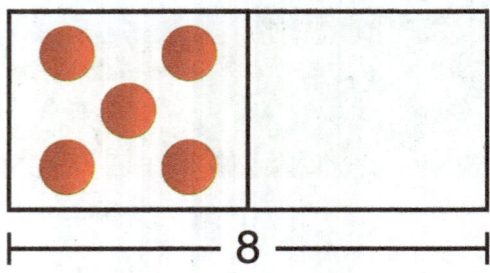

___ + ___ = ___

___ − ___ = ___

___ orange beads

Apply and Grow: Practice

2. You have 9 rings. 7 are green. The rest are orange. How many orange rings do you have?

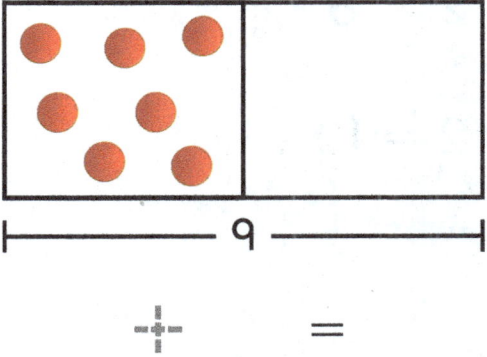

___ + ___ = ___

___ − ___ = ___

___ orange rings

3. There are 3 spiders in a tree. Some more are on the ground. There are 10 spiders in all. How many spiders are on the ground?

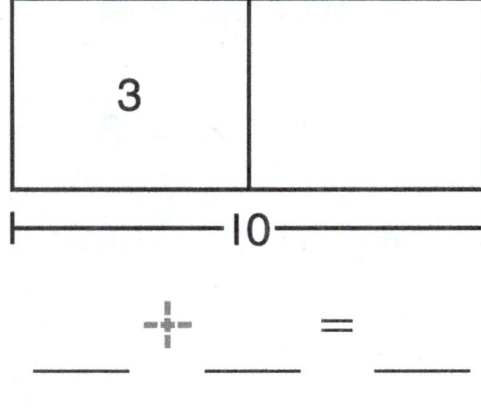

___ + ___ = ___

___ − ___ = ___

___ spiders

4. **Analyze a Problem** 10 students play instruments. 6 play drums. The rest play flutes. How many students play flutes? Use the model to write an equation and solve.

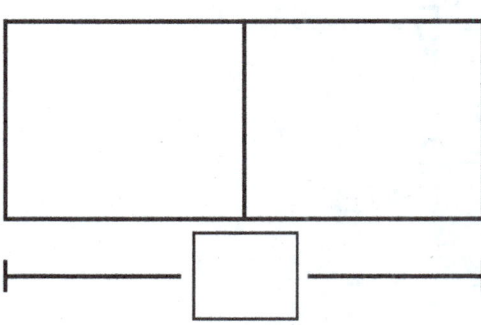

___ ○ ___ = ___

___ students

Think and Grow: Modeling Real Life

There are 8 students at a playground. 2 are on the slides. The rest are on the swings. How many students are on the swings?

Which equations match the story?

10 − 2 = 8   8 − 2 = 6

2 + 6 = 8   8 + 2 = 10

Show how you know:

_____ students are on the swings.

Show and Grow   I can think deeper!

5. Your teacher has 5 outdoor toys. 2 are flying discs. The rest are jump ropes. How many jump ropes are there?

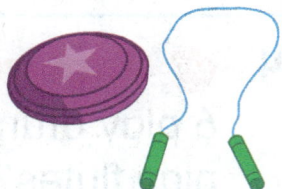

Which equations match the story?

5 + 2 = 7   7 − 2 = 5

2 + 3 = 5   5 − 2 = 3

Show how you know:

There are _____ jump ropes.

Name _____

Practice 1.9

Learning Target: Solve word problems that involve putting together and taking apart.

There are 7 cats. 3 are in a window. The rest are on a couch. How many cats are on the couch?

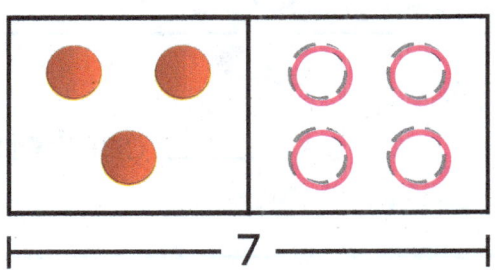

$\underline{3} + \underline{4} = \underline{7}$

$\underline{7} - \underline{3} = \underline{4}$

$\underline{4}$ cats

1. You have 8 markers. 2 are purple. The rest are blue. How many blue markers do you have?

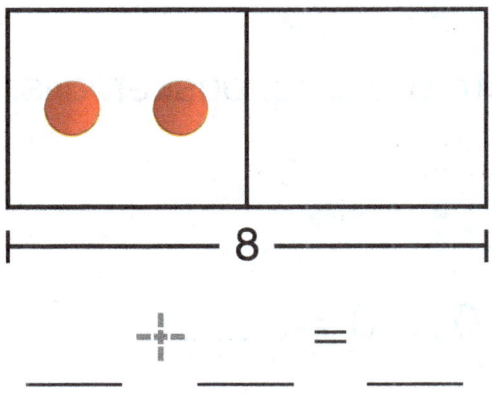

___ + ___ = ___

___ − ___ = ___

____ blue markers

2. There are 6 alligators. 3 are in a swamp. The rest are in the grass. How many alligators are in the grass?

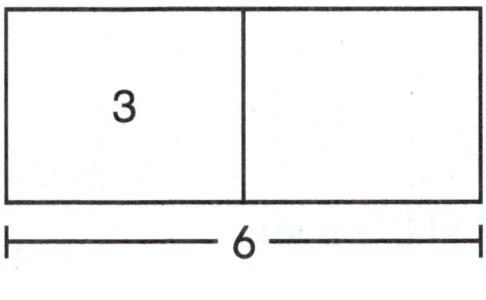

___ + ___ = ___

___ − ___ = ___

____ alligators

Chapter 1 | Lesson 9

fifty-five 55

3. **Analyze a Problem** There are 2 chickens inside a coop. Some more are outside the coop. There are 10 chickens in all. How many chickens are outside the coop? Use the model to write an equation and solve.

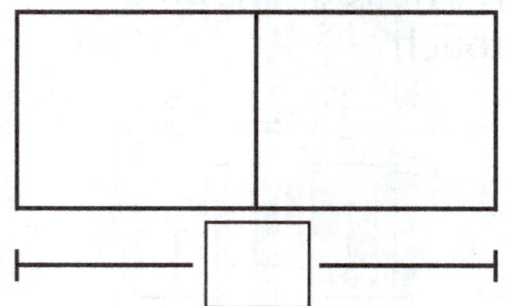

___ ◯ ___ = ___

___ chickens

4. **Modeling Real Life** Your teacher has 7 balls. 2 are soccer balls. The rest are basketballs. How many basketballs are there?

Which equations match the story?

$7 - 2 = 5$ $9 - 2 = 7$ $7 + 2 = 9$ $2 + 5 = 7$

Show how you know:

There are ___ basketballs.

Review & Refresh

Find the sum.

5. $6 + 0 =$ ___

6. $0 + 0 =$ ___

7. $5 + 1 =$ ___

8. $9 + 1 =$ ___

Name _____

Performance Task 1

1. 3 birds are on a wire. 5 birds are on a branch.

   a. 2 more birds land on the wire. How many birds are on the wire now?

   ____ birds

   b. 1 bird flies away from the branch. How many birds are on the branch now?

   ____ birds

   c. How many more birds are on the wire now than on the branch now?

   ____ more birds

2. **Use Equations** There are 6 birds. Draw some on the wire and some on the branch. Write an addition equation and a subtraction equation to match your picture.

____ ◯ ____ = ____   ____ ◯ ____ = ____

Three in a Row

To Play: Place the Three in a Row Game Cards in a pile. Players take turns. On your turn, flip over the top card and solve the problem. Place a counter on the answer. Your turn is over. Repeat until a player gets three in a row.

Name _____

Chapter Practice

1.1 Addition: Add To

1.
   There are 4 🐸.
   2 more 🐸 join them.
   Now there are ____ 🐸.

   ____ + ____ = ____

1.2 Solve Add To Problems

2. There are 5 🐙.
   3 more 🐙 join them.
   How many 🐙 are there now?

   ____ + ____ = ____

   ____ 🐙

3. **Modeling Real Life** You have 3 🖍. Your friend gives you 1 🖍. How many 🖍 do you have now?

   ____ 🖍

1.3 Solve *Put Together* Problems

4. You have 4 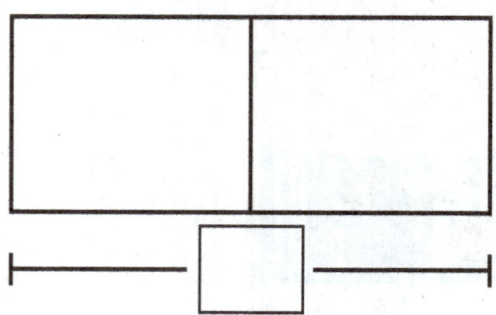 and 4 . How many flowers do you have in all?

___ + ___ = ___

___ flowers

1.4 Solve *Put Together* Problems with Both Addends Unknown

5. There are 10 . Some are standing up. The rest are knocked down. Draw two different pictures to show the .

___ = ___ + ___

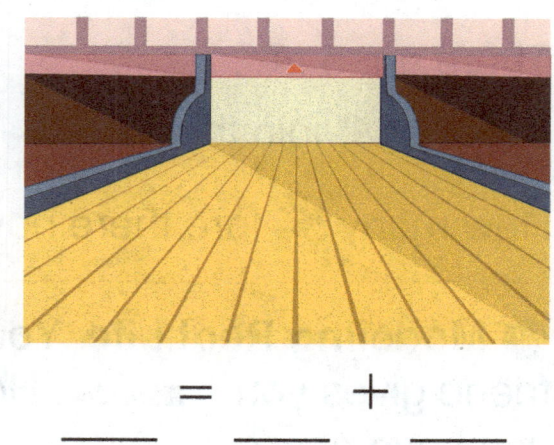

___ = ___ + ___

1.5 Solve *Take From* Problems

6. There are 7 .
3 swim away.
How many are left?

___ − ___ = ___

___

60   sixty

1.6 Solve *Compare* Problems: More

7. You have 6 whistles. Your friend has 3 whistles. How many more whistles do you have?

____ − ____ = ____

____ more whistles

8. There are 2 yellow blankets and 9 green blankets. Draw the missing blankets. How many more green blankets are there?

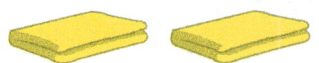

____ − ____ = ____

____ more green blankets

1.7 Solve *Compare* Problems: Fewer

9. You have 5 puzzles. Your friend has 7 puzzles. How many fewer puzzles do you have?

____ − ____ = ____

____ fewer puzzles

10. There are 8 red leaves and 4 orange leaves. Draw the missing leaves. How many fewer orange leaves are there?

____ − ____ = ____

____ fewer orange leaves

Solve *Add To* Problems with Change Unknown

11. You have 3 bracelets. Your friend gives you some more. Now you have 9. How many bracelets did your friend give you?

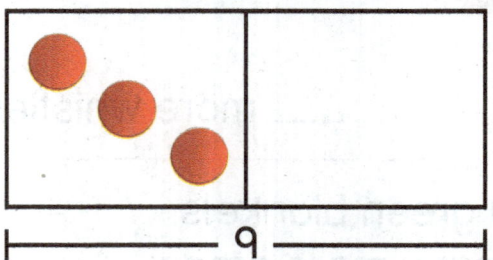

___ + ___ = ___

___ bracelets

12. You have 5 carrots. You buy some more. Now you have 10. How many carrots did you buy?

___ + ___ = ___

___ carrots

Connect *Put Together* and *Take Apart* Problems

13. You have 4 hats. 2 have polka dots. The rest have stripes. How many striped hats do you have?

___ + ___ = ___

___ — ___ = ___

___ striped hats

2 Fluency and Strategies within 10

- What is your favorite kind of flower?
- How many flowers do you see? If you pick 5 flowers, how many flowers will be left?

Chapter Learning Target:
Understand fluency and strategies.

Chapter Success Criteria:
- I can identify strategies.
- I can describe equations.
- I can explain rules.
- I can apply strategies.

sixty-three 63

2 Vocabulary

Review Words
addend
sum
difference

Organize It

Use the review words to complete the graphic organizer.

3 + 4 = 7

5 − 1 = 4

Define It

Use your vocabulary cards to match.

1. number line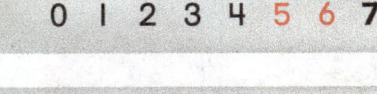

2. count on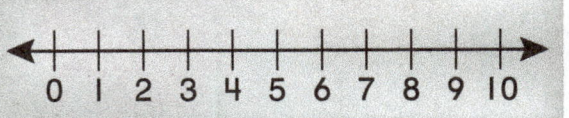

3. count back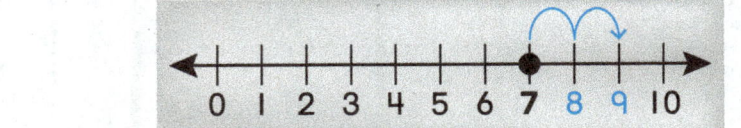

Chapter 2 Vocabulary Cards

count back	count on
doubles	doubles minus 1
doubles plus 1	number line

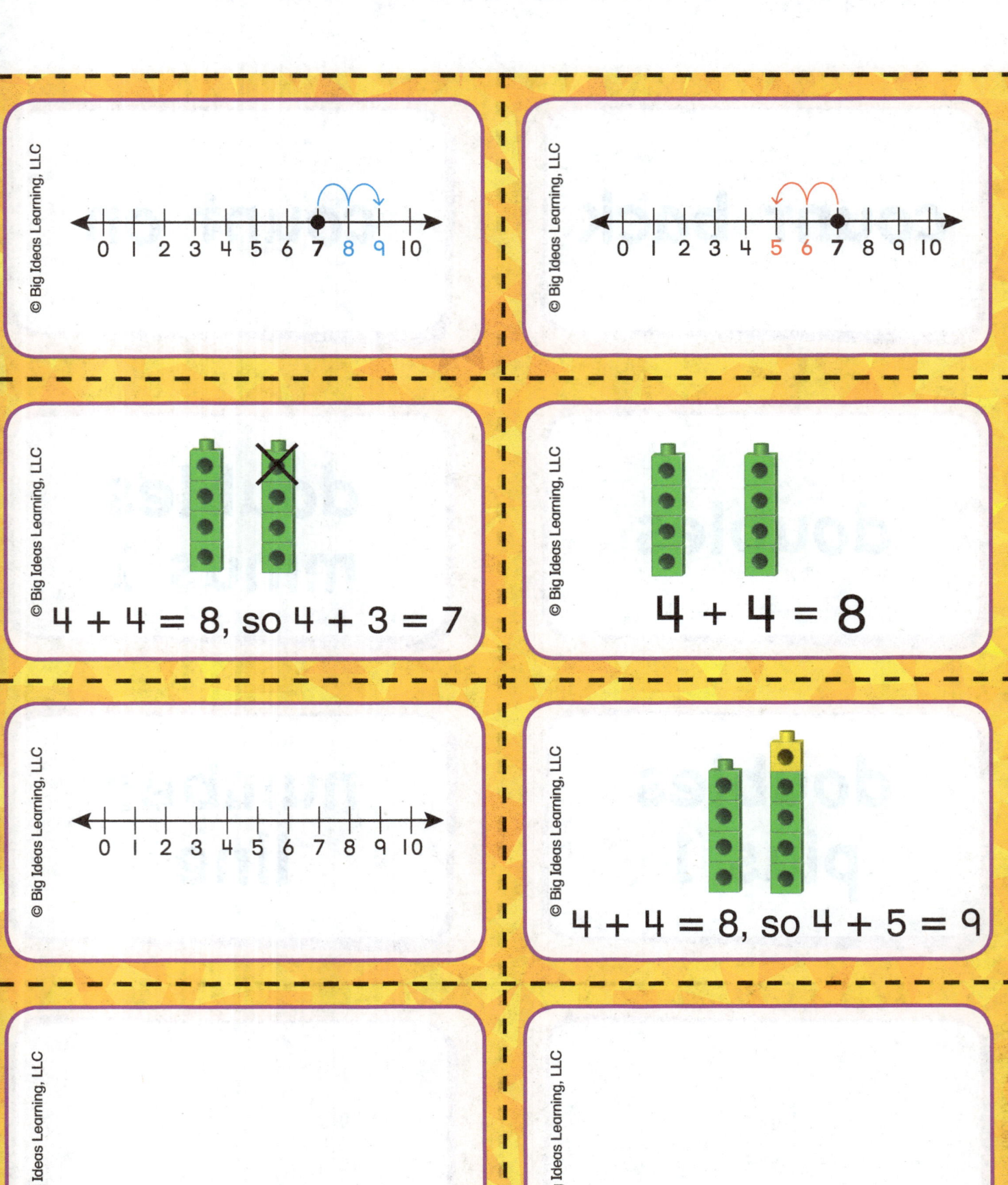

Name _____

Learning Target: Solve equations when an addend is 0.

Add 0 2.1

 Explore and Grow

Use linking cubes to model each story.

There are 6 ducks in the pond. 0 ducks join them. How many ducks are in the pond now?

_____ ducks

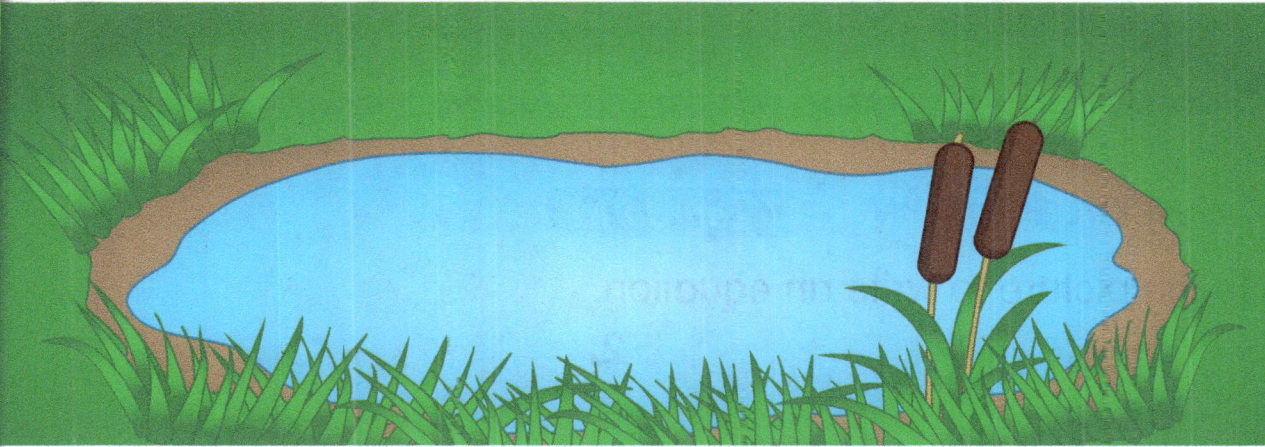

There are 0 ducks in the pond. 8 ducks go in the pond. How many ducks are in the pond now?

_____ ducks

Chapter 2 | Lesson 1

Think and Grow

When you add 0 to a number, the sum is that number.

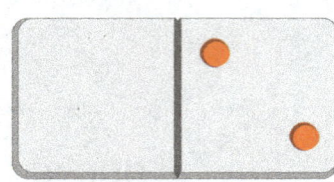

_5_ + 0 = _5_

0 + _2_ = _2_

When you add a number to 0, the sum is that number.

Show and Grow — I can do it!

Use the picture to write an equation.

1.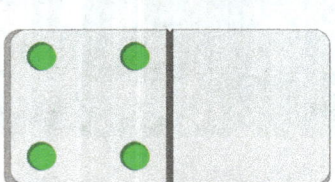

   ___ + 0 = ___

2.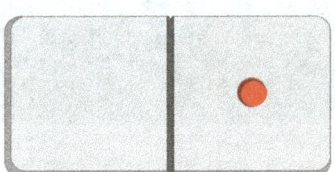

   0 + ___ = ___

3.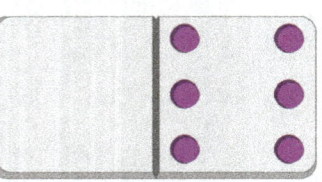

   0 + ___ = ___

4.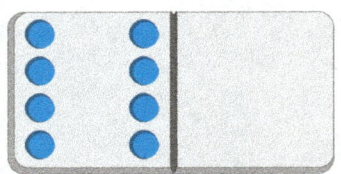

   ___ + 0 = ___

Name _____

✓ Apply and Grow: Practice

Use the picture to write an equation.

5.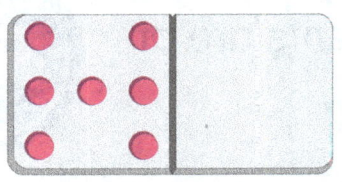

___ + 0 = ___

6.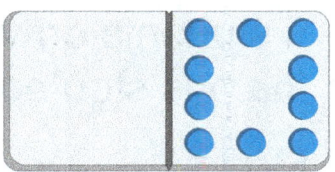

0 + ___ = ___

7. 9 + 0 = ___

8. 0 + 8 = ___

DIG DEEPER! Find each sum. Think: What do you notice?

9. 3 + 0 = ___

   0 + 3 = ___

10. 0 + 6 = ___

    6 + 0 = ___

11. **Logic** There are 7 penguins in all. How many penguins are inside the igloo?

____ penguins

Think and Grow: Modeling Real Life

There are no students at a bus stop. Then 9 students arrive. How many students are at the bus stop now?

Model:

Addition equation: _____

_____ students

Show and Grow   I can think deeper!

12. Your friend does not have any tokens. You give your friend 7 tokens. How many tokens does your friend have now?

Model:

Addition equation: _____

_____ tokens

Name _____

Practice 2.1

Learning Target: Solve equations when an addend is 0.

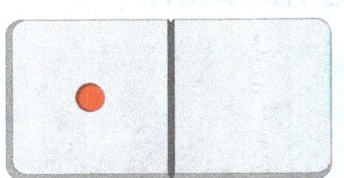

__1__ + 0 = __1__

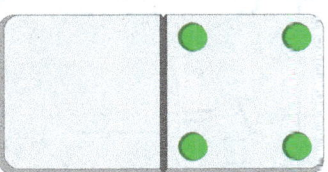

0 + __4__ = __4__

Use the picture to write an equation.

1.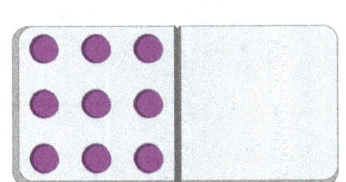

   ___ + 0 = ___

2.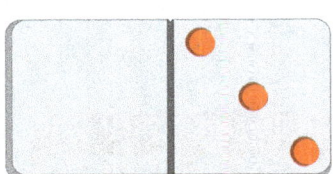

   0 + ___ = ___

3. $10 + 0 =$ ___

4. $0 + 5 =$ ___

5. $0 + 6 =$ ___

6. $0 + 0 =$ ___

Chapter 2 | Lesson 1

sixty-nine 69

7. DIG DEEPER! Find each sum. Think: What do you notice?

7 + 0 = ____

0 + 7 = ____

8. Logic There are 8 students in all. How many students are inside the museum?

____ students

9. Modeling Real Life There are no seals on the shore. Then 10 seals swim to the shore. How many seals are on the shore now?

____ seals

Review & Refresh

Write the number of goldfish.

10.  ____

11.  ____

12.  ____

13.  ____

Name _____

Learning Target: Subtract 0 and subtract all.

Subtract 0 and Subtract All 2.2

Explore and Grow

Use linking cubes to model each story.

There are 5 beavers on the log. None of the beavers leave. How many beavers are left?

____ beavers

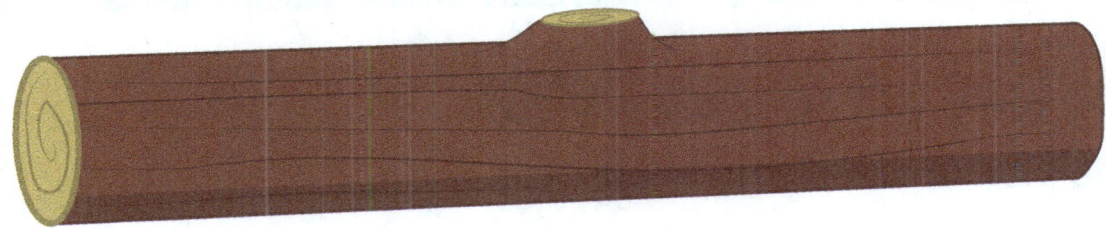

There are 5 beavers on the log. All of the beavers leave. How many beavers are left?

____ beavers

Chapter 2 | Lesson 2

seventy-one 71

Think and Grow

Number Sense
How is subtracting 0 like adding 0?

3 − 0 = 3

When you subtract a number from itself, the difference is 0.

3 − 3 = 0

Show and Grow — I can do it!

Use the picture to write an equation.

1.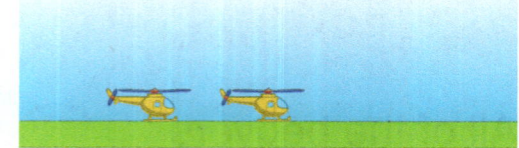

___ − 0 = ___

2.

___ − ___ = 0

3.

___ − 0 = ___

4.

___ − ___ = 0

Name _____

 Apply and Grow: Practice

Use the picture to write an equation.

5.

___ − 0 = ___

6.

___ − ___ = 0

7. 5 − 5 = ___

8. 6 − 0 = ___

9. 9 − 0 = ___

10. 7 − 7 = ___

11. **MP Structure** Complete the equation. Then use the words to complete the sentence.

4 − ___ = 4

When you _____ 0 from a number,

the _____ is that _____.

Words
difference
number
subtract

Chapter 2 | Lesson 2

Think and Grow: Modeling Real Life

Your friend has 7 pennies. You have 7 fewer pennies than your friend. How many do you have?

Draw a picture:

Subtraction equation:

_____ pennies

Show and Grow I can think deeper!

12. You have 6 pieces of chalk. You give all of your chalk to your friend. How many pieces do you have left?

Draw a picture:

Subtraction equation:

_____ pieces of chalk

Name _____

Practice 2.2

Learning Target: Subtract 0 and subtract all.

<u>6</u> − 0 = <u>6</u>

<u>6</u> − <u>6</u> = 0

Use the picture to write an equation.

1.

___ − 0 = ___

2.

___ − ___ = 0

3. 3 − 3 = ___

4. 1 − 0 = ___

5. 1 − 1 = ___

6. 7 − 0 = ___

Chapter 2 | Lesson 2

7. **Structure** Complete the equation. Then use the words to complete the sentence.

   9 − ___ = 0

   When you _____ a _____ from itself, the _____ is 0.

   Words
   difference
   number
   subtract

8. **Modeling Real Life** You have 4 stuffed animals. You give all of them to your friend. How many stuffed animals do you have left?

   ___ stuffed animals

9. **DIG DEEPER!** There are 8 turtle eggs in a nest. 5 eggs hatch. Then 3 more hatch. How many eggs are *not* hatched?

   ___ eggs

Review & Refresh

10. Write the number of dots you see on each domino. Then write the numbers in order.

    ___   ___   ___

    ___   ___   ___   ___

Name _____

Learning Target: Add and subtract 1.

Add and Subtract 1 **2.3**

Explore and Grow

Use linking cubes to model each story.

There are 7 kids on the bench. 1 kid joins them. How many kids are on the bench now?

_____ kids

There are 8 kids on the bench. 1 kid leaves. How many kids are left?

_____ kids

Chapter 2 | Lesson 3

Think and Grow

Find a Rule
When you add or subtract 1, what is true about the sum or difference?

4 + 1 = 5

4 - 1 = 3

Show and Grow — I can do it!

Use the picture to write an equation.

1.

___ - ___ = ___

2.

___ + ___ = ___

Apply and Grow: Practice

Use the picture to write an equation.

3.

___ + ___ = ___

4.

___ − ___ = ___

5. 5 − 1 = ___

6. 6 + 1 = ___

7. 8 + 1 = ___

8. 7 − 1 = ___

DIG DEEPER! Circle the problem with the greater sum or difference.

9.   2 − 1   2 + 1

10.   5 + 1   6 − 1

11. **YOU BE THE TEACHER** Circle to show who is correct. Show how you know.

3 + 1 = 2

3 + 1 = 4

Chapter 2 | Lesson 3

Think and Grow: Modeling Real Life

You have 9 action figures. Newton has 1 more than you. Descartes has 1 fewer than you. Who has more, Newton or Descartes?

Equations: Newton   Descartes

Who has more?   Newton   Descartes

Show and Grow — I can think deeper!

12. You have 5 video games. Newton has 1 fewer than you. Descartes has 1 more than you. Who has fewer, Newton or Descartes?

    Equations: Newton   Descartes

    Who has fewer?   Newton   Descartes

Name _____

Practice 2.3

Learning Target: Add and subtract 1.

$\underline{2} + \underline{1} = \underline{3}$

$\underline{2} - \underline{1} = \underline{1}$

Use the picture to write an equation.

1.

___ + ___ = ___

2.

___ − ___ = ___

3. 10 − 1 = ___

4. 7 + 1 = ___

DIG DEEPER! Circle the problem with the greater sum or difference.

5. 4 − 1   4 + 1 | 6. 7 + 1   8 − 1

7. **YOU BE THE TEACHER** Circle to show who is correct. Show how you know.

6 − 1 = _5_   6 − 1 = _7_

8. **Modeling Real Life** You have 3 karate belts. Newton has 1 fewer than you. Descartes has 1 more than you. Who has fewer, Newton or Descartes?

Who has fewer?   Newton   Descartes

Review & Refresh

9. Use the picture to complete the number bond.

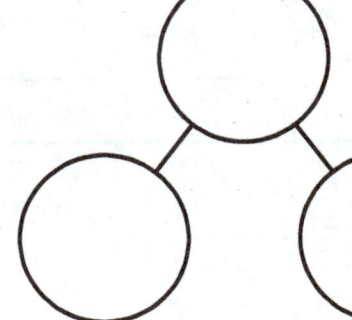

Name _____

Learning Target: Find the sum of doubles from 1 to 5.

Add Doubles from 1 to 5 **2.4**

 Explore and Grow

Use counters to model the story.

You have 3 balls. Your friend has 3 balls. How many balls are there in all?

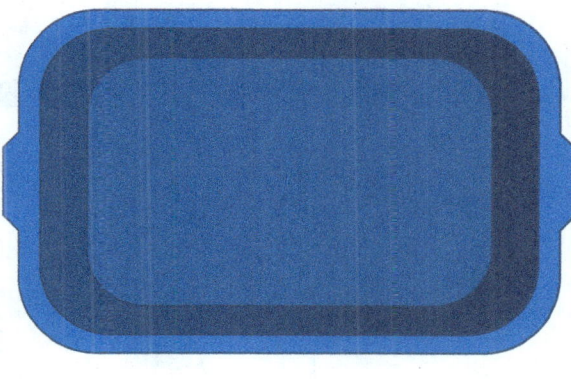

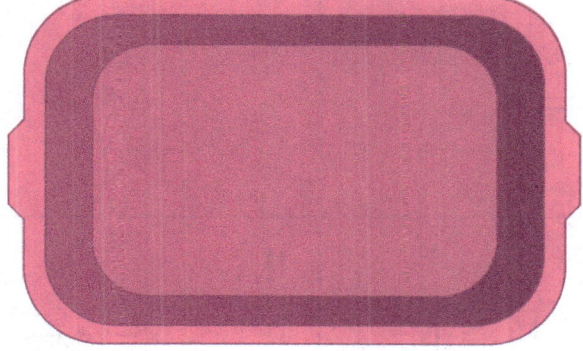

_____ balls

Chapter 2 | Lesson 4

eighty-three 83

 **Think and Grow**

The addends are the same.

3 + 3 = 6

 2
 + 2
___
4

2 + 2 and 3 + 3 are **doubles**.

Show and Grow — I can do it!

1.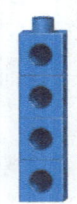

___ + ___ = ___

2.

___ + ___ = ___

3.

 + ▢ / ▢

4.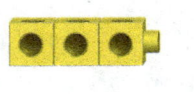

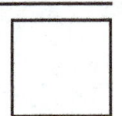 + ▢ / ▢

84 eighty-four

Name _____

✓ Apply and Grow: Practice

5.

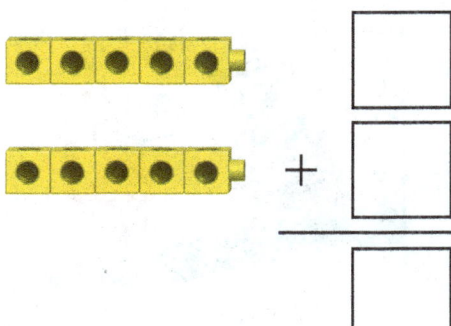

6.

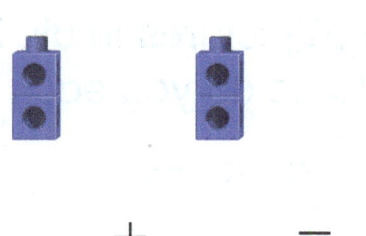

___ + ___ = ___

7. 2 + 2 = ___

8. 5 + 5 = ___

9.
```
    3
+   3
-----
   ☐
```

10.
```
    4
+   4
-----
   ☐
```

11. **DIG DEEPER!** Circle the equations you can complete using doubles.

___ + ___ = 6   ___ + ___ = 5

___ + ___ = 9   ___ + ___ = 2

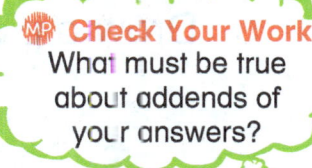
Check Your Work
What must be true about addends of your answers?

Think and Grow: Modeling Real Life

You and your friend color the same number of pictures. There are 10 pictures in all. How many pictures do you each color?

Draw a picture:

Addition equation:

_____ pictures

Show and Grow   I can think deeper!

12. You and your friend have the same number of flowers. There are 8 flowers in all. How many flowers do you each have?

Draw a picture:

Addition equation:

_____ flowers

Name _____

Practice  2.4

Learning Target: Find the sum of doubles from 1 to 5.

$\underline{1} + \underline{1} = \underline{2}$

$\begin{array}{r} 5 \\ + 5 \\ \hline 10 \end{array}$

1. ___ + ___ = ___

2. ___ + ___ = ___ (stacked)

3. $2 + 2 =$ ___

4. $4 + 4 =$ ___

5. $\begin{array}{r} 5 \\ + 5 \\ \hline \end{array}$

6. $\begin{array}{r} 3 \\ + 3 \\ \hline \end{array}$

Chapter 2 | Lesson 4

eighty-seven 87

7. **DIG DEEPER!** Circle the equations you can complete using doubles.

___ + ___ = 3   ___ + ___ = 8

___ + ___ = 4   ___ + ___ = 7

8. **Modeling Real Life** Newton and Descartes each have the same number of linking cubes. There are 6 linking cubes in all. How many linking cubes do Newton and Descartes each have?

_____ linking cubes

9. **DIG DEEPER!** You have 7 blocks. Your friend has 3 blocks. Draw to show how you can share the blocks equally.

Review & Refresh

Use the picture to write an equation.

10.

___ + ___ = ___

11.

___ + ___ = ___

Name _____

Use Doubles 2.5

Learning Target: Use the *doubles plus 1* and *doubles minus 1* strategies to find a sum.

Explore and Grow

Use counters to model the story.

You collect 4 shells. Your friend collects 4 shells. How many shells are there in all?

_____ shells

You collect 4 shells. Your friend collects 5 shells. How many shells are there in all?

_____ shells

Chapter 2 | Lesson 5

Think and Grow

Use the double 4 + 4 to find each sum.

4 + 5 = __9__   4 + 3 = __7__

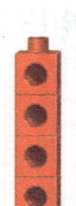 

doubles plus 1

4 + 5 is equal to 4 + 4 and 1 more.

doubles minus 1

4 + 3 is equal to 1 less than 4 + 4.

Show and Grow I can do it!

Use the double 3 + 3 to find each sum.

1. 3 + 4 = ____

```
   3
+  2
-----
```

Name _____

 **Apply and Grow: Practice**

Use the double 2 + 2 to find each sum.

2. 2 + 3 = ___

2 + 1 = ___

Find the sum. Write the double you used.

3. 3 + 4 = ___

___ + ___ = ___

4.
```
   5
 + 4
 ───
  □
```

```
   □
 + □
 ───
  □
```

5. **DIG DEEPER!** Use each card once to write two addition equations.

3   2   2
2   4   5

___ + ___ = ___

___ + ___ = ___

Chapter 2 | Lesson 5

Think and Grow: Modeling Real Life

You eat 4 grapes. Your friend eats 1 more than you. How many grapes do you and your friend eat in all?

Which doubles can you use to find the sum?

4 + 4   5 + 5   3 + 3

Addition equation:

_____ grapes

Show and Grow   I can think deeper!

6. You have 5 toy cars. Your friend has 1 fewer than you. How many cars do you and your friend have in all?

   Which doubles can you use to find the sum?

   4 + 4   6 + 6   5 + 5

   Addition equation:

   _____ toy cars

Name _____

Practice 2.5

Learning Target: Use the *doubles plus 1* and *doubles minus 1* strategies to find a sum.

Use the double 3 + 3 to find each sum.

3 + 4 = __7__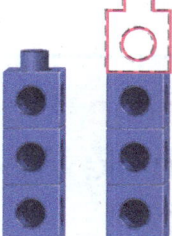

3 + 2 = __5__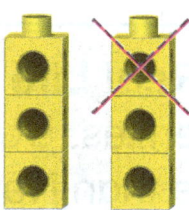

Use the double 4 + 4 to find each sum.

1. 4 + 5 = ____

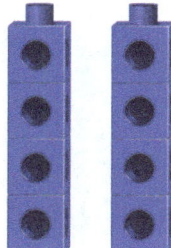

4 + 3 = ____

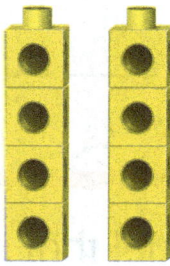

Find the sum. Write the double you used.

2. 1 + 2 = ____

___ + ___ = ___

3. 3 + 2 = ____

___ + ___ = ___

Chapter 2 | Lesson 5

ninety-three 93

4. **DIG DEEPER!** Use each card once to write two addition equations.

___ + ___ = ___

___ + ___ = ___

5. **Modeling Real Life** Newton catches 2 butterflies. Descartes catches 1 more than Newton. How many butterflies do Newton and Descartes catch in all?

Which doubles can you use to find the sum?

3 + 3   1 + 1   2 + 2

___ butterflies

6. **Patterns** Find the sums. Think: What do you notice?

4 + 5 = ___

4 + 4 = ___

5 + 5 = ___

Review & Refresh

7. Circle the model that shows the missing number.

2 + ___ = 5

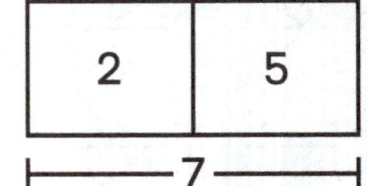

Name _____

Learning Target: Add in any order to find a sum.

Add in Any Order  2.6

Explore and Grow

Use counters to model each problem. What do you notice?

$$4 + 3 = \underline{}$$

$$3 + 4 = \underline{}$$

Chapter 2 | Lesson 6

ninety-five 95

 Think and Grow

$\underline{5} + \underline{3} = \underline{8}$

$\underline{3} + \underline{5} = \underline{8}$

Change the order of the addends.

MP Structure
Does the order of the addends change the sum?

Show and Grow I can do it!

1. ___ + ___ = ___   ___ + ___ = ___

2. ___ + ___ = ___   ___ + ___ = ___

3.  ☐ + ☐ = ☐    ☐ + ☐ = ☐

96 ninety-six

Name _____

✓ Apply and Grow: Practice

4.

___ + ___ = ___   ___ + ___ = ___

Find the sum. Then change the order of the addends. Write the new addition problem.

5.
```
   1
+  4
_____
  ☐
```
```
+  ☐
   ☐
_____
   ☐
```

6.
```
   5
+  2
_____
  ☐
```
```
+  ☐
   ☐
_____
   ☐
```

7. 2 + 6 = ___

___ + ___ = ___

8. ___ = 8 + 1

___ = ___ + ___

9. **MP Analyze a Problem** Use the numbers shown to write two addition equations.

4   9   5

___ + ___ = ___

___ + ___ = ___

MP Communicate Clearly
How did you choose the addends?

Think and Grow: Modeling Real Life

You have 7 shirts. 3 are green. The rest are blue. How many blue shirts do you have?

Which equations describe your shirts?

$3 + 4 = 7$ $3 + 7 = 10$

$7 + 3 = 10$ $4 + 3 = 7$

Show how you know:

You have _____ blue shirts.

Show and Grow   I can think deeper!

10. You have 5 cups. 2 are yellow. The rest are red. How many red cups do you have?

    Which equations describe your cups?

    $5 + 2 = 7$ $2 + 3 = 5$

    $2 + 5 = 7$ $3 + 2 = 5$

    Show how you know:

    You have _____ red cups.

98 ninety-eight

Name _____

Practice 2.6

Learning Target: Add in any order to find a sum.

1.

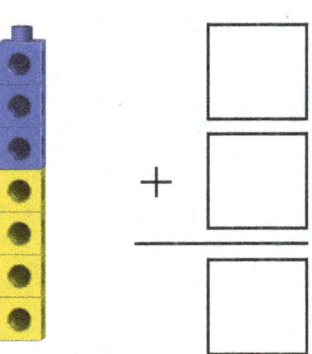

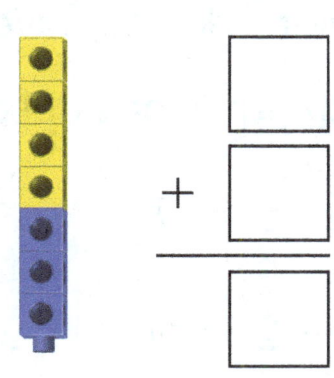

2.

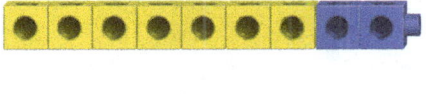

___ + ___ = ___   ___ + ___ = ___

Find the sum. Then change the order of the addends. Write the new addition problem.

3.

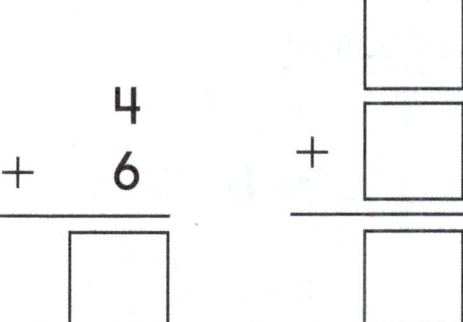

4.

___ = 5 + 1

___ = ___ + ___

Chapter 2 | Lesson 6

ninety-nine 99

5. **Analyze a Problem** Use the numbers shown to write two addition equations.

8   10   2

___ + ___ = ___

___ + ___ = ___

6. **Which One Doesn't Belong?** Which picture represents a different sum?

7. **Modeling Real Life** You have 7 tomatoes. 2 are red. The rest are yellow. How many yellow tomatoes do you have?

Which equations describe your tomatoes?

$2 + 5 = 7$ $5 + 2 = 7$

$7 + 2 = 9$ $2 + 7 = 9$

Show how you know:

You have ___ yellow tomatoes.

Review & Refresh

8. Use the ten frame to complete the equation.

$5 + $ ___ $= 8$

100   one hundred

Name _____

Learning Target: Use the *count on* strategy to find a sum.

Count On to Add 2.7

 Explore and Grow

Model the story.

There are 5 coins in a piggy bank. You put in 2 more. How many coins are in the bank now?

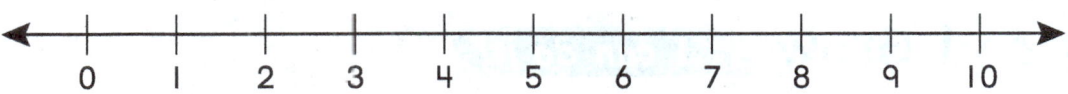

____ coins

Chapter 2 | Lesson 7

Think and Grow

To add, **count on**.

4 + 3 = __7__

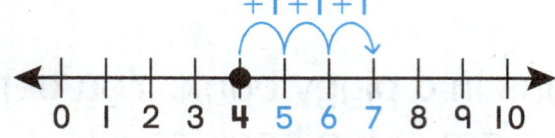

Start at 4. Count on 3.

This **number line** shows the numbers 0 through 10.

Show and Grow I can do it!

1. 7 + 2 = ____

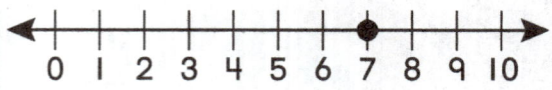

2. 3 + 1 = ____

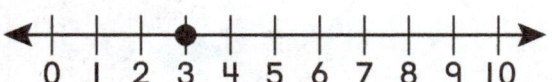

3. 4 + 6 = ____

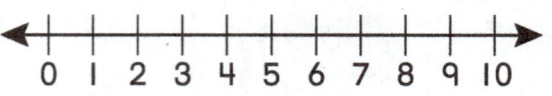

4. 0 + 5 = ____

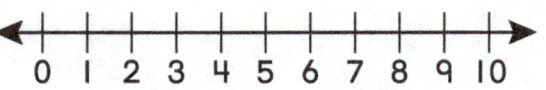

Name _____

✓ Apply and Grow: Practice

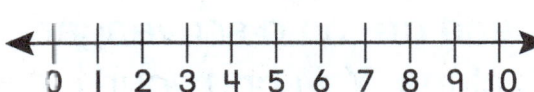

5. 4 + 2 = ___

6. 6 + 1 = ___

7.
     5
 + 4
  ☐

8.
     3
 + 2
  ☐

9. ___ = 0 + 7

10. ___ = 2 + 8

11. **DIG DEEPER!** Tell what problems Newton and Descartes solved. Think: How are the problems the same? How are they different?

  ___ + ___ = ___

 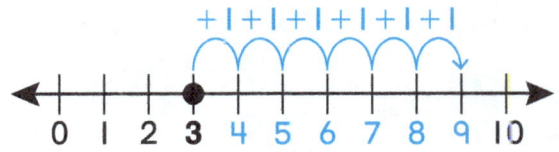 ___ + ___ = ___

Chapter 2 | Lesson 7   one hundred three **103**

Think and Grow: Modeling Real Life

You and your friend are on a scavenger hunt. You find 3 clues. You and your friend find 8 clues in all. How many clues does your friend find?

Model:

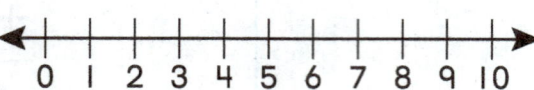

_____ clues

Show and Grow   I can think deeper!

12. Your friend collects 4 cans. You and your friend collect 10 cans in all. How many cans do you collect?

Model:

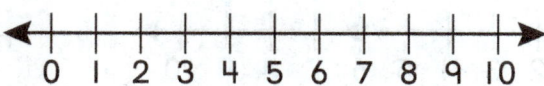

_____ cans

Name _____

Practice 2.7

Learning Target: Use the *count on* strategy to find a sum.

$8 + 2 = \underline{10}$

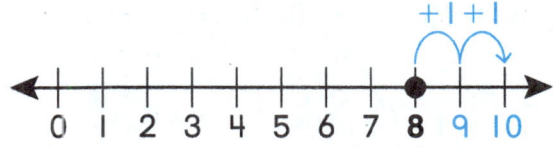

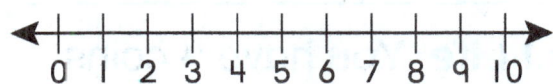

1. $4 + 3 =$ _____

2. $8 + 1 =$ _____

3. $6 + 2 =$ _____

4. $7 + 3 =$ _____

5.
```
     0
  +  9
  ─────
  ☐
```

6. _____ $= 1 + 5$

Chapter 2 | Lesson 7

7. **DIG DEEPER!** Tell what problems Newton and Descartes solved. Think: How are the problems the same? How are they different?

 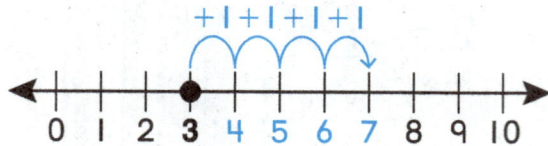   ___ + ___ = ___

 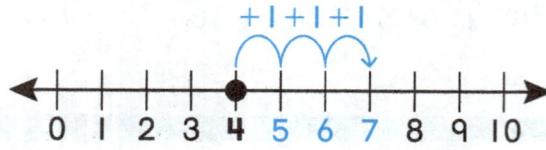   ___ + ___ = ___

8. **Modeling Real Life** You have 4 coins. You and your friend have 9 coins in all. How many coins does your friend have?

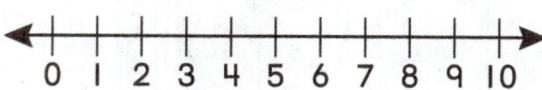

___ coins

Review & Refresh

Use the picture to write an equation.

9.

___ − ___ = ___

10.

___ − ___ = ___

Name _____

Learning Target: Use the *count back* strategy to find a difference.

Count Back to Subtract

Explore and Grow

Model the story.

There are 8 students in a line. 2 of them leave. How many students are left?

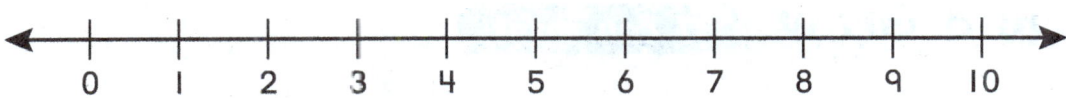

_____ students

Chapter 2 | Lesson 8

 **Think and Grow**

 To subtract, **count back**.

$8 - 3 = 5$

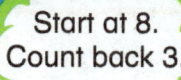 Start at 8. Count back 3.

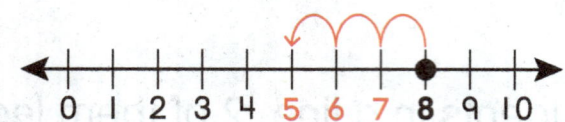

Show and Grow *I can do it!*

1. $5 - 4 =$ ___

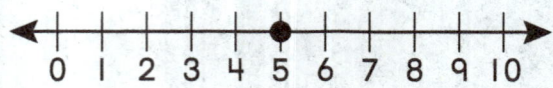

2. $7 - 3 =$ ___

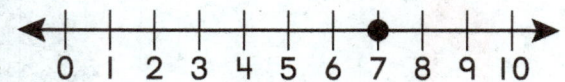

3. $6 - 1 =$ ___

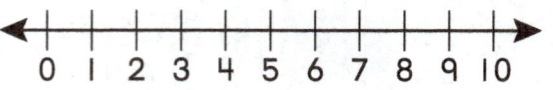

4. $10 - 8 =$ ___

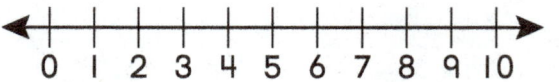

Name _____

 **Apply and Grow: Practice**

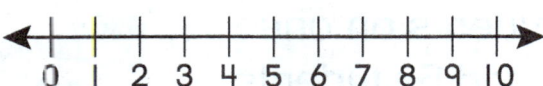

5. $10 - 6 =$ _____

6. $9 - 3 =$ _____

7. $\begin{array}{r} 5 \\ -2 \\ \hline \square \end{array}$

8. $\begin{array}{r} 8 \\ -0 \\ \hline \square \end{array}$

9. _____ $= 7 - 6$

10. _____ $= 4 - 1$

11. **Structure** Write the problem shown.

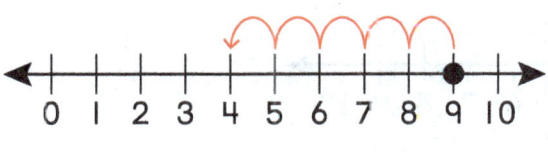

___ − ___ = ___

Use Math Tools
How does a number line help you add and subtract?

Chapter 2 | Lesson 8

Think and Grow: Modeling Real Life

There are 5 students on one side of a table and 5 students on the other. 7 students leave. How many students are left?

Model:

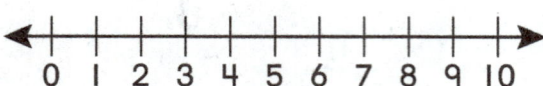

_____ students

Show and Grow   I can think deeper!

12. You have 4 board games and 4 card games. You give 3 games to your friend. How many games do you have left?

    Model:

    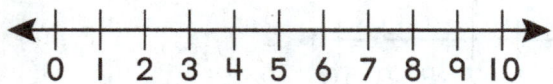

    _____ games

110   one hundred ten

Name _____

Practice 2.8

Learning Target: Use the *count back* strategy to find a difference.

$8 - 5 = \underline{3}$

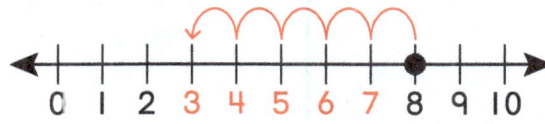

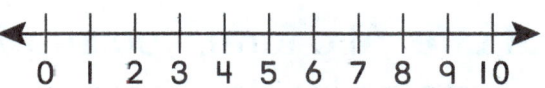

1. $5 - 4 = \underline{}$

2. $8 - 3 = \underline{}$

3. $9 - 1 = \underline{}$

4. $6 - 2 = \underline{}$

5.
$$\begin{array}{r} 7 \\ -5 \\ \hline \end{array}$$

6. $\underline{} = 10 - 5$

Chapter 2 | Lesson 8

7. Structure Write the problem shown.

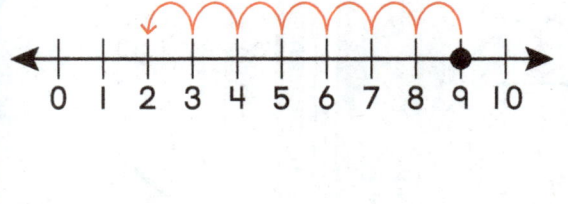

____ − ____ = ____

8. Modeling Real Life You have 4 star stickers and 4 heart stickers. You give 6 away. How many stickers do you have left?

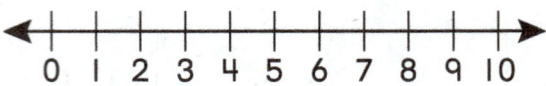

____ stickers

9. Modeling Real Life At a farm, you see 7 cows and 3 calves outside. Some go inside. There are 4 animals left. How many animals go inside?

____ animals

Review & Refresh

10. Use the pictures to write the related equations.

____ ○ ____ = ____   ____ ○ ____ = ____

Use Addition to Subtract 2.9

Learning Target: Use the *add to subtract* strategy to find a difference.

Explore and Grow

Use counters to model each problem.

$$4 + \underline{} = 7$$

$$7 - 4 = \underline{}$$

Chapter 2 | Lesson 9

Think and Grow

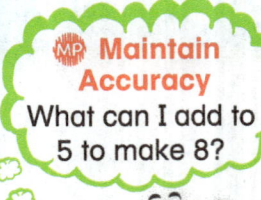

Maintain Accuracy
What can I add to 5 to make 8?

8 − 5 = ?

Count on 3 to make 8.

Think 5 + __3__ = 8. So, 8 − 5 = __3__.

Show and Grow   I can do it!

1.   5 − 4 = ?

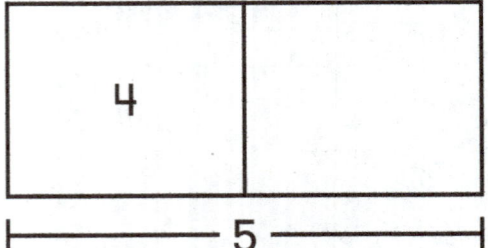

Think 4 + ____ = 5.

So, 5 − 4 = ____.

2.   6 − 3 = ?

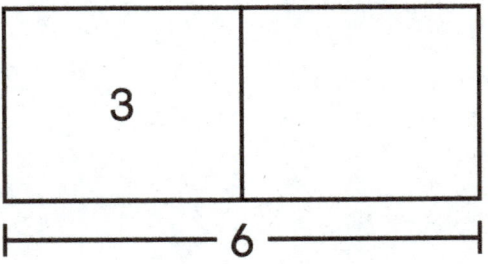

Think 3 + ____ = 6.

So, 6 − 3 = ____.

Name _____

 Apply and Grow: Practice

3.   8 − 4 = ?

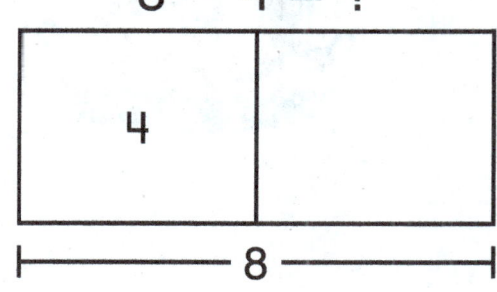

Think 4 + ____ = 8.

So, 8 − 4 = ____.

4.   7 − 5 = ?

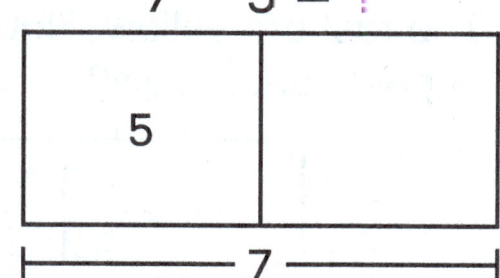

Think 5 + ____ = 7.

So, 7 − 5 = ____.

5.   6 − 4 = ?

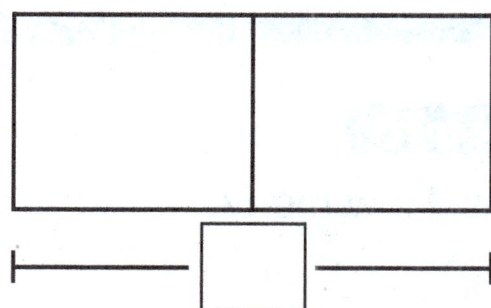

Think ____ + ____ = ____.

So, 6 − 4 = ____.

6.   9 − 6 = ?

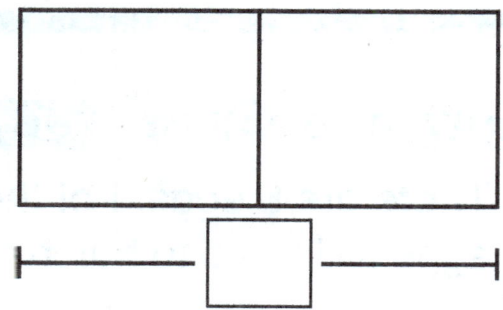

Think ____ + ____ = ____.

So, 9 − 6 = ____.

7. **YOU BE THE TEACHER** There are 8 goats. 2 of them leave. Newton uses addition to tell how many goats are left. Is he correct? Show how you know.

8 + 2 = 10
10 goats are left.

Chapter 2 | Lesson 9

Think and Grow: Modeling Real Life

There are 10 puppies. 7 are brown. The rest are yellow. How many puppies are yellow?

Model:

Subtraction equation:

_____ puppies

Show and Grow — I can think deeper!

8. There are 8 eggs. 1 of them hatches. How many eggs still need to hatch?

Model:

Subtraction equation:

_____ eggs

Name _____ Practice **2.9**

Learning Target: Use the *add to subtract* strategy to find a difference.

5 − 4 = ?

| 4 | ○ |

⊢——— 5 ———⊣

Think 4 + __1__ = 5.

So, 5 − 4 = __1__.

1. 3 − 2 = ?

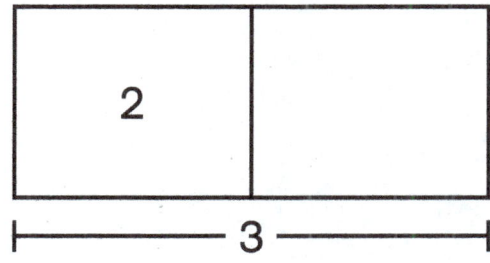

Think 2 + ____ = 3.

So, 3 − 2 = ____.

2. 10 − 5 = ?

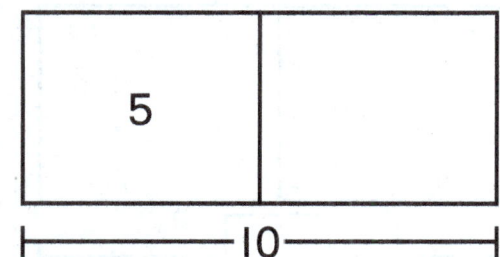

Think 5 + ____ = 10.

So, 10 − 5 = ____.

3. 9 − 5 = ?

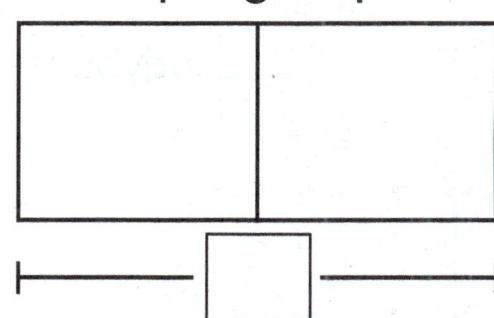

Think ____ + ____ = ____.

So, 9 − 5 = ____.

4. 7 − 6 = ?

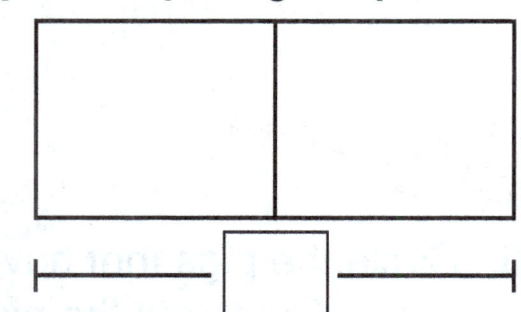

Think ____ + ____ = ____.

So, 7 − 6 = ____.

Chapter 2 | Lesson 9   one hundred seventeen **117**

5. **YOU BE THE TEACHER** There are 8 birds. 5 fly away. Descartes uses addition to tell how many birds are left. Is he correct? Show how you know.

5 + 3 = 8
3 birds are left.

6. **Modeling Real Life** There are 9 kittens. 7 are adopted. How many kittens still need to be adopted?

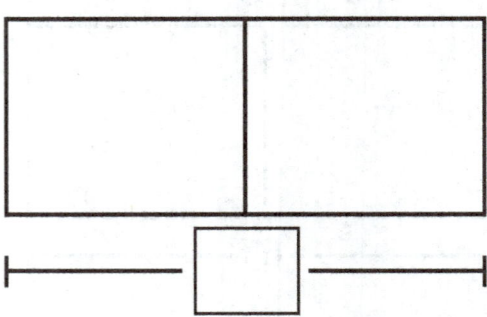

____ kittens

7. **DIG DEEPER!** You and your friend want to find 10 ladybugs. You find 5. Your friend finds 2. How many more ladybugs do you and your friend need to find?

____ ladybugs

Review & Refresh

8. Circle the pigs that have spots. Cross out the pigs that do *not* have spots.

Name _____

Performance Task 2

1. You plant 4 red flower seeds and 4 yellow flower seeds. Your friend plants 5 red flower seeds and 4 yellow flower seeds.

   a. 1 of your yellow seeds does not grow. How many of your flowers grow?

   _____ flowers

   b. 3 of your friend's red seeds do not grow. How many of your friend's flowers grow?

   _____ flowers

   c. Who has more flowers?

   You   Friend

   Make a Plan
   Read the question carefully. Which numbers should you use to solve?

   d. How many more red flowers do you have than your friend?

   _____ flowers

Chapter 2

Add or Subtract

To Play: Players take turns. On your turn, spin both spinners. Write the numbers on your Add or Subtract Recording Sheet. Decide whether you want to add or subtract the numbers you spin. Place a counter on your sum or difference. Your turn is over. Play until a player gets 4 counters in a row.

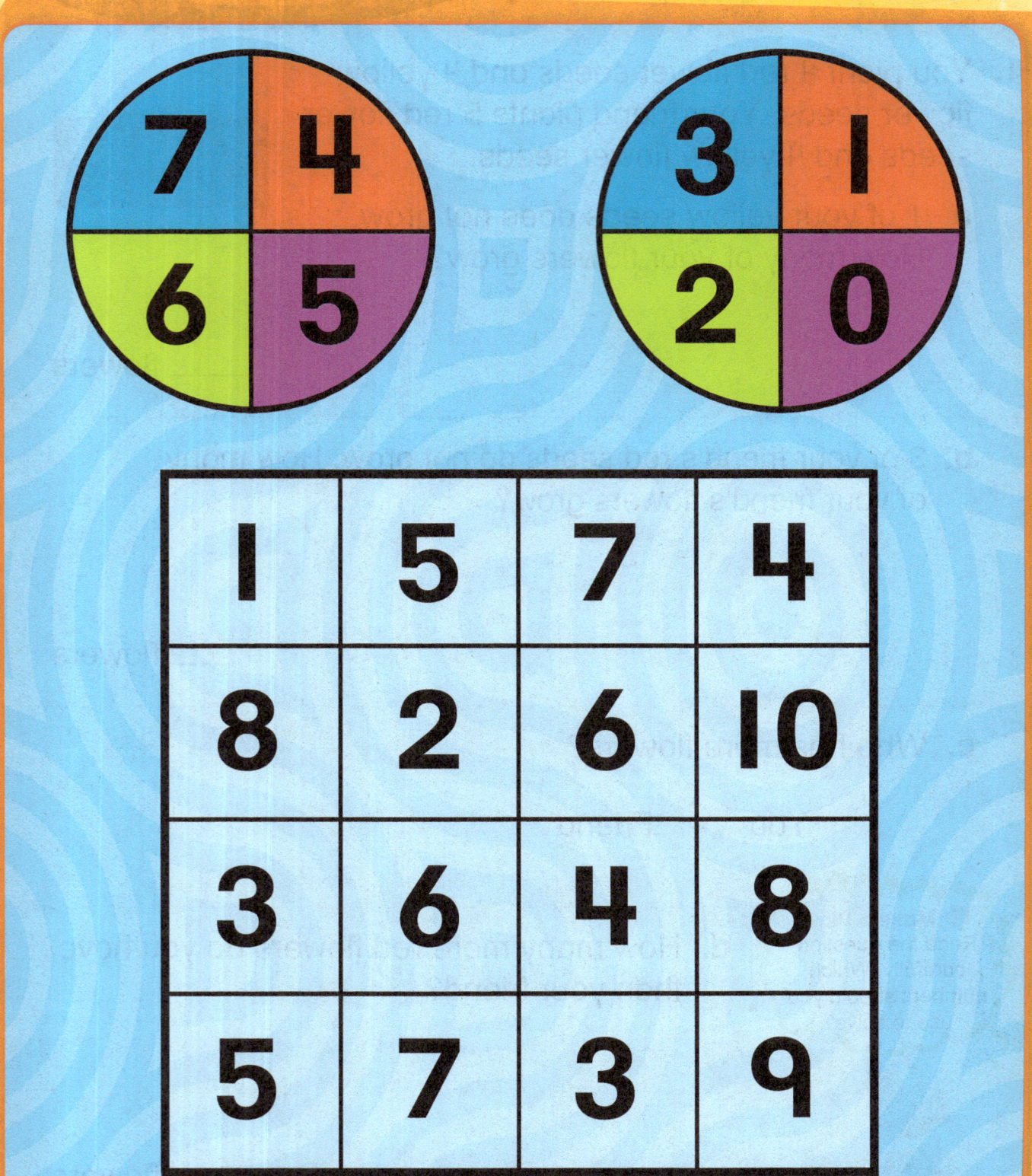

Chapter 2 Practice

2.1 Add 0

Use the picture to write an equation.

1.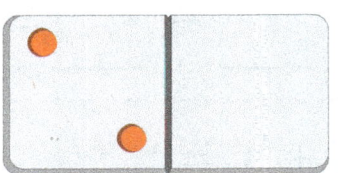

   ___ + 0 = ___

2.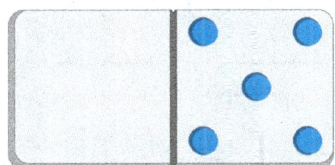

   0 + ___ = ___

3. 7 + 0 = ___

4. 0 + 6 = ___

2.2 Subtract 0 and Subtract All

Use the picture to write an equation.

5.

   ___ − 0 = ___

6.

   ___ − ___ = 0

7. 9 − 9 = ___

8. 8 − 0 = ___

2.3 Add and Subtract 1

Use the picture to write an equation.

9.

___ + ___ = ___

10.

___ − ___ = ___

11. 3 − 1 = ___

12. 5 + 1 = ___

2.4 Add Doubles from 1 to 5

13.

___ + ___ = ___

14.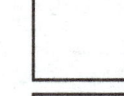

+

15. **Reasoning** Circle the equations you can complete using doubles.

___ + ___ = 10

___ + ___ = 3

___ + ___ = 6

___ + ___ = 7

2.5 Use Doubles

Use the double 2 + 2 to find each sum.

16. 2 + 3 = ___   2 + 1 = ___

Find the sum. Write the double you used.

17. 4 + 5 = ___

___ + ___ = ___

18.
$$\begin{array}{r} 4 \\ +\ 3 \\ \hline \end{array}$$

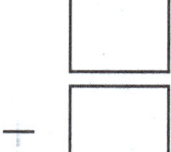

2.6 Add in Any Order

19.

___ + ___ = ___   ___ + ___ = ___

20. **Analyze a Problem** Use the numbers shown to write two addition equations.

9   6   3

___ + ___ = ___

___ + ___ = ___

2.7 Count On to Add

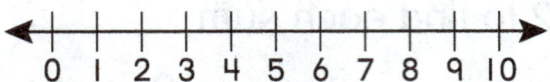

21. 5 + 2 = ___

22. 6 + 4 = ___

2.8 Count Back to Subtract

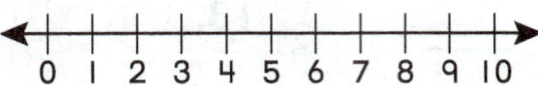

23. 9 − 7 = ___

24. 10 − 5 = ___

2.9 Use Addition to Subtract

25. 5 − 3 = ?

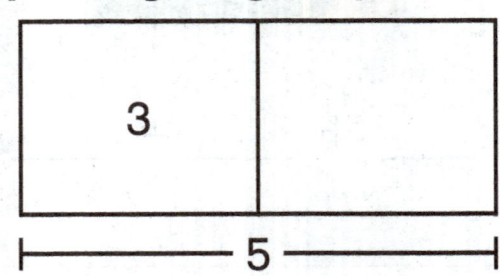

Think 3 + ___ = 5.

So, 5 − 3 = ___.

26. 9 − 8 = ?

Think 8 + ___ = 9.

So, 9 − 8 = ___.

Name _____

3 Vocabulary

Review Words
count on
number line

Organize It

Use the review words to complete the graphic organizer.

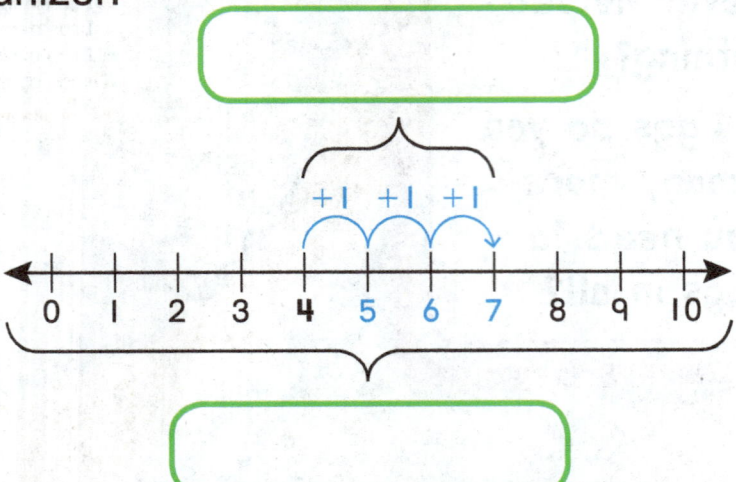

Define It

Use your vocabulary cards to identify the words.

2 + 3 = 5
3 + 2 = 5
5 − 2 = 3
5 − 3 = 2

126   one hundred twenty-six

Chapter 3 Vocabulary Cards

bar model

fact family

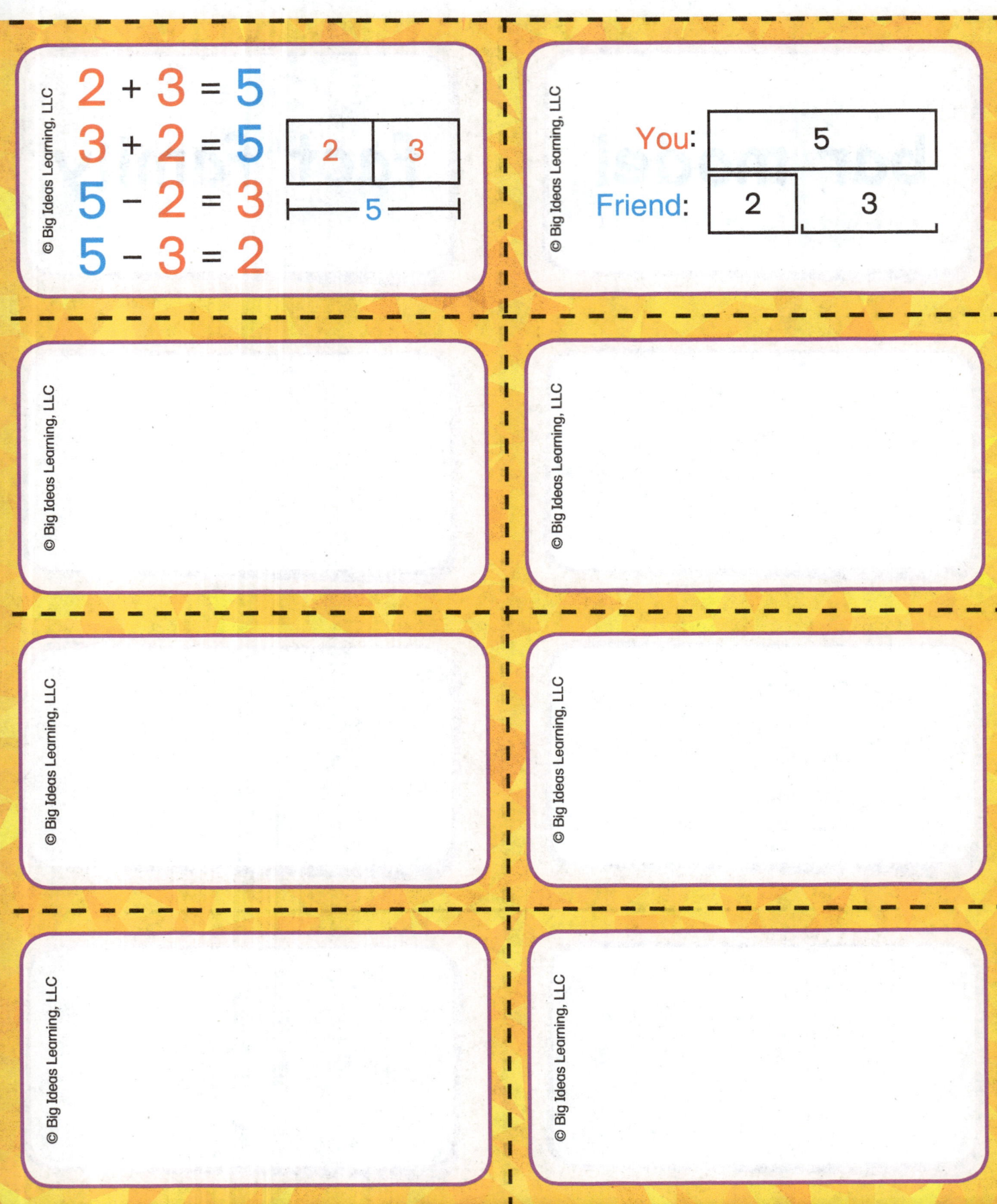

Name _____

Learning Target: Solve for a missing addend given an addend and the sum.

Solve *Add To* Problems with Start Unknown 3.1

Explore and Grow

Use counters to model each problem.

$$\begin{array}{r} 2 \\ + \ \square \\ \hline 5 \end{array}$$

$$\begin{array}{r} \square \\ + \ 2 \\ \hline 5 \end{array}$$

Chapter 3 | Lesson 1

one hundred twenty-seven 127

Think and Grow

? + 4 = 6

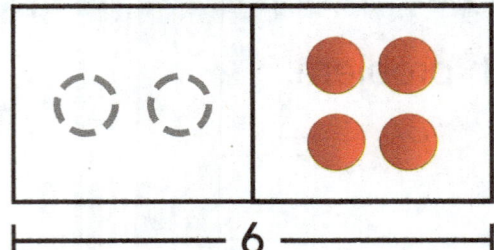

2 + 4 = 6

Draw more dots to make the whole.

Show and Grow I can do it!

1. ? + 5 = 8

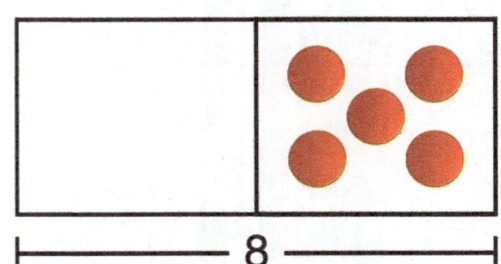

___ + 5 = 8

2. ? + 2 = 3

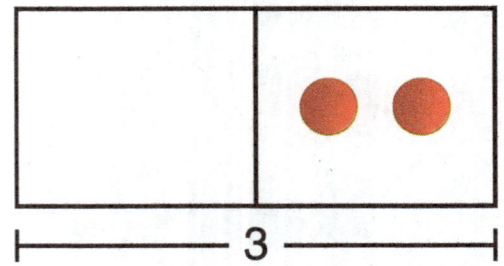

___ + 2 = 3

Name _____

 **Apply and Grow: Practice**

3. ? + 3 = 7

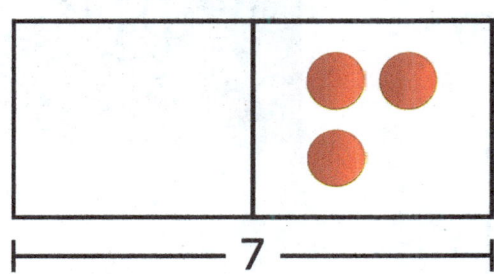

___ + 3 = 7

4. ? + 8 = 10

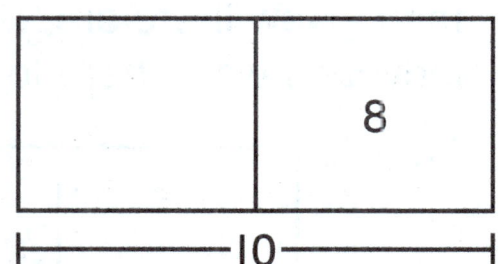

___ + 8 = 10

5. ___ + 4 = 9

6. ___ + 0 = 5

7. **DIG DEEPER!** Complete the model and the equation to match.

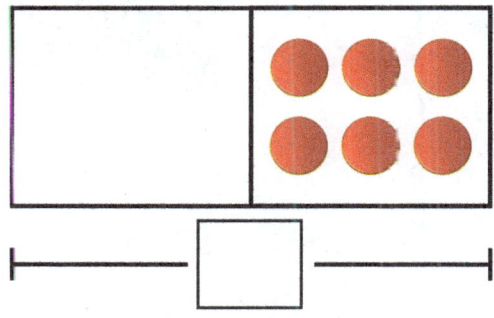

___ + ___ = 8

Communicate Clearly
In the model, what shows the addends? the sum?

Chapter 3 | Lesson 1

one hundred twenty-nine 129

Think and Grow: Modeling Real Life

There are some ladybugs. 2 more join them. Now there are 9. How many ladybugs were there to start?

Model:

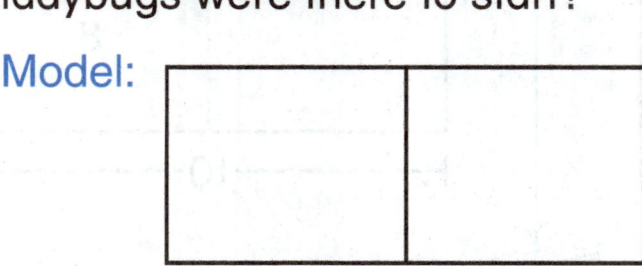

Addition equation: _____

_____ ladybugs

Show and Grow — I can think deeper!

8. You have some books. You get 4 more books. Now you have 10. How many books did you have to start?

Model:

Addition equation: _____

_____ books

Name _____   Practice **3.1**

Learning Target: Solve for a missing addend given an addend and the sum.

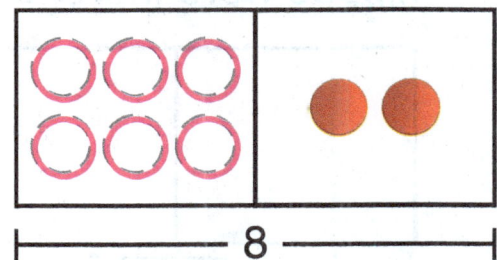
? + 2 = 8

Draw more dots to make the whole.

_6_ + 2 = 8

1. ? + 5 = 10
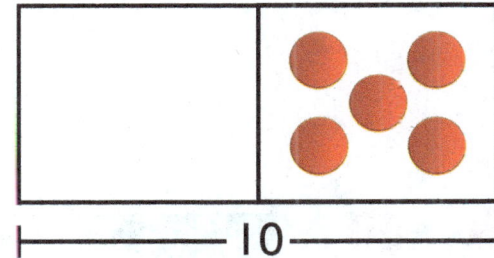
___ + 5 = 10

2. ? + 1 = 4
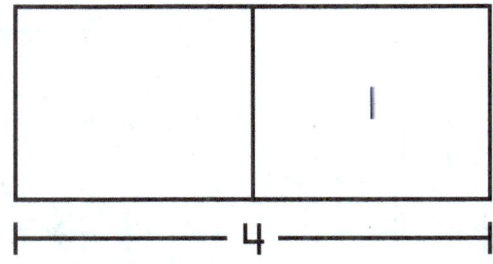
___ + 1 = 4

3. ___ + 2 = 7

4. ___ + 3 = 9

Chapter 3 | Lesson 1   one hundred thirty-one **131**

5. **DIG DEEPER!** Complete the model and the equation to match.

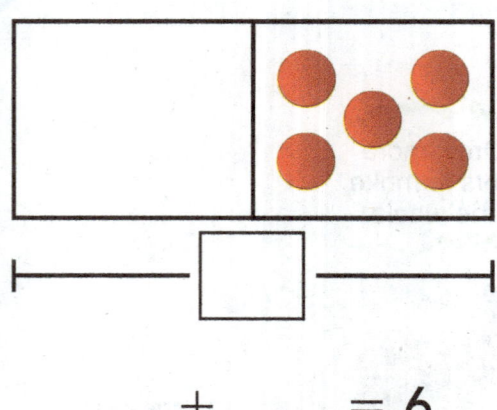

___ + ___ = 6

6. **Modeling Real Life** There are some hippos. 6 more join them. Now there are 9. How many hippos were there to start?

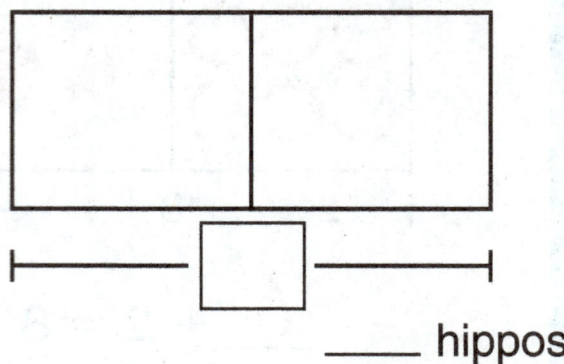

___ hippos

7. **DIG DEEPER!** Which model can you use to complete the equation?

___ + 1 = 5

Review & Refresh

8. You have 3 ⚽. You lose 1 ⚽. How many ⚽ do you have left?

___ − ___ = ___

___

Name _____

Learning Target: Solve a subtraction equation to find the missing part.

Solve *Take From* Problems with Change Unknown 3.2

Explore and Grow

Use counters to model each problem.

$$\begin{array}{r} 6 \\ -\ 2 \\ \hline \square \end{array}$$

$$\begin{array}{r} 6 \\ -\ \square \\ \hline 2 \end{array}$$

Chapter 3 | Lesson 2   one hundred thirty-three 133

# Think and Grow

$4 - ? = 1$

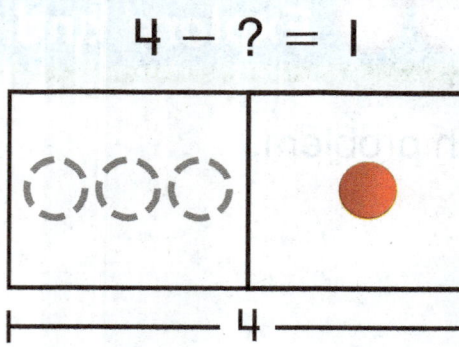

Draw more dots to make the whole.

$4 - \underline{3} = 1$

Show and Grow I can do it!

1. $7 - ? = 2$

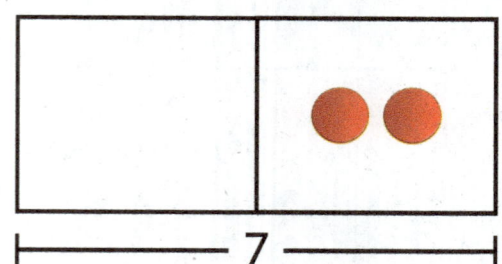

$7 - \underline{} = 2$

2. $5 - ? = 3$

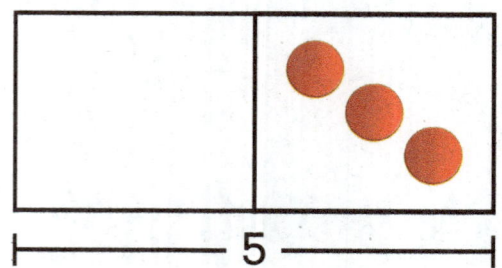

$5 - \underline{} = 3$

Name _____

 **Apply and Grow: Practice**

3. 8 − ? = 2

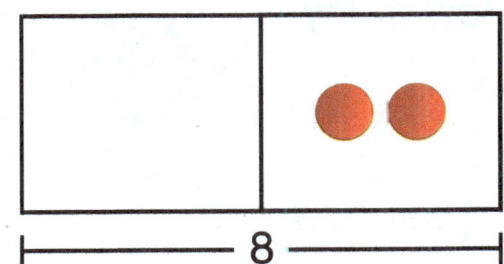

8 − ___ = 2

4. 9 − ? = 6

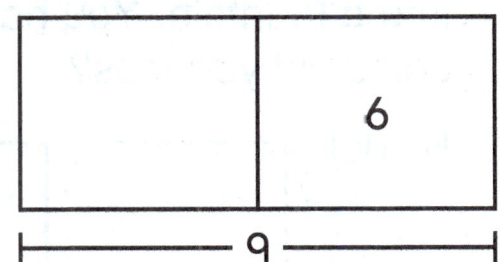

9 − ___ = 6

5. 3 − ___ = 0

6. 10 − ___ = 5

7. **Repeated Reasoning** Match each model with its correct equation.

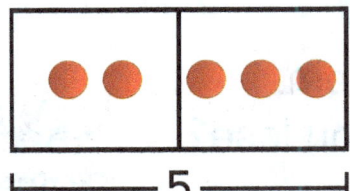

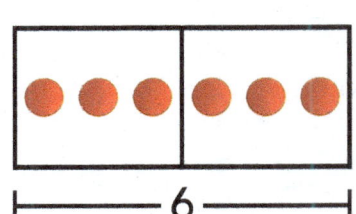

7 − 2 = 5

5 − 2 = 3

6 − 3 = 3

Chapter 3 | Lesson 2

# Think and Grow: Modeling Real Life

You have 9 coins. You toss some of them into a fountain. You have 5 left. How many coins did you toss?

Model: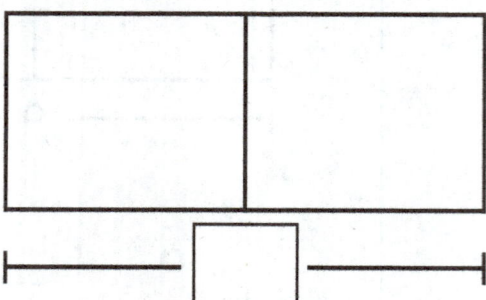

Subtraction equation: _____

_____ coins

Show and Grow   I can think deeper!

8. You have 8 crayons. You lose some of them. You have 2 left. How many crayons did you lose?

Model: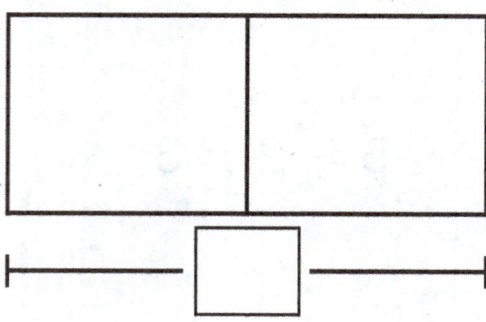

Subtraction equation: _____

_____ crayons

Name _____

Practice 3.2

Learning Target: Solve a subtraction equation to find the missing part.

6 − ? = 2

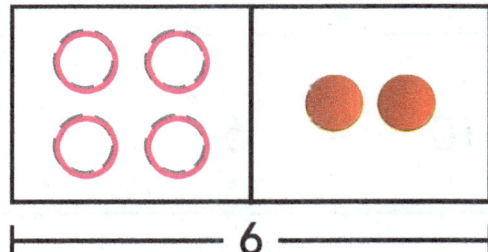

Draw more dots to make the whole.

6 − _4_ = 2

1. 8 − ? = 4

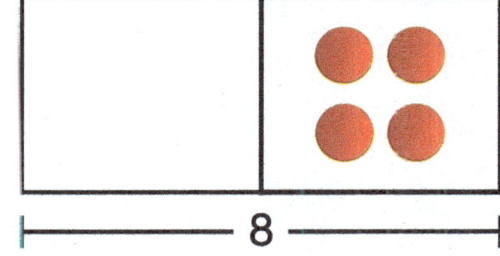

8 − ___ = 4

2. 7 − ? = 3

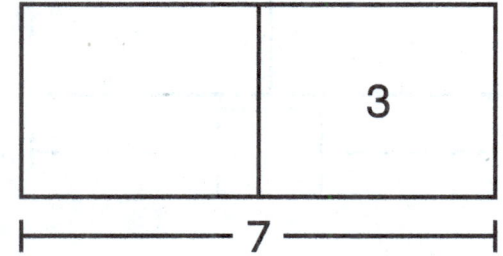

7 − ___ = 3

3. 5 − ___ = 4

4. 6 − ___ = 6

Chapter 3 | Lesson 2

5. **Repeated Reasoning** Match each model with its correct equation.

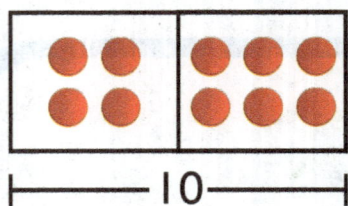

$10 - 7 = 3$

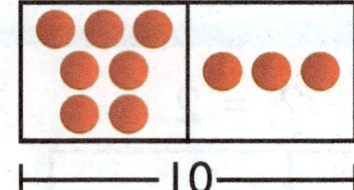

$10 - 4 = 6$

6. **Modeling Real Life** You have 10 toys. Your friend borrows some of them. You have 7 left. How many toys did your friend borrow?

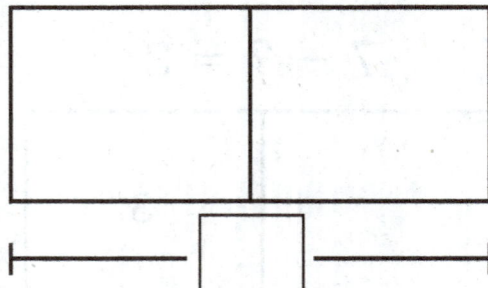

_____ toys

7. **DIG DEEPER!** There are 9 pigeons on a curb. 3 of them fly away, and some of them jump down to the street. There are 4 left. How many pigeons jumped down to the street?

_____ pigeons

Review & Refresh

8. You have 4 🖊. You buy 1 more 🖊. How many 🖊 do you have now?

___ + ___ = ___

___ 🖊

Solve Take From Problems with Start Unknown 3.3

Learning Target: Solve a subtraction equation to find the whole.

Explore and Grow

Use counters to model each problem.

$$3 + 4 = \underline{}$$

$$\underline{} - 3 = 4$$

Use a Similar Problem How are the equations related?

Chapter 3 | Lesson 3

Think and Grow

? − 3 = 2

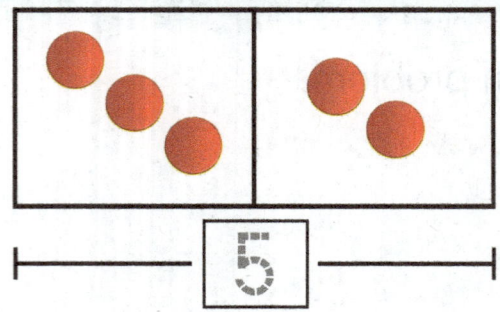

Think 3 + 2 = __5__.

So, __5__ − 3 = 2.

Add the parts to find the whole.

Show and Grow I can do it!

1. ? − 2 = 4

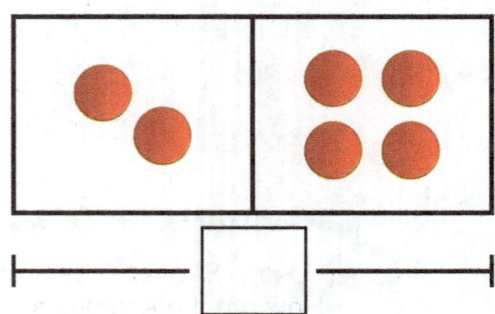

Think 2 + 4 = ____.

So, ____ − 2 = 4.

2. ? − 1 = 1

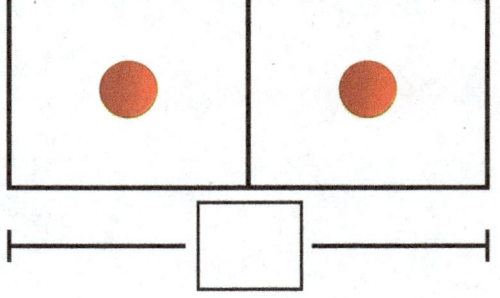

Think 1 + 1 = ____.

So, ____ − 1 = 1.

Name _____

Apply and Grow: Practice

3. ? − 2 = 5

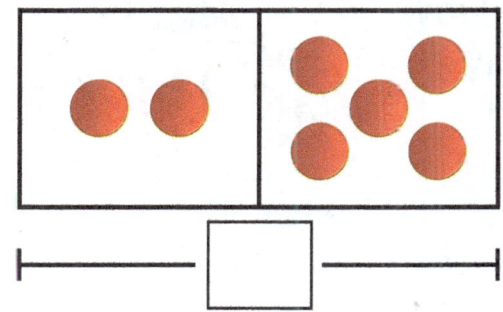

Think 2 + 5 = ____.

So, ____ − 2 = 5.

4. ? − 3 = 6

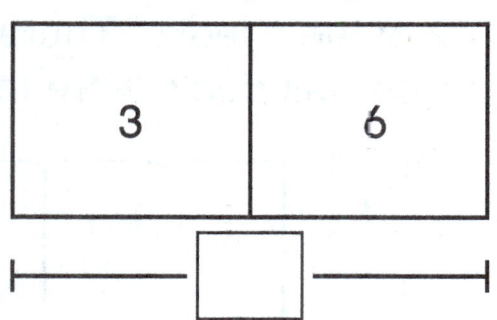

Think 3 + 6 = ____.

So, ____ − 3 = 6.

5. ? − 4 = 1

Think 4 + 1 = ____.

So, ____ − 4 = 1.

6. ? − 6 = 4

Think 6 + 4 = ____.

So, ____ − 6 = 4.

7. **Structure** Circle the equations that match the model.

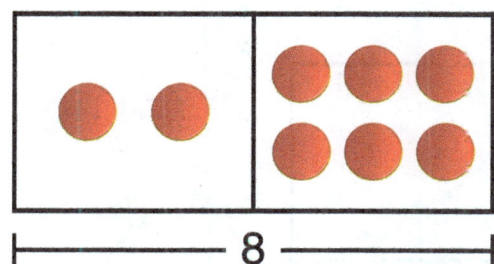

8 − 2 = 6   8 + 2 = 10

6 − 2 = 4   2 + 6 = 8

Think and Grow: Modeling Real Life

A group of students are at a playground. 2 of them leave. There are 8 left. How many students were there to start?

Model:

Subtraction equation:

_____ students

Show and Grow   I can think deeper!

8. You have some strawberries. You eat 9 of them. You have 0 left. How many strawberries did you have to start?

Model:

Subtraction equation:

_____ strawberries

Name _____

Practice 3.3

Learning Target: Solve a subtraction equation to find the whole.

? − 3 = 1

Think 3 + 1 = **4**.

So, **4** − 3 = 1.

[whole shown as 4]

1. ? − 7 = 2

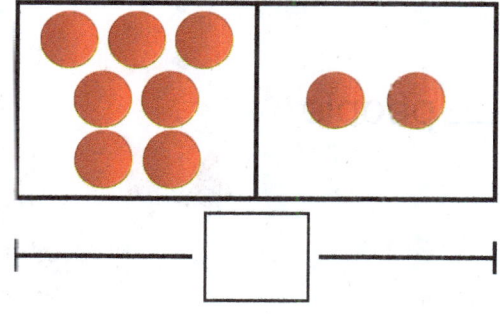

Think 7 + 2 = ____.

So, ____ − 7 = 2.

2. ? − 2 = 8

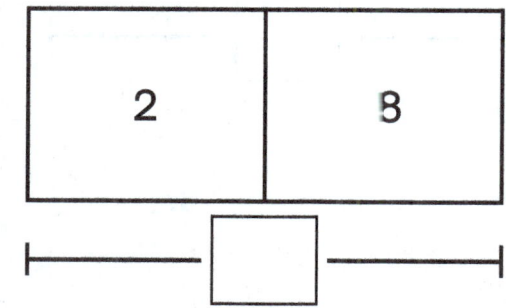

Think 2 + 8 = ____.

So, ____ − 2 = 8.

3. ? − 3 = 0

Think 3 + 0 = ____.

So, ____ − 3 = 0.

4. ? − 2 = 6

Think 2 + 6 = ____.

So, ____ − 2 = 6.

Chapter 3 | Lesson 3

5. **Structure** Circle the equations that match the model.

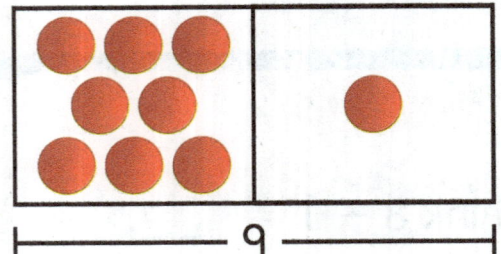

$8 - 1 = 7$ $9 + 1 = 10$

$9 - 8 = 1$ $8 + 1 = 9$

6. **Modeling Real Life** There are some people on a trolley. 4 of them exit. There are 4 people left. How many people were on the trolley to start?

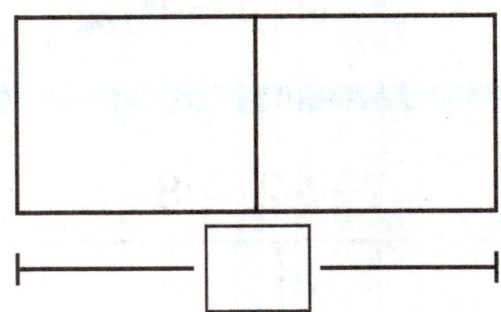

_____ people

Analyze a Problem Which words help you find the parts and the whole?

Review & Refresh

7. There are 5 blue balloons and 3 red balloons. How many more blue balloons are there?

____ − ____ = ____

_____ more blue balloons

144   one hundred forty-four

Name _____

Learning Target: Solve *compare* word problems when given how many more.

Compare Problems: Bigger Unknown 3.4

 Explore and Grow

Use counters to model the story.

Newton has 5 balls. Descartes has 2 more balls than Newton. How many balls does Descartes have?

Descartes

Newton

Descartes has ____ balls.

# Think and Grow

Your friend has 4 stickers. You have 1 more than your friend. How many stickers do you have?

bar model

You: 5

Friend: 4 | 1

4 + 1 = 5

5 stickers

Show and Grow — I can do it!

1. Your friend has 7 trading cards. You have 3 more than your friend. How many trading cards do you have?

   You:

   Friend: 7

   7 + ___ = ___

   ___ trading cards

Apply and Grow: Practice

2. Your friend has 1 soccer ball. You have 2 more than your friend. How many soccer balls do you have?

You: [   ]

Friend: [1]

1 + ___ = ___

___ soccer balls

3. Your friend swims 4 more laps than you. You swim 3 laps. How many laps does your friend swim?

Friend: [   ]

You: [   ]

___ + ___ = ___

___ laps

4. **Precision** Your friend catches 5 more fish than you. You catch 2 fish. How many fish does your friend catch? Circle the bar model that matches the problem.

Friend: [5]   You: [2] 3

Friend: [7]   You: [2] 5

Chapter 3 | Lesson 4

Think and Grow: Modeling Real Life

Your friend has 1 yellow flower and 2 red flowers. You have 3 more flowers than your friend. How many flowers do you have?

Model: You:
Friend:

Addition equation:

_____ flowers

Show and Grow   I can think deeper!

5. Your friend has 6 gray shirts and 2 blue shirts. You have 2 more shirts than your friend. How many shirts do you have?

Model: You:
Friend:

Addition equation:

_____ shirts

148   one hundred forty-eight

Name _____

Practice 3.4

Learning Target: Solve *compare* word problems when given how many more.

Your friend has 2 toy cars. You have 4 more than your friend. How many toy cars do you have?

You: | 6 |
Friend: | 2 | 4 |

2 + _4_ = _6_

_6_ toy cars

1. You have 3 key chains. Your friend has 5 more than you. How many key chains does your friend have?

Friend: [ ]
You: | 3 |

3 + ___ = ___

___ key chains

2. You have 8 more bracelets than your friend. Your friend has 2 bracelets. How many bracelets do you have?

You: [ ]
Friend: [ ]

___ + ___ = ___

___ bracelets

Chapter 3 | Lesson 4   one hundred forty-nine   149

3. **Precision** You have 1 seashell. Your friend has 8 more than you. How many seashells does your friend have? Circle the bar model that matches the problem.

| Friend: | 9 | | Friend: | 8 |
| You: | 1 | 8 | | You: | 1 | 7 |

4. **Modeling Real Life** Your friend has 2 comic books and 2 mystery books. You have 3 more books than your friend. How many books do you have?

You:
Friend:

_____ books

Review & Refresh

5. There are 2 blue crayons and 6 red crayons. How many fewer blue crayons are there?

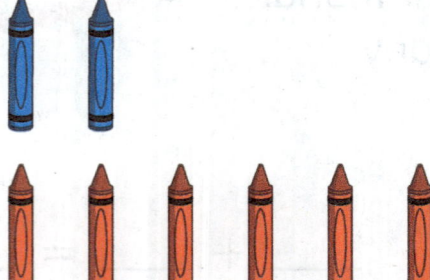

___ − ___ = ___

___ fewer blue crayons

Name _____

Learning Target: Solve *compare* word problems when given how many fewer.

Compare Problems: Smaller Unknown 3.5

Explore and Grow

Use counters to model the story.

Newton has 5 treats. Descartes has 2 fewer treats than Newton. How many treats does Descartes have?

Newton

Descartes

Descartes has ____ treats.

Think and Grow

Your friend builds 6 sand castles. You build 4 fewer than your friend. How many sand castles do you build?

Friend: 6

You: 2 | 4

You can subtract or add to find the missing part!

6 − 4 = 2

2 + 4 = 6

2 sand castles

Show and Grow — I can do it!

1. Your friend has 8 stones. You have 1 fewer than your friend. How many stones do you have?

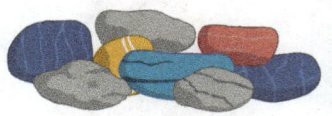

Friend:

You: _____ | 1

___ − ___ = ___

___ + ___ = ___

____ stones

152   one hundred fifty-two

Name _____

 **Apply and Grow: Practice**

2. You blow 5 bubbles. Your friend blows 2 fewer than you. How many bubbles does your friend blow?

You: [   ]
Friend: [| 2]

___ + ___ = ___

___ − ___ = ___

___ bubbles

3. You have 3 fewer oranges than your friend. Your friend has 9 oranges. How many oranges do you have?

Friend: [   ]
You: [|]

___ ◯ ___ = ___

___ oranges

4.  Complete the bar model. Do both equations match the bar model?

You: [8   ]
Friend: [| 3]

$8 - 3 = 5$

$5 + 3 = 8$

Yes   No

Chapter 3 | Lesson 5

Think and Grow: Modeling Real Life

Your friend has 2 blue markers and 7 yellow markers. You have 5 fewer markers than your friend. How many markers do you have?

Model: Friend:
You:

Equation:

_____ markers

Show and Grow   I can think deeper!

5. Your friend has 6 tennis balls and 1 baseball. You have 2 fewer balls than your friend. How many balls do you have?

Model: Friend:
You:

Equation:

_____ balls

Name _____   **Practice** 3.5

Learning Target: Solve *compare* word problems when given how many fewer.

You have 7 pencils. Your friend has 6 fewer than you. How many pencils does your friend have?

You: | 7 |
Friend: | 1 | 6 |

_7_ − 6 = _1_

_1_ + 6 = _7_

_1_ pencil

1. Your friend has 9 awards. You have 5 fewer than your friend. How many awards do you have?

   Friend: [   ]
   You: [| 5]

   ___ − ___ = ___

   ___ + ___ = ___

   ___ awards

2. Your friend finds 2 fewer bugs than you. You find 4 bugs. How many bugs does your friend find?

   You: [   ]
   Friend: [|]

   ___ ◯ ___ = ___

   ___ bugs

Chapter 3 | Lesson 5

3. **DIG DEEPER!** Complete the bar model. Do both equations match the bar model?

You: | 7 |
Friend: | | 4 |

7 − 4 = 3

7 + 3 = 10

Yes   No

4. **Modeling Real Life** Your friend has 8 black cats and 2 orange cats. You have 7 fewer cats than your friend. How many cats do you have?

Friend: | |
You: | |

_____ cats

Review & Refresh

5. Write the numbers of shirts and shorts. Are the numbers equal? Circle the thumbs up for *yes* or the thumbs down for *no*.

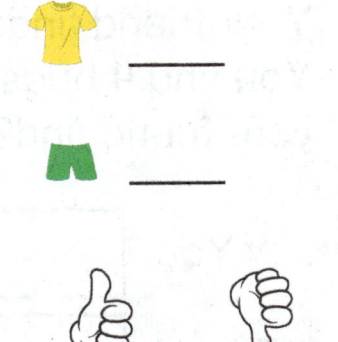

156   one hundred fifty-six

Name _____

Learning Target: Identify whether an equation is true or false.

True or False Equations

Explore and Grow

Color the flowers that have a sum or difference of 6.

Construct an Argument
Write an equation using two colored flowers. Is your equation true? How do you know?

Chapter 3 | Lesson 6

one hundred fifty-seven 157

Think and Grow

$7 + 1 \stackrel{?}{=} 4 + 4$

$7 + 1$: ○○○○○○○○

$4 + 4$: ○○○○○○○○

Both sides equal 8.

$8 \stackrel{?}{=} 8$

8 = 8 is true.

(True)   False

Show and Grow — I can do it!

Is the equation true or false?

1. $2 + 0 \stackrel{?}{=} 1 + 2$

   $2 + 0$: ___

   $1 + 2$: ___

   ___ $\stackrel{?}{=}$ ___

   True   False

2. $5 - 4 \stackrel{?}{=} 6 - 5$

   $5 - 4$: ___

   $6 - 5$: ___

   ___ $\stackrel{?}{=}$ ___

   True   False

Name _____

Apply and Grow: Practice

Is the equation true or false?

3. $4 + 1 \stackrel{?}{=} 2 + 2$

   $4 + 1:$

   $2 + 2:$

   $\underline{} \stackrel{?}{=} \underline{}$

   True   False

4. $7 + 2 \stackrel{?}{=} 3 + 6$

   $7 + 2:$

   $3 + 6:$

   $\underline{} \stackrel{?}{=} \underline{}$

   True   False

5. $10 - 4 \stackrel{?}{=} 6 - 0$

   $\underline{} \stackrel{?}{=} \underline{}$

   True   False

6. $5 - 2 \stackrel{?}{=} 7 - 4$

   $\underline{} \stackrel{?}{=} \underline{}$

   True   False

7. $6 + 1 \stackrel{?}{=} 6 - 1$

   $\underline{} \stackrel{?}{=} \underline{}$

   True   False

8. $3 - 1 \stackrel{?}{=} 1 + 2$

   $\underline{} \stackrel{?}{=} \underline{}$

   True   False

9. **Reasoning** Circle all of the equations that are true.

   $7 \stackrel{?}{=} 7$ $5 + 5 \stackrel{?}{=} 6 + 4$

   $10 - 4 \stackrel{?}{=} 8$ $4 + 2 \stackrel{?}{=} 9 - 3$

Chapter 3 | Lesson 6

Think and Grow: Modeling Real Life

You have 7 marbles. You lose 2 of them. Your friend has 4 marbles and finds 3 more. Do you and your friend have the same number of marbles?

Equation: ____ − ____ $\stackrel{?}{=}$ ____ + ____

____ $\stackrel{?}{=}$ ____

Yes   No

Show and Grow   I can think deeper!

10. You have 1 balloon. You blow up 3 more. Your friend has 5 balloons. 1 of your friend's balloons pops. Do you and your friend have the same number of balloons?

Equation: ____ + ____ $\stackrel{?}{=}$ ____ − ____

____ $\stackrel{?}{=}$ ____

Yes   No

Communicate Clearly
How do you read the equations you wrote?

Name _____ Practice 3.6

Learning Target: Identify whether an equation is true or false.

$5 + 2 \stackrel{?}{=} 3 + 3$

$5 + 2:$ ◯ ◯ ◯ ◯ ◯ ◯ ◯

$3 + 3:$ ◯ ◯ ◯ ◯ ◯ ◯

$\underline{7} \stackrel{?}{=} \underline{6}$ True (False)

Is the equation true or false?

1. $7 + 0 \stackrel{?}{=} 2 + 4$

   $7 + 0:$

   $2 + 4:$

   ___ $\stackrel{?}{=}$ ___

   True False

2. $8 - 1 \stackrel{?}{=} 9 - 2$

   $8 - 1:$

   $9 - 2:$

   ___ $\stackrel{?}{=}$ ___

   True False

3. $9 - 5 \stackrel{?}{=} 1 + 3$

   ___ $\stackrel{?}{=}$ ___

   True False

4. $8 - 1 \stackrel{?}{=} 4 + 4$

   ___ $\stackrel{?}{=}$ ___

   True False

Chapter 3 | Lesson 6

5. **Reasoning** Circle all of the equations that are false.

$2 \stackrel{?}{=} 4$ $4 + 5 \stackrel{?}{=} 6 - 2$

$4 + 4 \stackrel{?}{=} 10 - 2$ $9 \stackrel{?}{=} 9 - 0$

6. **Modeling Real Life** You have 5 crayons. You find 3 more. Your friend has 7 crayons and finds 1 more. Do you and your friend have the same number of crayons?

___ + ___ $\stackrel{?}{=}$ ___ + ___

___ $\stackrel{?}{=}$ ___

Yes   No

7. **DIG DEEPER!** You have 2 purple poppers, 1 pink popper, and 5 blue poppers. Your friend has 3 yellow poppers and 4 red poppers. Do you and your friend have the same number of poppers? Think: How do you know?

Yes   No

Review & Refresh

8. Circle the triangles.

    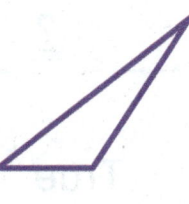

Name _____

Find Numbers That Make 10 — 3.7

Learning Target: Find the missing addend that makes 10.

Explore and Grow

Place some red counters on the ten frame. Add yellow counters to fill the frame. Write an equation to match.

Choose Tools
Why is it helpful to use red *and* yellow counters?

___ + ___ = ___

Chapter 3 | **Lesson 7**

Think and Grow

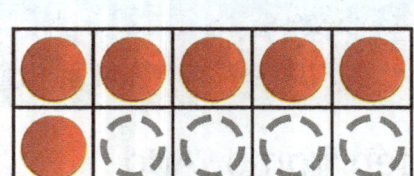

6 + __4__ = 10

Draw 4 more circles to make 10.

Show and Grow *I can do it!*

1.

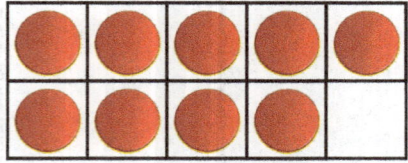

9 + ___ = 10

2.

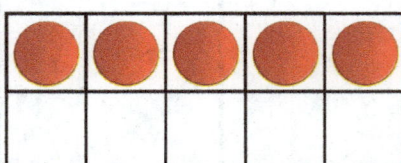

5 + ___ = 10

3.

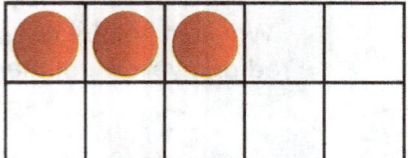

3 + ___ = 10

4.

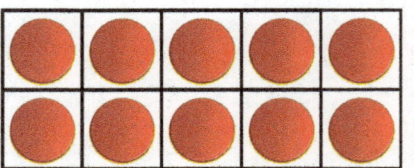

10 + ___ = 10

Name _____

✓ Apply and Grow: Practice

5.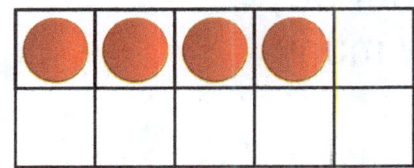

   $4 + \underline{} = 10$

6.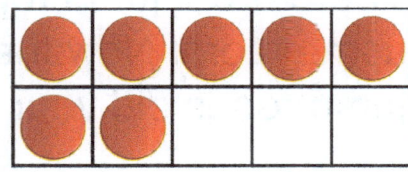

   $7 + \underline{} = 10$

7. $1 + \underline{} = 10$

8. $8 + \underline{} = 10$

9. $\underline{} + 2 = 10$

10. $\underline{} + 5 = 10$

11. $\underline{} + 3 = 10$

12. $\underline{} + 0 = 10$

13. **DIG DEEPER!** Match the numbers that have a sum of 10.

    4   3   5   1

    5   7   6   9

Chapter 3 | Lesson 7

Think and Grow: Modeling Real Life

There are 7 jump ropes. Your teacher buys some more. Now there are 10. How many jump ropes did your teacher buy?

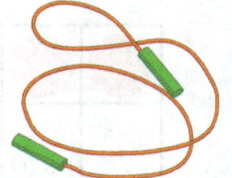

Model:

Addition equation:

_____ jump ropes

Show and Grow   I can think deeper!

14. There are 2 penguins. Some more join them. Now there are 10. How many more penguins joined them?

Model:

Addition equation:

_____ penguins

Name _____

Practice 3.7

Learning Target: Find the missing addend that makes 10.

Draw 3 more circles to make 10.

7 + _3_ = 10

1.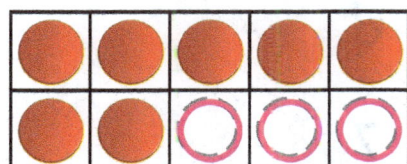

   8 + ___ = 10

2.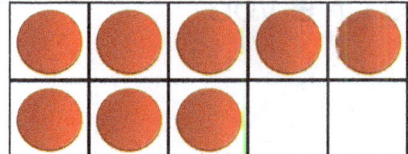

   1 + ___ = 10

3. 10 + ___ = 10

4. 5 + ___ = 10

5. ___ + 4 = 10

6. ___ + 0 = 10

Chapter 3 | Lesson 7   one hundred sixty-seven   167

7. DIG DEEPER! Match the numbers that have a sum of 10.

2   8

4   9

3   7

1   6

8. **Modeling Real Life** You have 3 baseball cards. Your friend gives you some more. Now you have 10. How many baseball cards did your friend give you?

_____ baseball cards

Review & Refresh

Find the sum. Then change the order of the addends. Write the new addition problem.

9.   4
   + 2
   ☐

☐
+ ☐
☐

10.   7
   + 1
   ☐

☐
+ ☐
☐

Name _____

Fact Families 3.8

Learning Target: Write related addition and subtraction equations to complete a fact family.

Explore and Grow

Use linking cubes to model the equations.

4 + 5 = ___

5 + 4 = ___

9 − 4 = ___

9 − 5 = ___

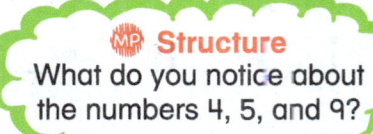

Structure
What do you notice about the numbers 4, 5, and 9?

Chapter 3 | Lesson 8

Think and Grow

Add the parts in any order.

Subract each part from the whole.

2	3

⊢———— 5 ————⊣

fact family

2 + 3 = 5   5 − 2 = 3

3 + 2 = 5   5 − 3 = 2

Show and Grow — I can do it!

1. Complete the fact family.

1	8

⊢———— 9 ————⊣

1 + 8 = ___   9 − ___ = ___

___ + ___ = ___   9 − ___ = ___

170   one hundred seventy

Name _____

 **Apply and Grow: Practice**

Complete the fact family.

2.

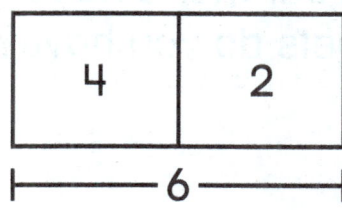

4 + 2 = ___   6 − ___ = ___

___ + ___ = ___   6 − ___ = ___

3.

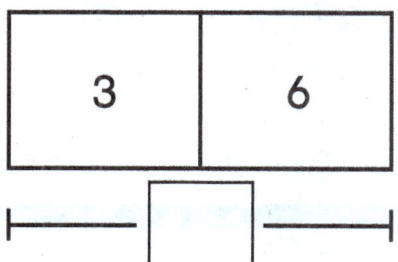

3 + 6 = ___   ___ − 6 = 3

___ + ___ = ___   ___ − ___ = ___

4. 7 + 1 = ___   ___ − 7 = ___

___ + ___ = ___   ___ − 1 = ___

5. **Which One Doesn't Belong?** Cross out the equation that does *not* belong in the fact family.

5 + 3 = 8   5 − 3 = 2

3 + 5 = 8   8 − 5 = 3

Chapter 3 | Lesson 8   one hundred seventy-one 171

Think and Grow: Modeling Real Life

You have 3 puppets. Your friend has 7 puppets. How many fewer puppets do you have?

Model:

Equation:

_____ fewer puppets

Show and Grow I can think deeper!

6. There are 2 spoons and 8 forks. How many more forks are there?

Model:

Equation:

_____ more forks

172   one hundred seventy-two

Name _____

Practice 3.8

Learning Target: Write related addition and subtraction equations to complete a fact family.

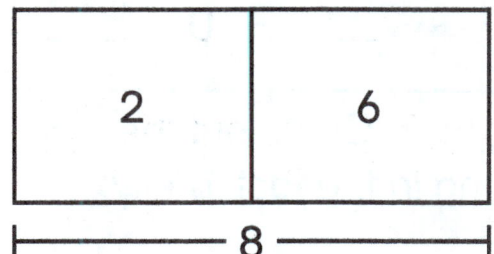

2 + 6 = __8__   8 − __6__ = __2__

__6__ + __2__ = __8__   8 − __2__ = __6__

Complete the fact family.

1.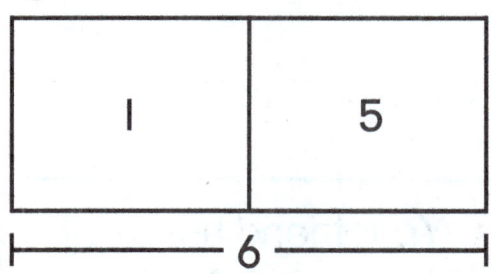

   1 + 5 = ___   6 − ___ = ___

   ___ + ___ = ___   6 − ___ = ___

2. 3 + 7 = ___   ___ − 7 = 3

   ___ + ___ = ___   ___ − ___ = ___

Chapter 3 | Lesson 8   one hundred seventy-three 173

3. Complete the fact family.

3 + 0 = ___   ___ − 3 = ___

___ + ___ = ___   ___ − 0 = ___

4. Which One Doesn't Belong? Cross out the equation that does *not* belong in the fact family.

6 + 4 = 10   10 − 6 = 4

4 + 6 = 10   6 − 4 = 2

5. Modeling Real Life There are 7 fish and 2 frogs. How many fewer frogs are there?

___ fewer frogs

6. Use Equations Your friend uses only 2 equations to write the fact family for the model. Is this reasonable?

| 2 | 2 |

├──── 4 ────┤

Review & Refresh

7. 3 + 3 = ___

8. 5 + 5 = ___

Name _____

Performance Task 3

1. You and your friend bake banana bread and raisin bread. You have 8 loaves of bread. 3 of them are raisin bread. Your friend has 10 loaves of bread. 6 of them are banana bread. How many more loaves of banana bread does your friend have than you?

   _____ loaf

2. You give away 3 loaves of banana bread and 3 loaves of raisin bread. Your friend gives away 1 more loaf of bread than you. How many loaves of bread does your friend give away?

   _____ loaves

3. You and your friend make boxes of muffins. Does each box have the same number of muffins?

   3 apple
   7 lemon

   5 apple
   4 lemon

   Yes   No

Number Land

To Play: Put the Addition and Subtraction Cards in a pile. Start at Newton. Take turns drawing a card and moving your piece to the missing number in the equation. Repeat this process until a player gets back to Newton.

Name _____

Chapter 3 Practice

3.1 Solve *Add To* Problems with Start Unknown

1. ? + 4 = 6

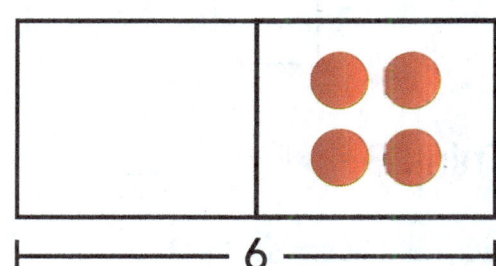

___ + 4 = 6

2. ? + 2 = 8

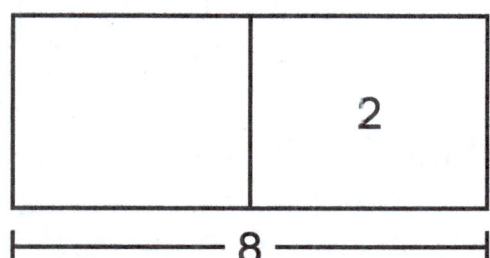

___ + 2 = 8

3.2 Solve *Take From* Problems with Change Unknown

3. 5 − ? = 4

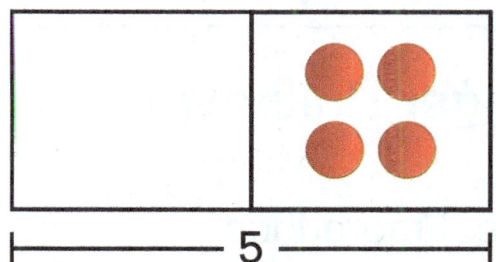

5 − ___ = 4

4. 7 − ? = 7

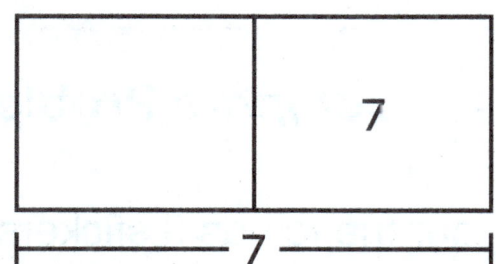

7 − ___ = 7

3.3 Solve Take From Problems with Start Unknown

5. ? − 6 = 3

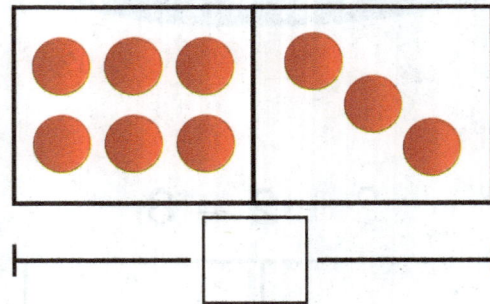

Think 6 + 3 = ____.

So, ____ − 6 = 3.

6. ? − 3 = 1

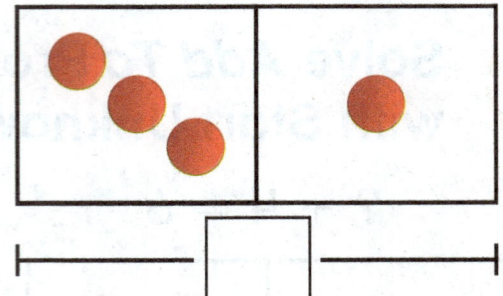

Think 3 + 1 = ____.

So, ____ − 3 = 1.

7. 🔶 **Structure** Circle the equation that matches the model.

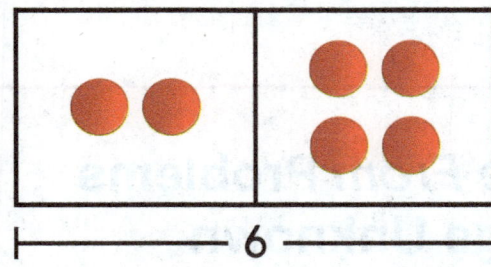

6 − 6 = 0   4 − 2 = 2   6 − 2 = 4

3.4 Compare Problems: Bigger Unknown

8. Your friend has 3 stickers. You have 4 more than your friend. How many stickers do you have?

You:
Friend: 3

3 + ____ = ____

____ stickers

3.5 Compare Problems: Smaller Unknown

9. Your friend has 5 stuffed animals. You have 2 fewer than your friend. How many stuffed animals do you have?

Friend:
You:

___ ◯ ___ = ___

___ stuffed animals

10. **Modeling Real Life** Your friend has 4 dogs and 2 cats. You have 1 fewer pet than your friend. How many pets do you have?

Friend:
You:

___ pets

3.6 True or False Equations

Is the equation true or false?

11. $5 + 3 \stackrel{?}{=} 10 - 2$

___ $\stackrel{?}{=}$ ___

True   False

12. $7 - 1 \stackrel{?}{=} 6 + 1$

___ $\stackrel{?}{=}$ ___

True   False

13. **Reasoning** Circle all of the equations that are true.

$$8 \stackrel{?}{=} 2 \qquad\qquad 1 + 1 \stackrel{?}{=} 4 - 2$$

$$6 + 4 \stackrel{?}{=} 10 \qquad\qquad 3 + 2 \stackrel{?}{=} 3 + 3$$

3.7 Find Numbers That Make 10

14.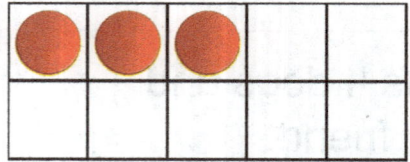

3 + ___ = 10

15.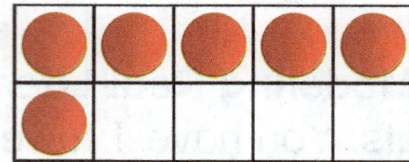

6 + ___ = 10

3.8 Fact Families

16. Complete the fact family.

8 + 1 = ___   ___ − 8 = 1

___ + ___ = ___   ___ − ___ = ___

17. **Modeling Real Life** There are 2 slides and 6 swings on a playground. How many more swings are there?

___ more swings

180   one hundred eighty

Name _____

Cumulative Practice 1-3

1. Shade the circle next to the answer.

   $4 + 4 = $ _____

   ○ 4   ○ 6
   ○ 9   ○ 8

2. Shade the circle next to the addition equation that you can use to solve $8 - 3$.

   ○ $8 + 3 = 11$

   ○ $3 + 5 = 8$

   ○ $1 + 8 = 9$

   ○ $5 + 2 = 7$

3. Circle the equation that matches the bar model.

   You: | 3 |
   Friend: | 2 | 1 |

   $3 + 1 = 4$

   $2 + 1 = 3$

Chapter 3   one hundred eighty-one   181

4. You take 10 pictures. Your friend takes 3 pictures. Shade the circle next to the equation that shows how many more pictures you take.

○ 3 + 3 = 6

○ 10 − 3 = 7

○ 10 + 3 = 13

○ 3 − 1 = 2

5. Shade the circle next to the number that completes the addition equation.

___ + 7 = 9

○ 1

○ 2

○ 3

○ 4

6. There are 6 🐠.

3 more 🐠 join them.

How many 🐠 are there now?

___ + ___ = ___

___ 🐠

7. Is each equation true or false?

$0 + 1 \stackrel{?}{=} 0 + 8$ True   False

$1 + 5 \stackrel{?}{=} 9 - 5$ True   False

$10 - 8 \stackrel{?}{=} 7 - 5$ True   False

$4 - 3 \stackrel{?}{=} 4 + 3$ True   False

8. Use the picture to write a subtraction equation.

____ − 0 = ____

9. You have 8 beads. 5 are orange. The rest are blue. Shade the circles next to the equations that describe the beads.

○ $3 + 5 = 8$

○ $8 - 2 = 6$

○ $4 + 4 = 8$

○ $8 - 5 = 3$

Chapter 3   one hundred eighty-three   183

10. Use the numbers shown to write two equations.

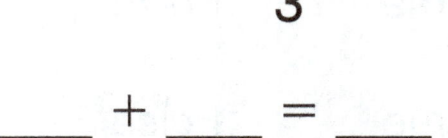

 3   8   5

___ + ___ = ___   ___ + ___ = ___

11. Shade the circle next to the equation that does *not* belong in the fact family.

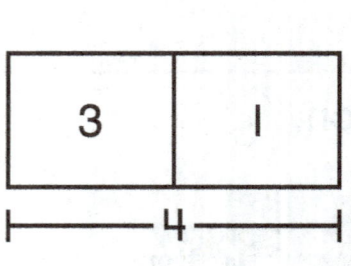

○ 3 + 1 = 4

○ 4 − 3 = 1

○ 1 + 3 = 4

○ 3 − 1 = 2

12. There are 3 rabbits. 3 more join them. Shade the circle next to the equation that shows how many rabbits there are in all.

○ 3 + 2 = 5

○ 3 + 4 = 7

○ 4 + 1 = 5

○ 3 + 3 = 6

184   one hundred eighty-four

4 Add Numbers within 20

- How would you describe the weather today?
- How many sunny or cloudy days do you see in the forecast?

Chapter Learning Target:
Understand counting strategies.

Chapter Success Criteria:
- I can identify counting strategies.
- I can describe equations.
- I can explain the strategy I used.
- I can apply strategies to solve word problems.

one hundred eighty-five

Vocabulary

Organize It

Use the review words to complete the graphic organizer.

Review Words
addend
doubles
doubles minus 1
doubles plus 1
sum

_____

_____

_____

Define It

Match the review word to its definition.

1. addend

2. sum

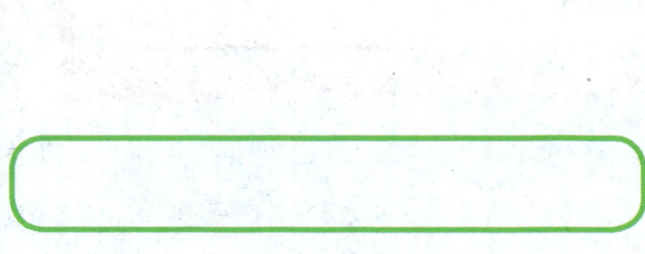

Name _____

Learning Target: Find the sum of doubles from 6 to 10.

Use counters to model the story.

You have 7 marbles. Your friend has 7 marbles. How many marbles are there in all?

_____ marbles

Chapter 4 | Lesson 1

 **Think and Grow**

$\underline{6} + \underline{6} = \underline{12}$

The addends are the same, so these are doubles.

$$\begin{array}{r} 7 \\ +\ 7 \\ \hline 14 \end{array}$$

Show and Grow I can do it!

1.

   ___ + ___ = ___

2.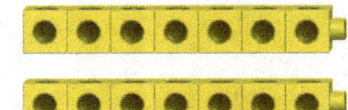

   ___ + ___ = ___

3.

   $$\begin{array}{r} \square \\ +\ \square \\ \hline \square \end{array}$$

4.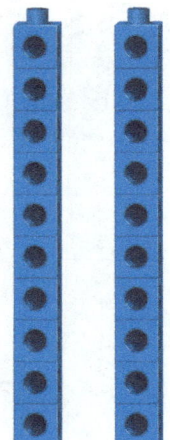

   $$\begin{array}{r} \square \\ +\ \square \\ \hline \square \end{array}$$

Name _____

 Apply and Grow: Practice

5.

___ + ___ = ___

6.

___ + ___ = ___

7. 7 + 7 = ___

8. 10 + 10 = ___

9. 9
     + 9
     ____

10. 8
      + 8
      ____

11. **Reasoning** You and your friend each read 6 books. How many books do you and your friend read in all?

____ books

Chapter 4 | Lesson 1

 **Think and Grow: Modeling Real Life**

You and your friend have the same number of video games. There are 16 in all. How many video games do you have?

Draw a picture:

Addition equation:

_____ video games

Show and Grow   I can think deeper!

12. 2 friends give you the same number of pictures. You have 12 in all. How many pictures does each friend give you?

Draw a picture:

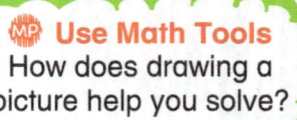 How does drawing a picture help you solve?

Addition equation:

_____ pictures

Name _____

Practice  4.1

Learning Target: Find the sum of doubles from 6 to 10.

8 + 8 = 16

7 + 7 = 14

1. ___ + ___ = ___

2. ___ + ___ = ___

3. 9
  + 9
  ___
  ☐

4. 10
  + 10
  ___
  ☐

Chapter 4 | Lesson 1

one hundred ninety-one 191

5. **Reasoning** You and your friend each do 7 jumping jacks. How many jumping jacks do you and your friend do in all?

_____ jumping jacks

6. **Modeling Real Life** Newton and Descartes each have the same number of treats. They have 18 treats in all. How many treats does Newton have?

_____ treats

7. **Graph Data** Complete the weather chart to show an equal number of sunny days and rainy days. Write an equation to show how many sunny days and rainy days there are in all.

SUN	MON	TUE	WED	THU	FRI	SAT

____ + ____ = ____

Review & Refresh

8. $7 - 0 =$ ____

9. $5 - 0 =$ ____

Name _____

Learning Target: Use the *doubles plus 1* and *doubles minus 1* strategies to find a sum.

Use Doubles within 20

Explore and Grow

Use counters to model the story.

You collect 8 leaves. Your friend collects 8 leaves. How many leaves are there in all?

_____ leaves

You collect 1 more leaf. How many leaves are there now?

_____ leaves

Chapter 4 | Lesson 2

Think and Grow

Use the double 8 + 8 to find each sum.

8 + 9 = 17

doubles plus 1

8 + 9 is equal to 8 + 8 and 1 more.

8 + 7 = 15

doubles minus 1

8 + 7 is equal to 1 less than 8 + 8.

Show and Grow — I can do it!

1. Use the double 6 + 6 to find each sum.

   6 + 7 = ___

   6 + 5 = ___

Name _____

 **Apply and Grow: Practice**

Use the double 7 + 7 to find each sum.

2. 7 + 8 = ____   7 + 6 = ____

Find the sum. Write the double you used.

3. 5 + 6 = ____

___ ◯ ___ = ___

4. 9 + 8 = ____

___ ◯ ___ = ___

5. **DIG DEEPER!** Circle two ways you can solve 9 + 10. Show how you know.

9 + 9 and 1 more

9 + 9 and 1 less

10 + 10 and 1 more

10 + 10 and 1 less

Chapter 4 | Lesson 2

Think and Grow: Modeling Real Life

A music room has 7 keyboards. There is 1 more recorder than keyboards. How many instruments are there?

Which doubles can you use to find the sum?

7 + 7   8 + 8   6 + 6

Equation: _____

_____ instruments

Show and Grow   *I can think deeper!*

6. A museum has 10 paintings. There is 1 fewer sculpture than paintings. How many art pieces are there?

Which doubles can you use to find the sum?

8 + 8   9 + 9   10 + 10

Equation: _____

_____ art pieces

Name _____

Practice

Learning Target: Use the *doubles plus 1* and *doubles minus 1* strategies to find a sum.

Use the double 5 + 5 to find each sum.

5 + 6 = 11   5 + 4 = 9

Use the double 9 + 9 to find each sum.

1. 9 + 10 = ____   9 + 8 = ____

Find the sum. Write the double you used.

2. 10 + 9 = ____

___ ◯ ___ = ___

3. 7 + 8 = ____

___ ◯ ___ = ___

Chapter 4 | Lesson 2

4. **DIG DEEPER!** Circle two ways you can solve 8 + 9. Show how you know.

   8 + 8 and 1 more

   8 + 8 and 1 less

   9 + 9 and 1 more

   9 + 9 and 1 less

5. **Modeling Real Life** There are 6 balls. There is 1 more toy hoop than balls. How many toys are there?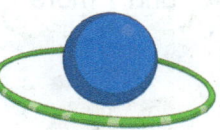

   Which doubles can you use to find the sum?

   7 + 7   8 + 8   6 + 6

   _____ toys

Review & Refresh

Use the picture to write an equation.

6.

   ____ – ____ = ____

7.

   ____ – ____ = ____

Name _____

Count On to Add within 20 4.3

Learning Target: Use the *count on* strategy to find a sum.

Model the story.

There are 8 coins in a piggy bank. You put in 5 more. How many coins are in the bank now?

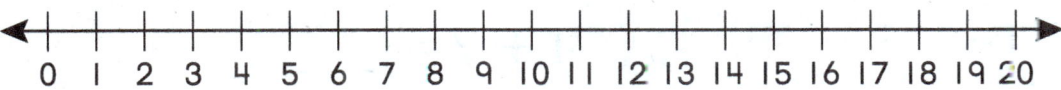

_____ coins

Chapter 4 | Lesson 3

Think and Grow

One Way:

Start at 7. Count on 9.

7 + 9 = 16

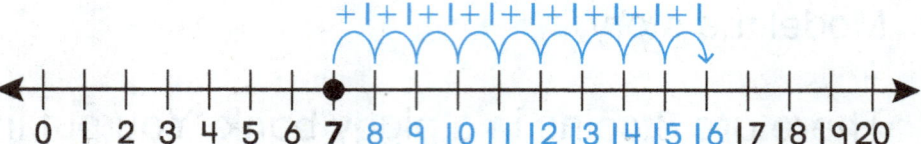

The order of the addends changes, but the sum stays the same!

Another Way:

Start at 9. Count on 7.

9 + 7 = 16

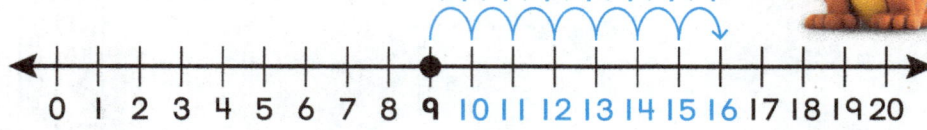

Show and Grow — I can do it!

1. 8 + 4 = ___

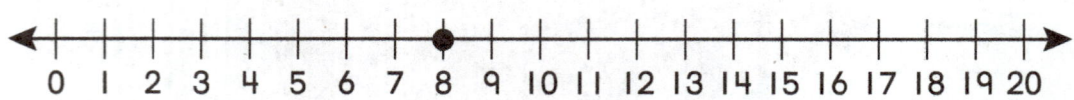

2. 5 + 10 = ___

200 two hundred

Name _____

Apply and Grow: Practice

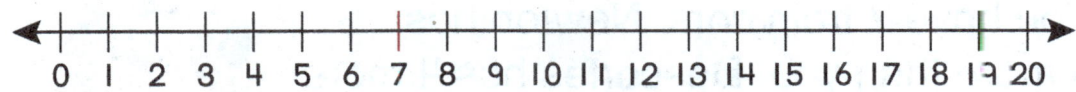

3. $6 + 8 = $ _____

4. $12 + 5 = $ _____

5. $7 + 8 = $ _____

6. $10 + 9 = $ _____

7. _____ $= 0 + 11$

8. _____ $= 4 + 9$

 **Construct an Argument** Why might you switch the order of the addends before counting on?

9. **Structure** Write the equation shown by the number line. Then write the equation another way.

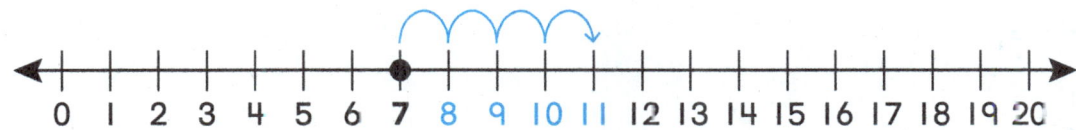

___ + ___ = ___   ___ + ___ = ___

Chapter 4 | Lesson 3

Think and Grow: Modeling Real Life

You have 7 train cars. Newton has 5 more than you. Descartes has 4 more than you. Who has more train cars, Newton or Descartes?

Model:

Equations: _____ Newton _____ Descartes

Who has more?   Newton   Descartes

Show and Grow   *I can think deeper!*

10. You have 6 comic books. Newton has 5 more than you. Descartes has 6 more than you. Who has more comic books, Newton or Descartes?

Model:

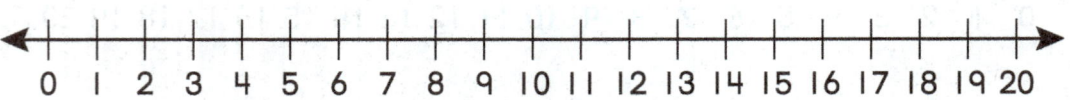

Equations: _____ Newton _____ Descartes

Who has more?   Newton   Descartes

Name _____

Practice 4.3

Learning Target: Use the *count on* strategy to find a sum.

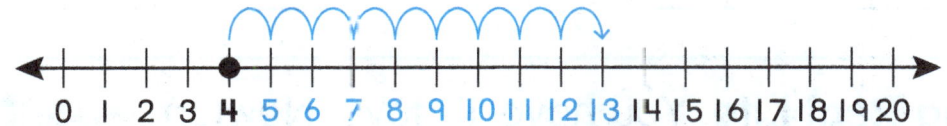

$4 + 9 = \underline{13}$

1. $10 + 7 = \underline{}$

2. $8 + 9 = \underline{}$

3. $\underline{} = 6 + 9$

4. $\underline{} = 12 + 4$

Chapter 4 | Lesson 3

5. **Structure** Write the equation shown by the number line. Then write the equation another way.

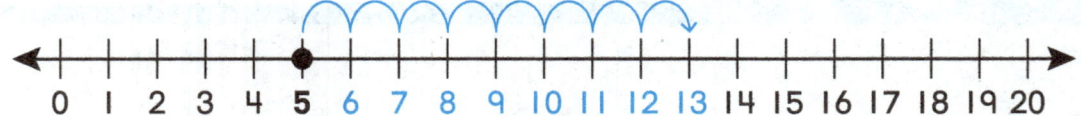

___ + ___ = ___   ___ + ___ = ___

6. **Modeling Real Life** You have 11 toys. Newton has 3 more than you. Descartes has 6 more than you. Who has more toys, Newton or Descartes?

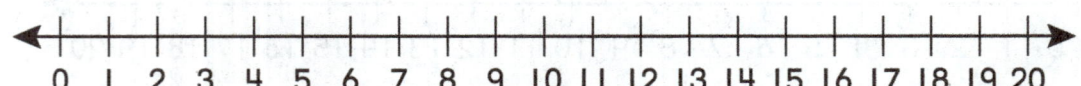

Newton   Descartes

7. **Maintain Accuracy** In Exercise 6, you, Newton, and Descartes each get 2 more toys. How many toys do you each have now?

You	Newton	Descartes
___ toys	___ toys	___ toys

Review & Refresh

8. Circle the cube. Draw a rectangle around the sphere.

Name _____

Learning Target: Add three numbers.

Add Three Numbers 4.4

Explore and Grow

Use linking cubes to model the story.

You have 5 red pencils, 4 yellow pencils, and 3 blue pencils. How many pencils do you have in all?

_____ pencils

Chapter 4 | Lesson 4

Think and Grow

You can add any 2 numbers first.

The sum is always the same.

4 + 1 + 5 = ?

④ + ① + 5 = 10
   \ /
    5

④ + 1 + ⑤ = 10
   \   /
     9

4 + ① + ⑤ = 10
   \   /
     6

Show and Grow — I can do it!

1.

②+⑤+ 6 = ___   2 +⑤+⑥= ___   ②+ 5 +⑥= ___

2.

④+ 3 +④= ___   4 +③+④= ___   ④+③+ 4 = ___

Name _____

 Apply and Grow: Practice

3.

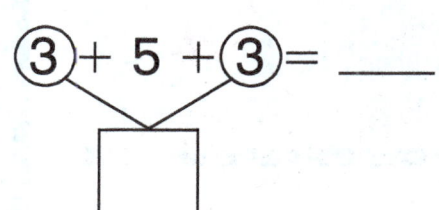 ③ + 5 + ③ = ___   ③+⑤+ 3 = ___   3 +⑤+③= ___

4.	**5.**	**6.**
3 + 1 + 2 = ___	7 + 5 + 5 = ___	4 + 5 + 2 = ___
□	□	□
7.	**8.**	**9.**
7 + 8 + 1 = ___	8 + 6 + 2 = ___	4 + 9 + 4 = ___

10. **DIG DEEPER!** Complete the number puzzle so that each branch has a sum of 14.

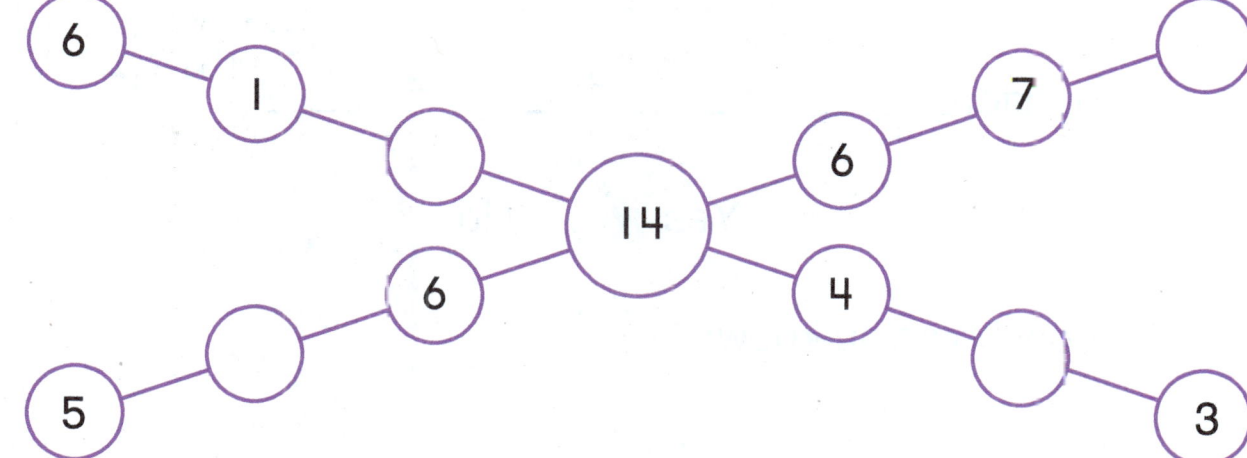

Chapter 4 | Lesson 4   two hundred seven   **207**

Think and Grow: Modeling Real Life

You have 6 goldfish, 7 minnows, and 6 guppies. Will the tank hold all of your fish?

Equation: ___ + ___ + ___ = ___

Yes   No

Show how you know:

Show and Grow — I can think deeper!

11. You have 2 lovebirds, 4 canaries, and 3 finches. Will the cage hold all of your birds?

Equation: ___ + ___ + ___ = ___

Yes   No

Show how you know:

Name _____

Practice

Learning Target: Add three numbers.

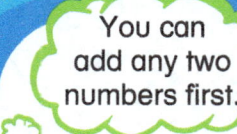 You can add any two numbers first.

6 + 5 + 1 = ?

6 + ⑤ + 1 = 12   6 + ⑤ + ① = 12
   | |
  11   6

1.

6 + ② + ② = ___   ⑥ + ② + 2 = ___   ⑥ + 2 + ② = ___

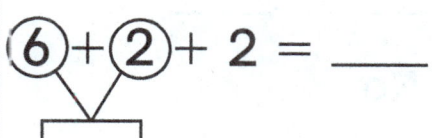

2. 6 + 5 + 6 = ___

3. 8 + 7 + 4 = ___

4. 9 + 10 + 1 = ___

5. 3 + 4 + 5 = ___

6. 7 + 5 + 5 = ___

7. 8 + 4 + 8 = ___

8. **DIG DEEPER!** Complete the number puzzle so that each branch has the sum of 13.

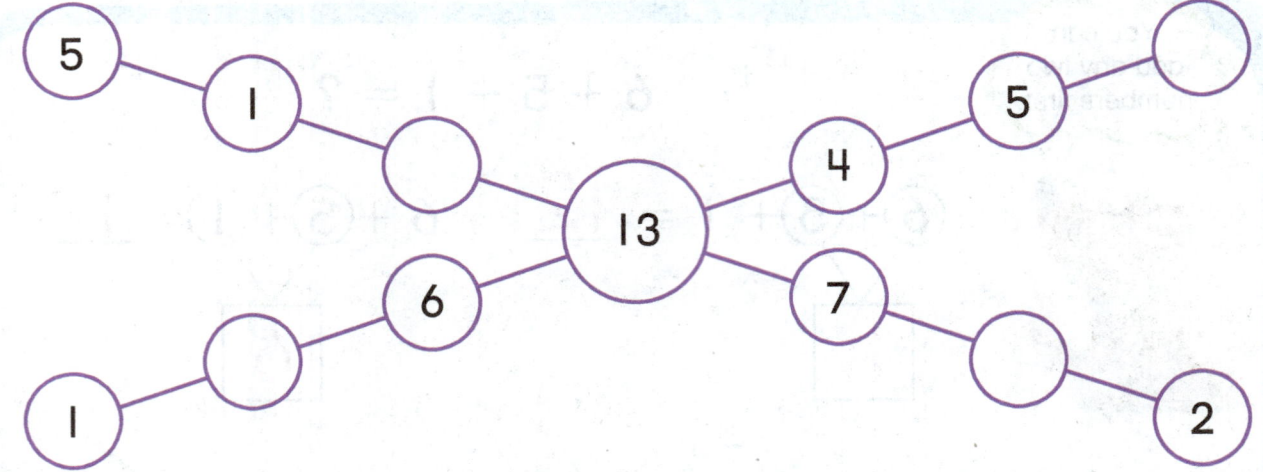

9. **Modeling Real Life** You have 7 white chickens, 1 black chicken, and 8 brown chickens. Will the chicken coop hold all of your chickens?

___ + ___ + ___ = ___

Yes   No

Show how you know:

Review & Refresh

10. $5 + \underline{} = 10$

11. $10 = 6 + \underline{}$

12. $8 + \underline{} = 10$

13. $10 = 3 + \underline{}$

Name _____

Learning Target: Use the *make a 10* strategy to add three numbers.

Add Three Numbers by Making a 10 **4.5**

Explore and Grow

Show three ways to find a sum.

$4 + 3 + 7 = \underline{}$

$4 + 3 + 7 = \underline{}$

$4 + 3 + 7 = \underline{}$

Chapter 4 | Lesson 5

Think and Grow

Find two addends whose sum is 10. Add those numbers first.

$3 + 7 + 5 = \underline{15}$

10

Making a 10 can help you add three numbers.

```
   8
   4
+  6    10
  ___
  18
```

Show and Grow — I can do it!

Make a 10 to add.

1. $9 + 1 + 3 = \underline{}$ 10

2. $4 + 2 + 8 = \underline{}$ 10

3.
```
    2
    3
+   7    10
  ___
  [  ]
```

4.
```
    5
    5
+   9    10
  ___
  [  ]
```

Name _____

 **Apply and Grow: Practice**

Make a 10 to add.

5. $3 + 7 + 3 =$ ___

   $\boxed{10}$

6. $8 + 6 + 2 =$ ___

   $\boxed{10}$

7. 6
    7    $\boxed{10}$
  + 4
   ☐

8. 8
    5    $\boxed{10}$
  + 5
   ☐

9. $4 + 6 + 2 =$ ___

10. $5 + 9 + 1 =$ ___

11. **DIG DEEPER!** What do you know about the missing addends and the sum?

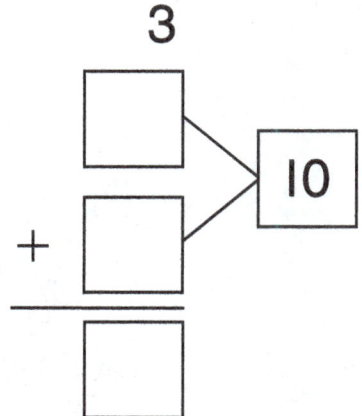

Chapter 4 | Lesson 5

Think and Grow: Modeling Real Life

You need to knock down 20 pins to win. Do you win?

Equation: ___ + ___ + ___ = ___

Yes   No

Show how you know:

Pins
6
3
7

Show and Grow *I can think deeper!*

12. Your hockey team needs 12 goals to break a record. Does your team break the record?

    Equation: ___ + ___ + ___ = ___

    Yes   No

    Show how you know:

Goals
5
6
4

214 two hundred fourteen

Practice 4.5

Name _____

Learning Target: Use the *make a 10* strategy to add three numbers.

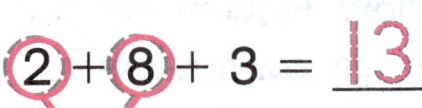= 13

10

Find 2 addends whose sum is 10. Add those numbers first.

6
9
+ 1

10

16

Making a 10 can help you add 3 numbers.

Make a 10 to add.

1. 6 + 8 + 4 = ___

   10

2.
   3
   7
   + 4
   ____
   ☐

   10

3. 5 + 8 + 2 = ___

4. 1 + 9 + 7 = ___

Chapter 4 | Lesson 5

5. **DIG DEEPER!** What do you know about the missing addends and the sum?

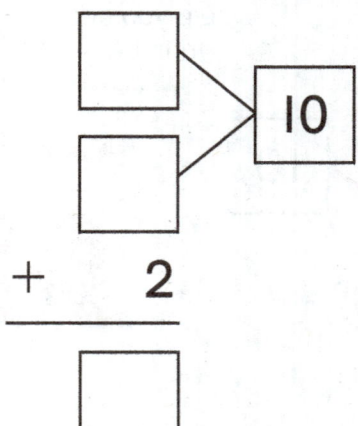

6. **Open-Ended** You pick 12 flowers. 4 of them are pink. The rest are purple and yellow. How many purple and yellow flowers could you have picked?

7. **Modeling Real Life** Your baseball team needs 15 runs to break a record. Does your team break the record?

Runs
6
4
6

___ + ___ + ___ = ___

Yes   No

Show how you know:

Review & Refresh

Circle the heavier object.

8.

9.

216   two hundred sixteen

Name _____

Learning Target: Use the *make a 10* strategy when adding 9.

Use counters and the ten frames to find the sum. Show how you can make a 10 to solve.

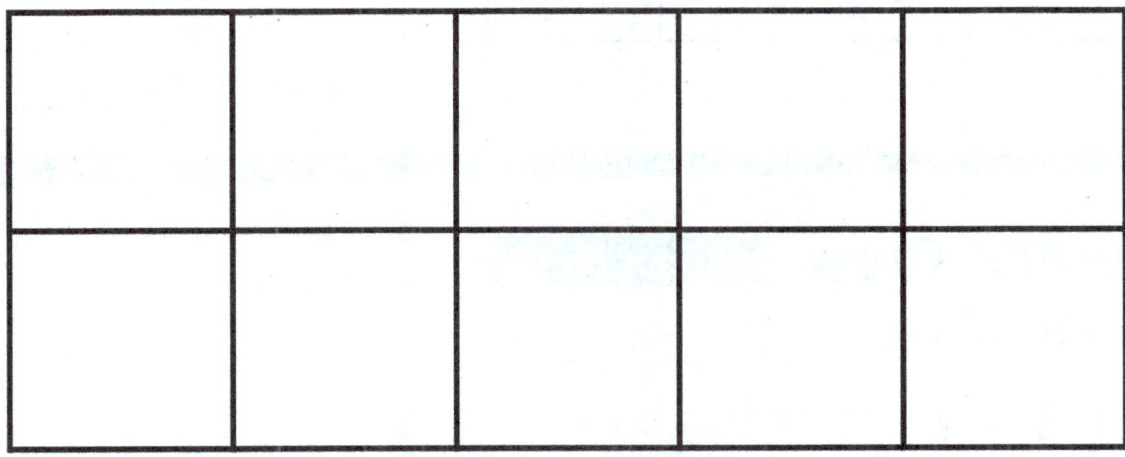

9 + 5 = ___

Chapter 4 | **Lesson 6**

two hundred seventeen 217

Think and Grow

$9 + 4 = ?$

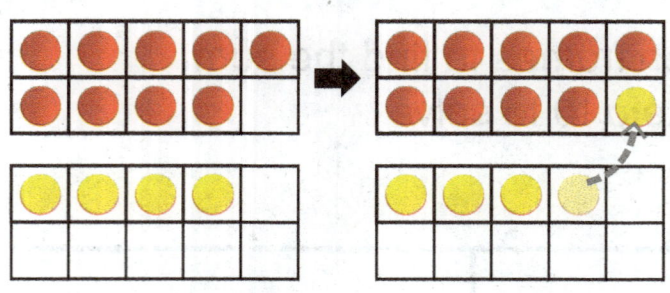

$9 + 4$

$9 + \underline{1} + \underline{3}$

$10 + \underline{3} = \underline{13}$

So, $9 + 4 = \underline{13}$.

Show and Grow I can do it!

Make a 10 to add.

1. $9 + 3 = ?$

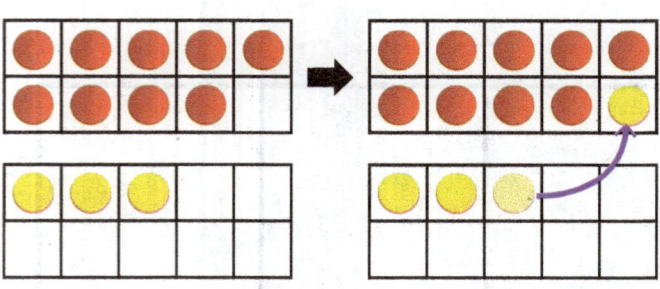

$9 + 3$

$9 + \underline{} + \underline{}$

$10 + \underline{} = \underline{}$

So, $9 + 3 = \underline{}$.

2. $9 + 6 = ?$

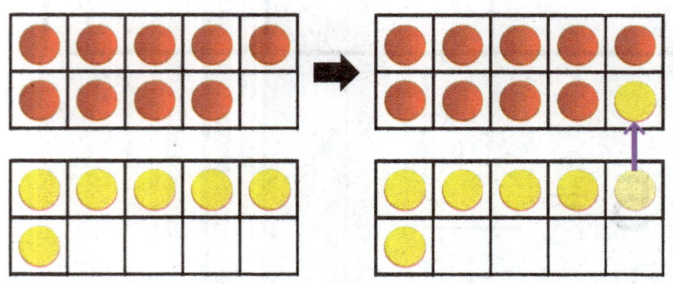

$9 + 6$

$9 + \underline{} + \underline{}$

$10 + \underline{} = \underline{}$

So, $9 + 6 = \underline{}$.

Apply and Grow: Practice

Make a 10 to add.

3. 9 + 2 = ?

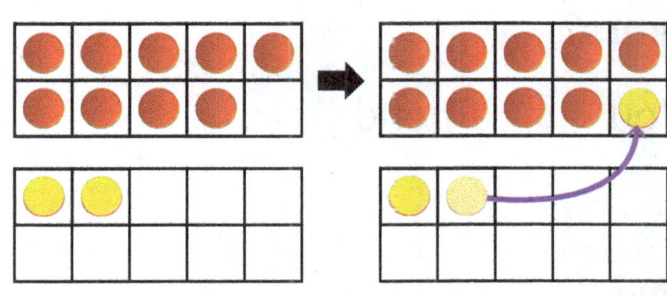

9 + 2

9 + ___ + ___

10 + ___ = ___

So, 9 + 2 = ___.

4. 9 + 9 = ?

9 + 9

9 + ___ + ___

10 + ___ = ___

So, 9 + 9 = ___.

5. 9 + 5 = ?

9 + 5

9 + ___ + ___

10 + ___ = ___

So, 9 + 5 = ___.

Find a Rule How do you break apart the second addend each time? Why?

6. **DIG DEEPER!** Use the ten frame to complete the equations.

9 + ? = 17

10 + ___ = 17

So, 9 + ___ = 17.

Chapter 4 | Lesson 6

two hundred nineteen 219

Think and Grow: Modeling Real Life

You have 9 stickers and earn 5 more. Your friend has 6 stickers and earns 10 more. Do you and your friend have the same number of stickers?

Addition equations: You   Friend

Yes   No

Show how you know:

Show and Grow — I can think deeper!

7. Your friend has 9 magnets and finds 6 more. You have 5 magnets and find 10 more. Do you and your friend have the same number of magnets?

Addition equations: You   Friend

Yes   No

Show how you know:

Name _____

Practice 4.6

Learning Target: Use the *make a 10* strategy when adding 9.

9 + 5 = ?

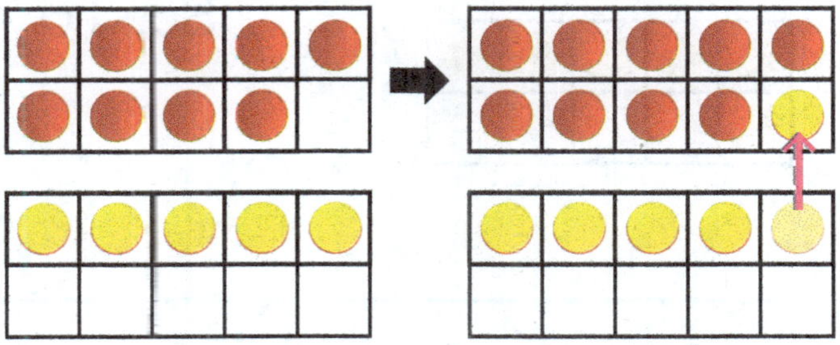

Make a 10 by thinking of 5 as 1 + 4.

9 + 5

9 + __1__ + __4__

10 + __4__ = __14__

So, 9 + 5 = __14__.

Make a 10 to add.

1. 9 + 3 = ?

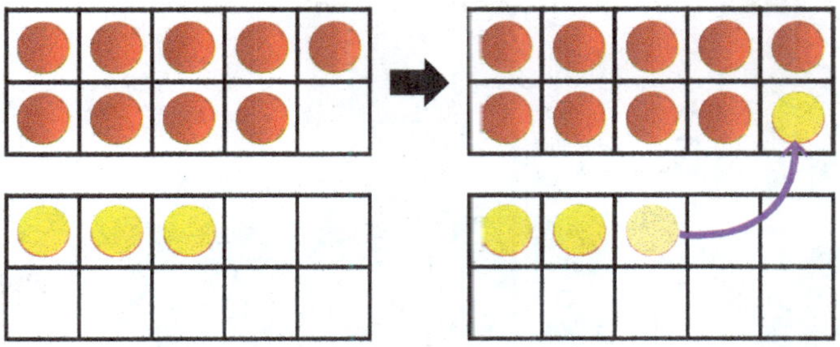

9 + 3

9 + ___ + ___

10 + ___ = ___

So, 9 + 3 = ___.

Chapter 4 | Lesson 6   two hundred twenty-one   **221**

2. **DIG DEEPER!** Use the ten frame to complete the equations.

   16 = ? + ?

   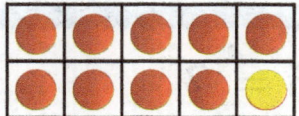

   10 + ___ = ___

   So, 16 = ___ + ___.

3. **Modeling Real Life** You have 9 rocks and collect 7 more. Your friend has 8 rocks and collects 8 more. Do you and your friend have the same number of rocks?

   Yes   No

   Show how you know:

Review & Refresh

Circle the longer object.

4.

5.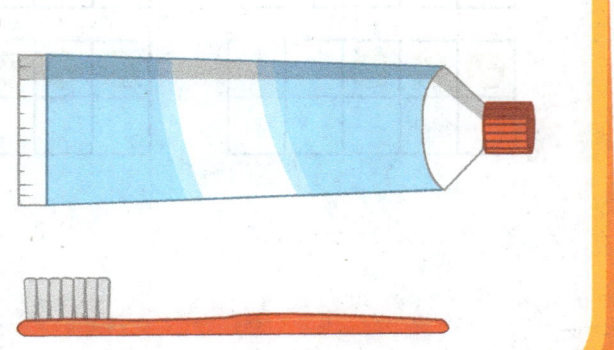

Name _____

Learning Target: Use the *make a 10* strategy to add two numbers.

Make a 10 to Add  4.7

Explore and Grow

Use counters and the ten frame to find the sum. Show how you can make a 10 to solve.

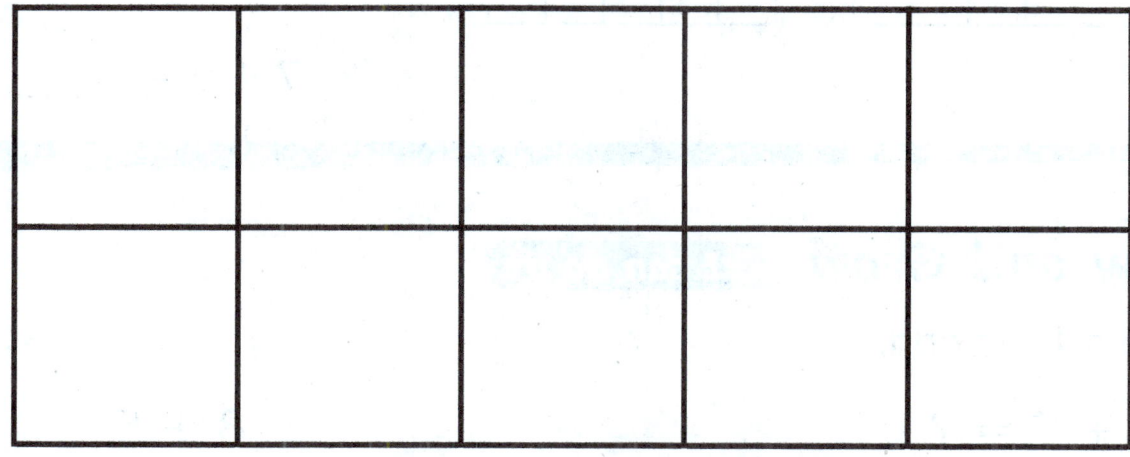

8 + 6 = ___

Chapter 4 | Lesson 7

Think and Grow

$7 + 5 = ?$

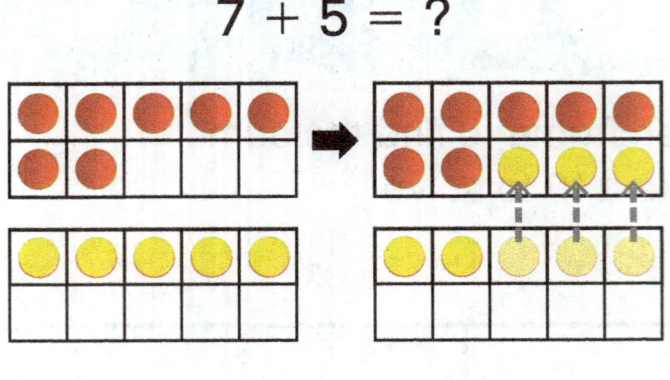

$7 + 5$

$7 + \underline{3} + \underline{2}$

$10 + \underline{2} = \underline{12}$

So, $7 + 5 = \underline{12}$.

Show and Grow I can do it!

Make a 10 to add.

1. $8 + 5 = ?$

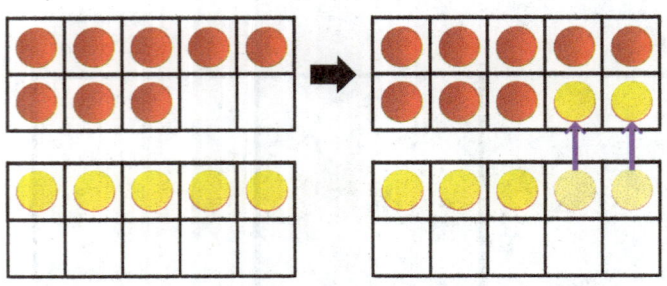

$8 + 5$

$8 + \underline{} + \underline{}$

$10 + \underline{} = \underline{}$

So, $8 + 5 = \underline{}$.

2. $7 + 7 = ?$

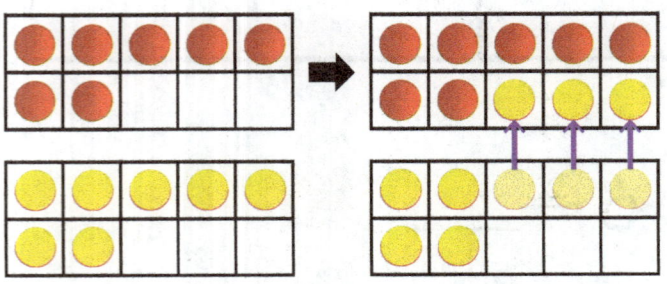

$7 + 7$

$7 + \underline{} + \underline{}$

$10 + \underline{} = \underline{}$

So, $7 + 7 = \underline{}$.

Name _____

✓ Apply and Grow: Practice

Make a 10 to add.

3. 7 + 6 = ?

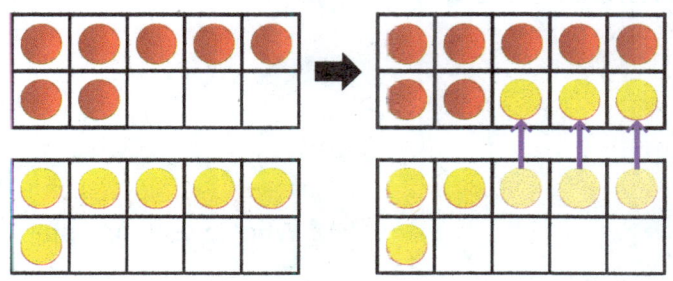

7 + 6
7 + ___ + ___
10 + ___ = ___

So, 7 + 6 = ___.

4. 7 + 4 = ?

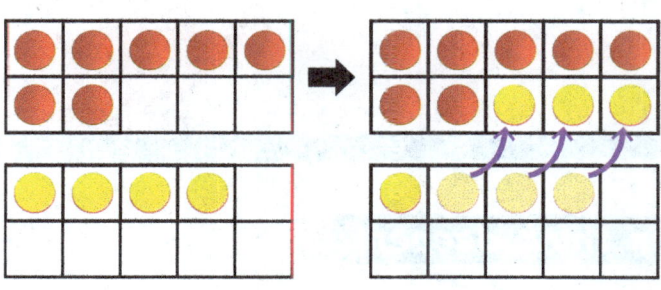

7 + 4
7 + ___ + ___
10 + ___ = ___

So, 7 + 4 = ___.

5. 8 + 7
8 + ___ + ___
10 + ___ = ___

So, 8 + 7 = ___.

6. 6 + 6
6 + ___ + ___
10 + ___ = ___

So, 6 + 6 = ___.

7. **MP Number Sense** Use 4, 7, and 10 to complete the sentence.

7 + ___ has the same sum as ___ + ___.

Chapter 4 | Lesson 7

Think and Grow: Modeling Real Life

There are 8 crabs. 7 more join them. There are 10 turtles. 5 more join them. Is the number of crabs the same as the number of turtles?

Addition equations:

Make a Plan
What is your first step?

Yes   No

Show how you know:

Show and Grow — I can think deeper!

8. There are 6 squirrels. 6 more join them. There are 10 birds. 2 more join them. Is the number of squirrels the same as the number of birds?

Addition equations:

Yes   No

Show how you know:

Practice 4.7

Learning Target: Use the *make a 10* strategy to add two numbers.

$8 + 3 = ?$

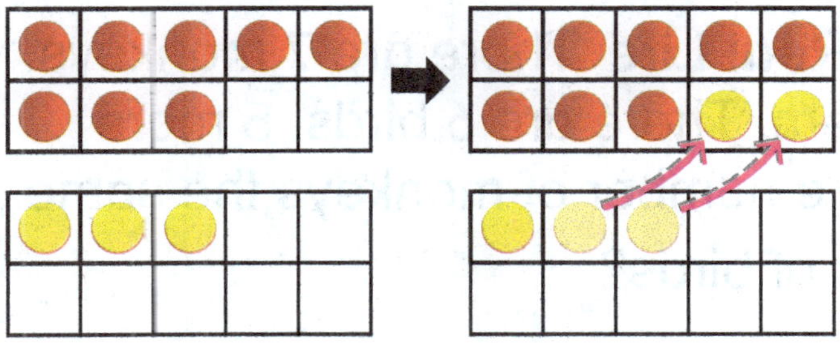

Make a 10 by thinking of 3 as 2 + 1.

$8 + 3$

$8 + \underline{2} + \underline{1}$

$10 + \underline{1} = \underline{11}$

So, $8 + 3 = \underline{11}$.

Make a 10 to add.

1. $6 + 5 = ?$

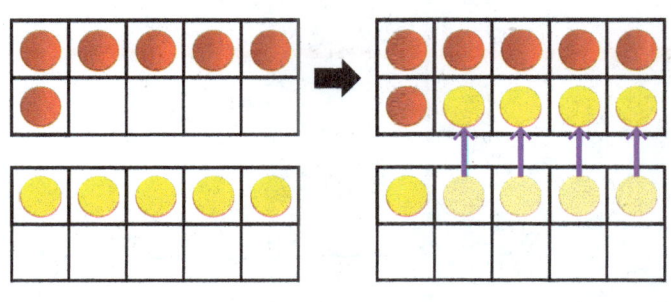

$6 + 5$

$6 + \underline{} + \underline{}$

$10 + \underline{} = \underline{}$

So, $6 + 5 = \underline{}$.

Chapter 4 | Lesson 7

two hundred twenty-seven 227

2. **Number Sense** Use 2, 6, and 10 to complete the sentence.

   ___ + ___ has the same sum as ___ + 6.

3. **Modeling Real Life** There are 7 monkeys. 4 more join them. There are 6 birds. 5 more join them. Is the number of monkeys the same as the number of birds?

   Yes   No

   Show how you know:

4. **DIG DEEPER!** In Exercise 3, you have a bunch of 4 bananas and a bunch of 6 bananas. How many more bananas do you need to feed one to each monkey?

Review & Refresh

5. There are 3 ✈.

   2 more ✈ join them.

   How many ✈ are there now?

   ___ + ___ = ___

   ___

Problem Solving: Addition within 20

4.8

Learning Target: Solve addition word problems.

Explore and Grow

Newton has 9 red crayons, 3 blue crayons, and 1 yellow crayon. How many crayons does he have in all?

____ crayons

Think and Grow

There are 8 girls and 6 boys in your class. How many students are in your class?

Circle what you know.

Underline what you need to find.

Solve:

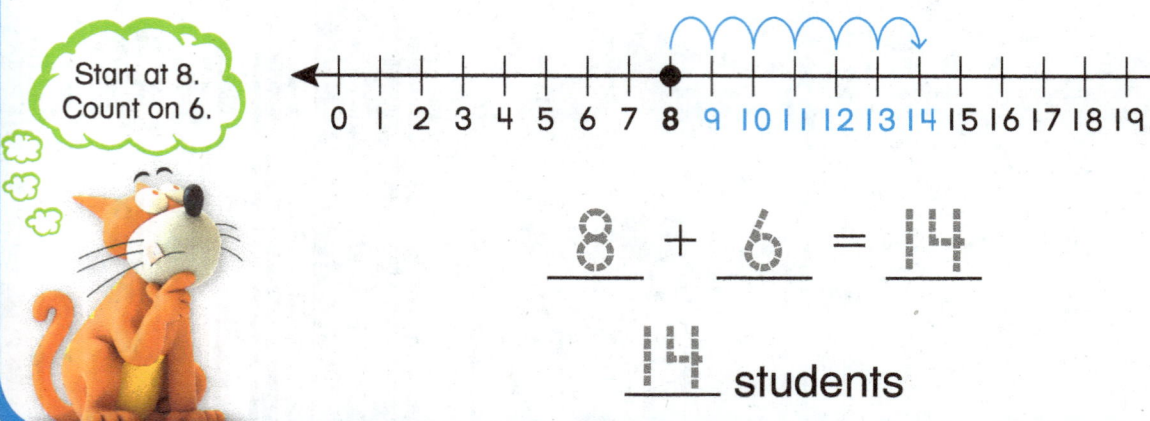

Start at 8. Count on 6.

$\underline{8} + \underline{6} = \underline{14}$

$\underline{14}$ students

Show and Grow — I can do it!

1. You have 6 notebooks. You buy 5 more. How many notebooks do you have now?

Circle what you know.

Underline what you need to find.

Solve:

____ ◯ ____ = ____   ____ notebooks

Name _____

✓ Apply and Grow: Practice

2. There are 6 soccer balls, 10 basketballs, and 4 volleyballs. How many balls are there in all?

   Circle what you know.   Underline what you need to find.

   Solve:

   ___ ◯ ___ ◯ ___ = ___

   [ ]

   ___ balls

3. You do 8 push-ups. Your friend does 1 fewer than you. How many push-ups do you and your friend do in all?

   ___ push-ups

4. **YOU BE THE TEACHER** Newton has 9 magnets. Descartes has 8 more than Newton. Your friend uses a bar model to show how many magnets Descartes has. Is your friend correct? Show how you know.

   Newton: | 9 |

   Descartes: | 8 | 1 |

   8 + 1 = 9

   9 magnets

Chapter 4 | Lesson 8

Think and Grow: Modeling Real Life

You have 5 bracelets. You have 7 fewer than your friend. How many bracelets does your friend have?

Circle what you know.

Underline what you need to find.

Solve: Friend: [   ]

You: [   ]

___ + ___ = ___   ___ bracelets

Show and Grow   I can think deeper!

5. Your friend finds 9 seashells. You find 6 more than your friend. How many seashells do you find?

Circle what you know.

Underline what you need to find.

Solve:

___ + ___ = ___   ___ seashells

Name _____

Practice 4.8

Learning Target: Solve addition word problems.

You have 6 keys. Your friend has 1 more than you. How many keys do you and your friend have in all?

6 + 7 is equal to 6 + 6 and 1 more.

Circle what you know.   Underline what you need to find.

Solve:

$\underline{6} \oplus \underline{7} = \underline{13}$

$\underline{13}$ keys

1. You have 5 robots. Your friend gives you more. Now you have 14. How many robots did your friend give you?

Circle what you know.   Underline what you need to find.

Solve:

___ ◯ ___ = ___

___ robots

2. There are some plates on a table. You add 8 more. Now there are 12. How many plates were on the table to start?

___ plates

Chapter 4 | Lesson 8

3. **YOU BE THE TEACHER** Newton has 8 tickets. Descartes has 5 more than Newton. Your friend uses a number line to show how many tickets Descartes has. Is your friend correct? Show how you know.

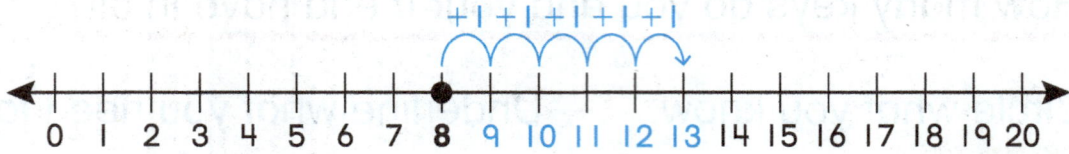

13 tickets

4. **Modeling Real Life** You have 9 medals. You have 9 fewer than your friend. How many medals does your friend have?

_____ medals

5. **Does It Make Sense?** Descartes has 2 rings and finds 9 more. You have 9 rings. Newton says Descartes has more rings than you. Without adding, does Newton's statement make sense? Think: Why?

Yes   No

Review & Refresh

6. 4 − 3 = _____

7. 5 − 2 = _____

Name _____

Performance Task 4

1. You track the weather for a few weeks. Each week has 7 days.

   a. **Maintain Accuracy** You track the weather every day for the first week. But you miss 1 day in the second week. How many days do you track the weather?

   _____ days

   b. You track the weather for 1 more week. How many days in all do you track the weather?

   _____ days

2. Your friend also tracks the weather. She records 9 sunny days and 5 cloudy days. How many days does your friend track the weather?

   _____ days

3. You record 10 rainy days in the first three weeks. Is the number of rainy days the same as the number of sunny days?

Week	Sunny Days
1	4
2	3
3	4

   Yes   No

   Show how you know:

Roll and Cover

To Play: Roll 3 dice and find the sum. Place a counter on a fish with the sum. Take turns until all of the fish have been covered.

Name _____

Chapter 4 Practice

4.1 Add Doubles from 6 to 10

1.

___ + ___ = ___

2.

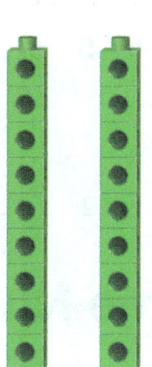 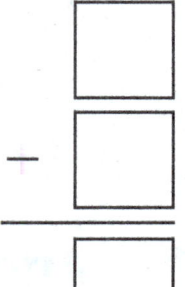

4.2 Use Doubles within 20

Use the double 6 + 6 to find each sum.

3. 6 + 7 = ___

6 + 5 = ___

Find the sum. Write the double you used.

4. 7 + 8 = ___

___ ◯ ___ = ___

5. 10 + 9 = ___

___ ◯ ___ = ___

Chapter 4   two hundred thirty-seven   237

4.3 Count On to Add within 20

6. 11 + 6 = ___

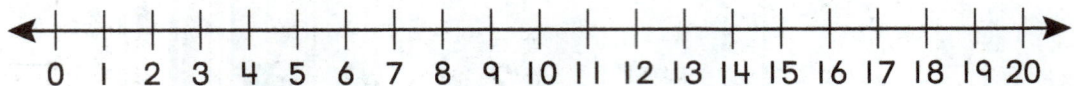

4.4 Add Three Numbers

7.

6 + ④ + ④ = ___ | ⑥ + ④ + 4 = ___ | ⑥ + 4 + ④ = ___

8. 7 + 8 + 5 = ___

9. 9 + 8 + 1 = ___

10. 2 + 3 + 5 = ___

238   two hundred thirty-eight

4.5 Add Three Numbers by Making a 10

Make a 10 to add.

11. 7 + 9 + 3 = ____

12. 4 + 9 + 1 = ____

13. **Number Sense** What do you know about the missing addends and the sum?

4.6 Add 9

14. Make a 10 to add 9 + 4.

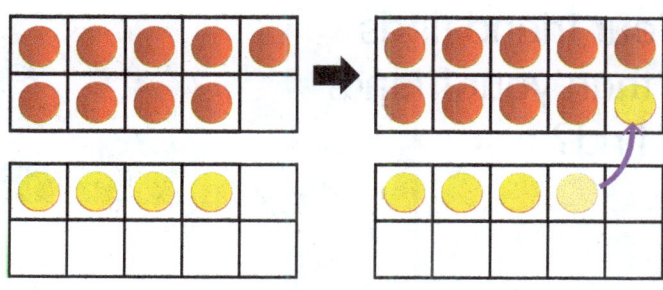

9 + ____ + ____

10 + ____ = ____

So, 9 + 4 = ____.

 **4.7 Make a 10 to Add**

15. Make a 10 to add 8 + 5.

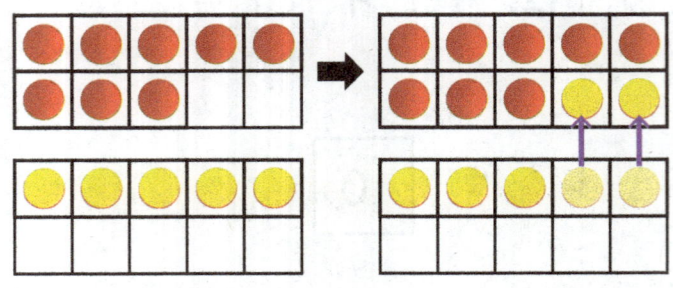

8 + 5

8 + ___ + ___

10 + ___ = ___

So, 8 + 5 = ___.

16. 7 + 7 = ?

7 + 7

7 + ___ + ___

10 + ___ = ___

So, 7 + 7 = ___.

17. 9 + 8 = ?

9 + 8

9 + ___ + ___

10 + ___ = ___

So, 9 + 8 = ___.

 **4.8 Problem Solving: Addition within 20**

18. **Modeling Real Life** Your friend finds 7 insects. You find 9 more than your friend. How many insects do you find?

___ insects

240 two hundred forty

5 Subtract Numbers within 20

- What do bees make?
- How many bees do you see? 7 of them fly away. How many bees are left?

Chapter Learning Target:
Understand subtraction strategies.

Chapter Success Criteria:
- I can identify counting back strategies.
- I can describe subtraction equations.
- I can explain the subtraction strategy I used.
- I can compare addition and subtraction strategies.

5 Vocabulary

Review Words
bar model
difference
minus
part-part-whole model
subtraction equation

Organize It

Use the review words to complete the graphic organizer.

$8 - 3 = 5$

Define It

Match the review word to its definition.

1. bar model

2. part-part-whole model

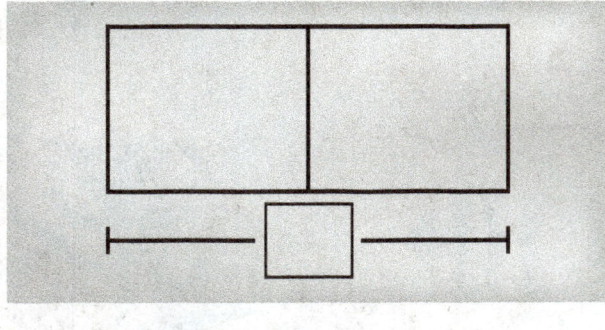

Friend:
You:

Name _____

Learning Target: Use the *count back* strategy to find a difference.

Count Back to Subtract within 20

5.1

Explore and Grow

Model the story.

You are on floor number 12. You go down 4 floors. What floor are you on now?

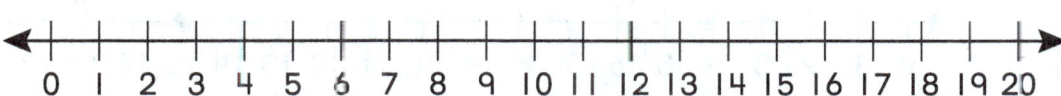

Use Math Tools
How does the number line help you solve?

floor number ____

Chapter 5 | **Lesson 1**

two hundred forty-three 243

Think and Grow

Start at 13. Count back 5.

13 − 5 = __8__

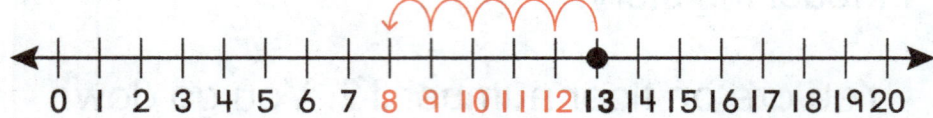

Show and Grow   I can do it!

1. 15 − 8 = ____

2. 12 − 3 = ____

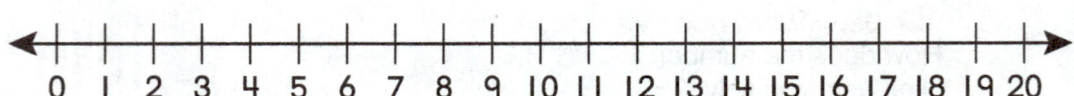

3. 17 − 9 = ____

Name _____

 **Apply and Grow: Practice**

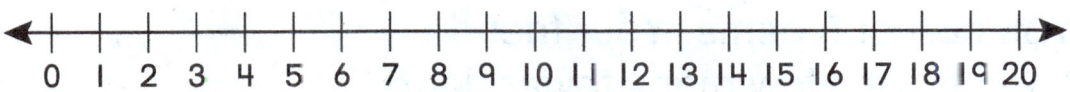

4. 11 − 6 = ___

5. 13 − 7 = ___

6. 18 − 9 = ___

7. 20 − 10 = ___

8. 17 − 8 = ___

9. 18 − 3 = ___

10. ___ = 16 − 4

11. ___ = 14 − 8

12. **DIG DEEPER!** Write the equation shown by the number line.

___ − ___ = ___

Think and Grow: Modeling Real Life

You collect 6 gems. Your friend collects 14. How many fewer gems do you collect?

Model:

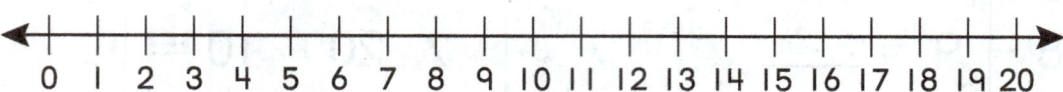

Subtraction equation:

_____ fewer gems

Show and Grow I can think deeper!

13. Your friend finds 16 gold bars. You find 9. How many fewer gold bars do you find?

Model:

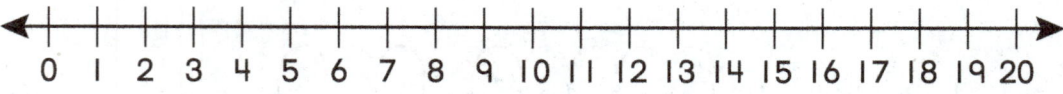

Subtraction equation:

_____ gold bars

Name _____

Practice 5.1

Learning Target: Use the *count back* strategy to find a difference.

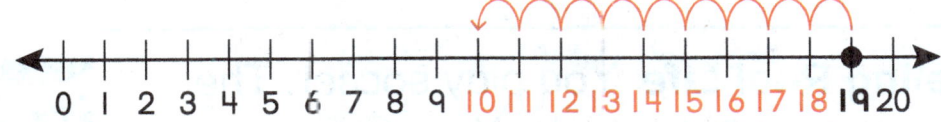

$19 - 9 = \underline{10}$

1. $12 - 5 = \underline{}$

2. $15 - 7 = \underline{}$

3. $13 - 6 = \underline{}$

4. $14 - 5 = \underline{}$

5. $11 - 5 = \underline{}$

6. $15 - 4 = \underline{}$

7. $\underline{} = 18 - 8$

8. $\underline{} = 12 - 8$

Chapter 5 | Lesson 1 two hundred forty-seven 247

9. **Structure** Write the equation shown by the number line.

10. **Modeling Real Life** You play soccer. The visiting team scores 12 goals. Your team scores 4 fewer. How many goals does your team score?

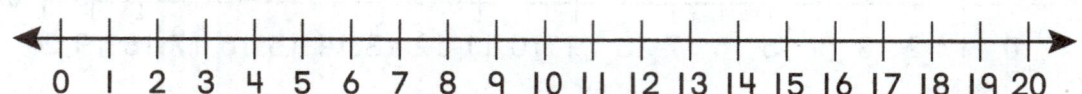

_____ goals

11. **DIG DEEPER!** You have 13 honey pots in a video game. A honey badger steals 4 of them. Then you find 6 more. How many honey pots do you have now?

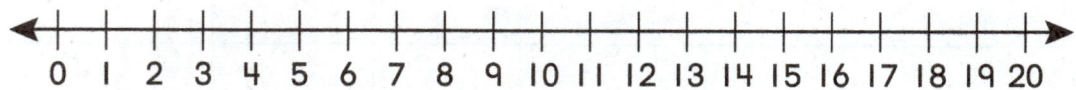

_____ honey pots

Review & Refresh

12. $6 + 2 =$ _____

13. $4 + 3 =$ _____

Name _____

Learning Target: Use the *add to subtract* strategy to find a difference.

Use Addition to Subtract within 20 5.2

Explore and Grow

Model the story.

Your class needs to make 15 scrapbook pages. 8 are already made. How many more pages does your class need to make?

Repeated Reasoning
Explain to your partner how you used the number line to solve.

_____ more pages

Chapter 5 | Lesson 2

two hundred forty-nine   249

Think and Grow

Start at 9. Count on 5 to get to 14.

$14 - 9 = ?$

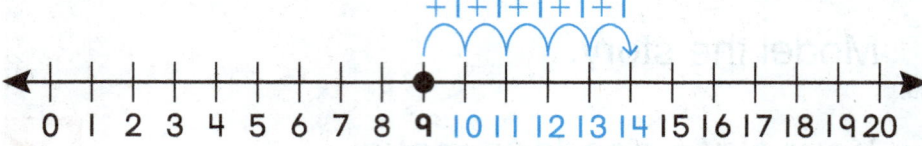

Think $9 + \underline{5} = 14$.

So, $14 - 9 = \underline{5}$.

Show and Grow — I can do it!

1. $11 - 7 = ?$

Think $7 + \underline{} = 11$.   So, $11 - 7 = \underline{}$.

2. $16 - 8 = ?$

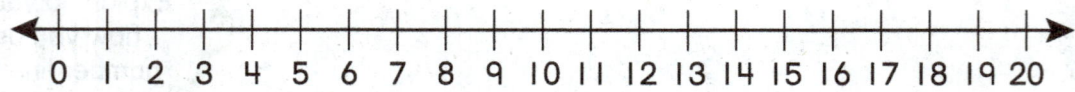

Think $8 + \underline{} = 16$.   So, $16 - 8 = \underline{}$.

3. $13 - 10 = ?$

Think $10 + \underline{} = 13$.   So, $13 - 10 = \underline{}$.

Name _____

 **Apply and Grow: Practice**

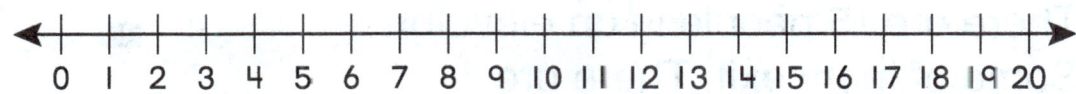

4. 12 − 7 = ?

Think 7 + ____ = 12.

So, 12 − 7 = ____.

5. 17 − 8 = ?

Think 8 + ____ = 17.

So, 17 − 8 = ____.

6. 11 − 2 = ____

7. ____ = 19 − 5

8. **DIG DEEPER!** Tell what subtraction problem Newton and Descartes solved. Think: What strategies did they use?

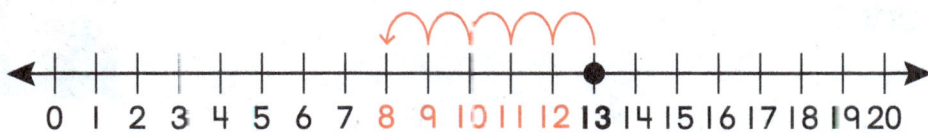

____ − ____ = ____

Chapter 5 | Lesson 2

Think and Grow: Modeling Real Life

There are 15 people in an elevator. Some of them exit. There are 7 left. How many people exit?

Model:

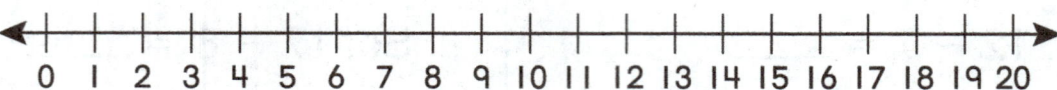

Subtraction equation:

_____ people

Show and Grow I can think deeper!

9. There are 18 people in a subway car. Some of them exit. There are 9 left. How many people exit?

Model:

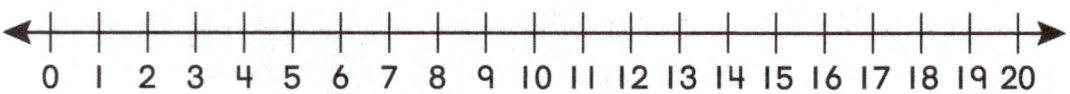

Subtraction equation:

_____ people

Name _____

Practice 5.2

Learning Target: Use the *add to subtract* strategy to find a difference.

$12 - 5 = ?$

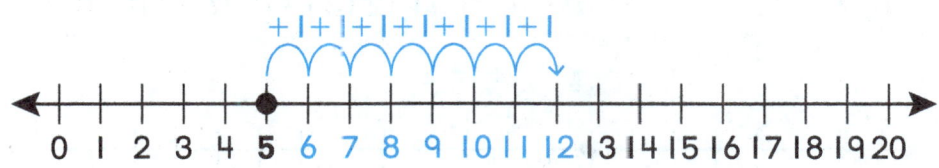

Think $5 + \underline{7} = 12$.

So, $12 - 5 = \underline{7}$.

> Start at 5. Count on 7 to get to 12.

1. $13 - 9 = ?$

   Think $9 + \underline{} = 13$.

   So, $13 - 9 = \underline{}$.

2. $17 - 8 = ?$

   Think $8 + \underline{} = 17$.

   So, $17 - 8 = \underline{}$.

3. $14 - 7 = \underline{}$

4. $\underline{} = 17 - 4$

Chapter 5 | Lesson 2

5. **DIG DEEPER!** Tell what subtraction problem Newton and Descartes solved. Think: What strategies did they use?

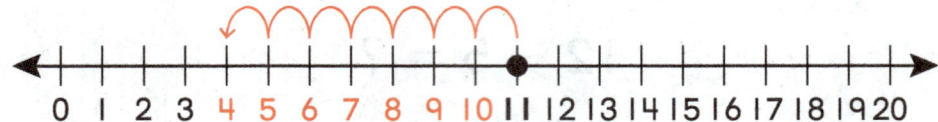

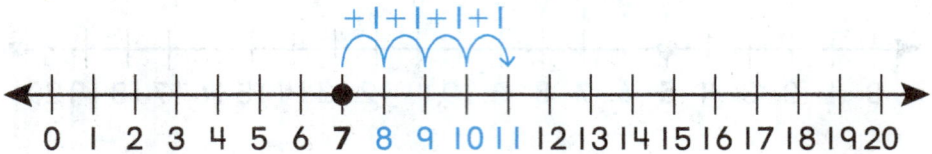

____ − ____ = ____

6. **Modeling Real Life** There are 13 people on a train. Some of them exit. There are 6 left. How many people exit?

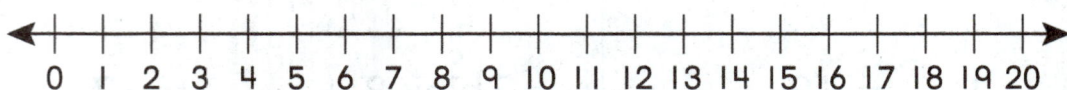

____ people

Review & Refresh

7. 10 − 9 = ____

8. 9 − 9 = ____

Name _____

Learning Target: Use the *get to 10* strategy when subtracting 9.

Subtract 9 5.3

Explore and Grow

Use counters to find each difference.

15 − 10 = ___   15 − 9 = ___

Chapter 5 | Lesson 3

two hundred fifty-five 255

Think and Grow

Start at 13. Subtract 3 to get to 10. 9 = 3 + 6, so subtract 6 more.

13 − 9 = ?

13 − **3** = 10

10 − **6** = **4**

So, 13 − 9 = **4**.

Show and Grow   I can do it!

Get to 10 to subtract.

1. 17 − 9 = ?

   17 − ___ = 10

   10 − ___ = ___

   So, 17 − 9 = ___.

2. 14 − 9 = ?

   14 − ___ = 10

   10 − ___ = ___

   So, 14 − 9 = ___.

Name _____

 Apply and Grow: Practice

3. 16 − 9 = ?

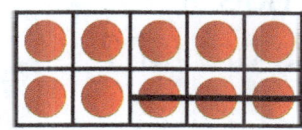

16 − ___ = 10

10 − ___ = ___

So, 16 − 9 = ___.

4. 11 − 9 = ?

11 − ___ = 10

10 − ___ = ___

So, 11 − 9 = ___.

5. 15 − 9 = ?

15 − ___ = 10

10 − ___ = ___

So, 15 − 9 = ___.

6. **Structure** Which models show 12 − 9?

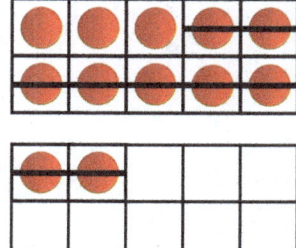 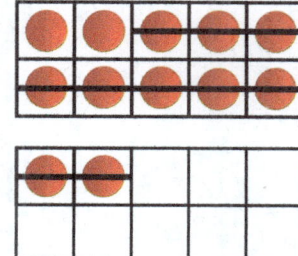 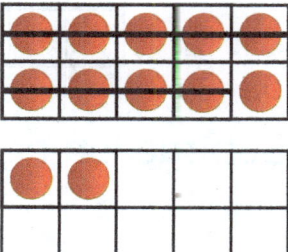

Chapter 5 | Lesson 3

Think and Grow: Modeling Real Life

You have 12 eggs. You use 9 of them. How many eggs are left?

Model:

Subtraction equation: _____

_____ eggs

Show and Grow   I can think deeper!

7. An egg carton has 18 eggs. You crack 9 of them. How many eggs are *not* cracked?

Model:

Subtraction equation: _____

_____ eggs

Name _____   **Practice** 5.3

Learning Target: Use the *get to 10* strategy when subtracting 9.

15 − 9 = ?

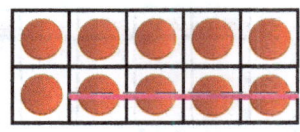

15 − **5** = 10

10 − **4** = **6**

So, 15 − 9 = **6**.

Get to 10 to subtract.

1. 18 − 9 = ?

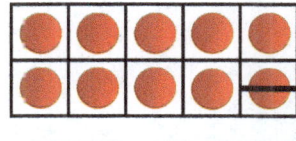

18 − ___ = 10

10 − ___ = ___

So, 18 − 9 = ___.

2. 12 − 9 = ?

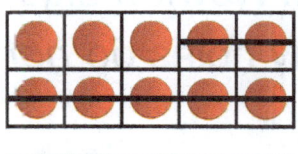

12 − ___ = 10

10 − ___ = ___

So, 12 − 9 = ___.

3. 19 − 9 = ?

19 − ___ = 10

10 − ___ = ___

So, 19 − 9 = ___.

Chapter 5 | Lesson 3

4. **Structure** Which models show 16 − 9?

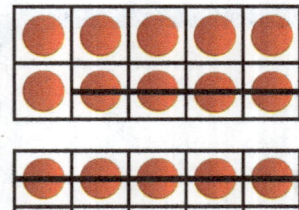 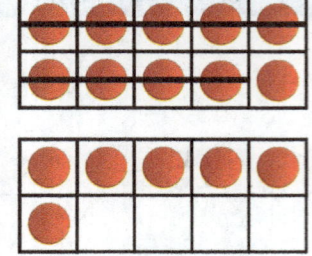 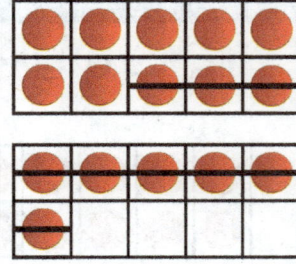

5. **Modeling Real Life** You have 14 water balloons. You break 9 of them. How many water balloons are left?

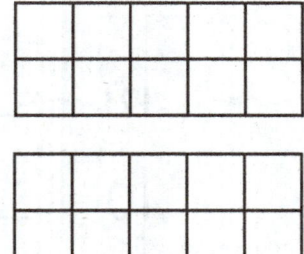

_____ water balloons

6. **DIG DEEPER!** You dig 6 holes. Newton digs 7. You fill 9 of the holes with plants. How many holes do *not* have plants?

_____ holes

Review & Refresh

7. Complete the fact family.

4 + 3 = _____   ___ − 3 = ___

___ + ___ = ___   ___ − ___ = ___

260 two hundred sixty

Name _____

Learning Target: Use the *get to 10* strategy to subtract.

Get to 10 to Subtract 5.4

Explore and Grow

Use counters to find the difference. Show how you can make a 10 to solve.

14 − 6 = ___

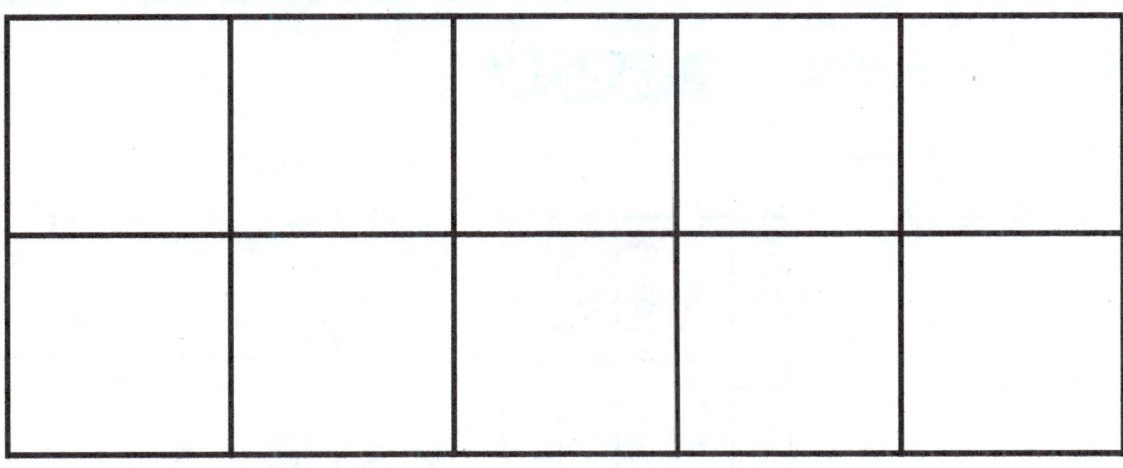

Chapter 5 | Lesson 4

Think and Grow

Start at 15. Subtract 5 to make a 10. 7 = 5 + 2, so subtract 2 more.

15 − 7 = ?

15 − **5** = 10

10 − **2** = **8**

So, 15 − 7 = **8**.

Show and Grow — I can do it!

Get to 10 to subtract.

1. 12 − 5 = ?

   12 − ___ = 10

   10 − ___ = ___

   So, 12 − 5 = ___.

2. 17 − 8 = ?

   17 − ___ = 10

   10 − ___ = ___

   So, 17 − 8 = ___.

262   two hundred sixty-two

Apply and Grow: Practice

Get to 10 to subtract.

3. 16 − 7 = ?

   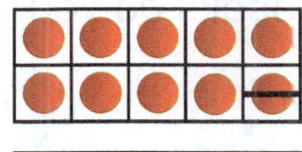

   16 − ___ = 10

   10 − ___ = ___

   So, 16 − 7 = ___.

4. 11 − 4 = ?

   11 − ___ = 10

   10 − ___ = ___

   So, 11 − 4 = ___.

5. 13 − 5 = ?

   13 − ___ = 10

   10 − ___ = ___

   So, 13 − 5 = ___.

6. **Number Sense** Which equations did Newton use to solve the problem?

   ○ 17 − 7 = 10,   10 − 7 = 3

   ○ 17 − 2 = 15,   15 − 4 = 11

   ○ 12 − 2 = 10,   10 − 4 = 6

Chapter 5 | Lesson 4

Think and Grow: Modeling Real Life

Your friend checks out 13 books. You check out 4 fewer. How many books do you check out?

Model: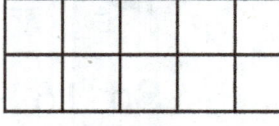

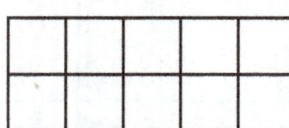

Subtraction equation:

_____ books

Show and Grow   I can think deeper!

7. Your friend skips 16 stones. You skip 8 fewer. How many stones do you skip?

Model: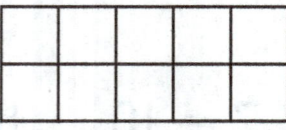

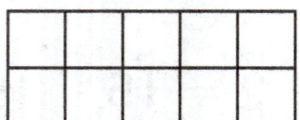

Subtraction equation:

_____ stones

Name _____   **Practice** 5.4

Learning Target: Use the *get to 10* strategy to subtract.

11 − 5 = ?

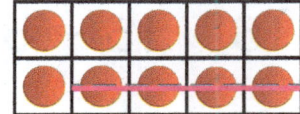

11 − __1__ = 10

10 − __4__ = __6__

So, 11 − 5 = __6__.

Get to 10 to subtract.

1. 15 − 6 = ?

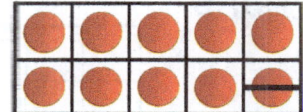

15 − ___ = 10

10 − ___ = ___

So, 15 − 6 = ___.

2. 12 − 4 = ?

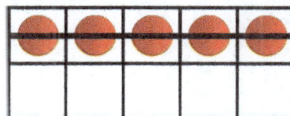

12 − ___ = 10

10 − ___ = ___

So, 12 − 4 = ___.

3. 13 − 7 = ?

13 − ___ = 10

10 − ___ = ___

So, 13 − 7 = ___.

4. 14 − 8 = ?

14 − ___ = 10

10 − ___ = ___

So, 14 − 8 = ___.

Chapter 5 | Lesson 4

5. **Number Sense** Which equations did Descartes use to solve the problem?

○ $15 - 5 = 10, \quad 10 - 4 = 6$

○ $20 - 5 = 15, \quad 15 - 5 = 10$

○ $20 - 4 = 16, \quad 16 - 5 = 11$

6. **Modeling Real Life** Your friend recycles 14 cans. You recycle 7 fewer. How many cans do you recycle?

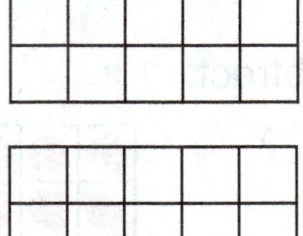

_____ cans

7. **DIG DEEPER!** 16 sand sculptors sign up for a festival. 9 drop out. Then 5 more sign up. How many sculptors participate in the festival?

_____ sculptors

Review & Refresh

Is the equation true or false?

8. $3 + 2 \stackrel{?}{=} 5 + 0$

_____ $\stackrel{?}{=}$ _____

True   False

Name _____

Learning Target: Identify whether an equation is true or false.

More True or False Equations 5.5

Explore and Grow

Color the stars that have a sum or difference equal to 19 − 5.

9 + 5

20 − 6

12 + 1 + 1

13 − 1

16 − 2

___ ○ ___

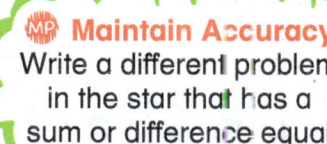

Maintain Accuracy
Write a different problem in the star that has a sum or difference equal to 19 − 5.

Chapter 5 | **Lesson 5**

two hundred sixty-seven **267**

 **Think and Grow**

$$15 - 8 \stackrel{?}{=} 11 - 4$$

15 − 8: 11 − 4:

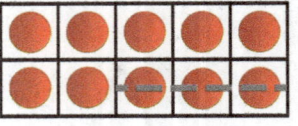 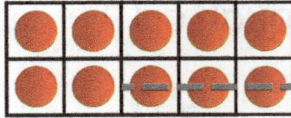

$$7 \stackrel{?}{=} 7$$

(True)   False

Show and Grow — I can do it!

Is the equation true or false?

1. $17 - 9 \stackrel{?}{=} 14 - 5$ 17 − 9:   14 − 5:

   ___ $\stackrel{?}{=}$ ___

   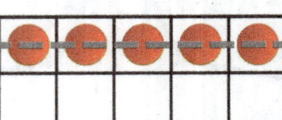

   True   False

2. $6 + 5 \stackrel{?}{=} 18 - 7$ 6 + 5:   18 − 7:

   ___ $\stackrel{?}{=}$ ___

   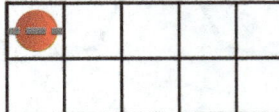

   True   False

Apply and Grow: Practice

Is the equation true or false?

3. $5 + 7 \stackrel{?}{=} 3 + 8$ $5 + 7:$ $3 + 8:$

   ___ $\stackrel{?}{=}$ ___

   True   False

4. $4 + 9 \stackrel{?}{=} 5 + 3 + 5$ $4 + 9:$ $5 + 3 + 5:$

   ___ $\stackrel{?}{=}$ ___

   True   False

5. $12 - 7 \stackrel{?}{=} 13 - 5$

   ___ $\stackrel{?}{=}$ ___

   True   False

6. $14 - 8 \stackrel{?}{=} 12 - 6$

   ___ $\stackrel{?}{=}$ ___

   True   False

7. $1 + 8 \stackrel{?}{=} 16 - 7$

   ___ $\stackrel{?}{=}$ ___

   True   False

8. $18 - 9 \stackrel{?}{=} 5 + 1 + 4$

   ___ $\stackrel{?}{=}$ ___

   True   False

9. **Reasoning** Circle all of the equations that are true.

   $20 \stackrel{?}{=} 2$ $19 - 7 \stackrel{?}{=} 12$ $6 + 6 + 3 \stackrel{?}{=} 7 + 8$

Chapter 5 | Lesson 5

# Think and Grow: Modeling Real Life

You have 12 lemons. You use 4 of them. Your friend has 3 lemons and buys 4 more. Do you each have the same number of lemons?

Equation: ____ − ____ $\overset{?}{=}$ ____ + ____

____ $\overset{?}{=}$ ____

Yes   No

Show and Grow   I can think deeper!

10. You have 14 grapes. You eat 7 of them. Your friend has 10 grapes and eats 3 of them. Do you each have the same number of grapes?

Equation: ____ − ____ $\overset{?}{=}$ ____ − ____

____ $\overset{?}{=}$ ____

Choose Tools
What math tool can you use to help solve?

Yes   No

Name _____

Practice 5.5

Learning Target: Identify whether an equation is true or false.

$5 + 9 \stackrel{?}{=} 7 + 8$

5 + 9:

7 + 8:

$\underline{14} \stackrel{?}{=} \underline{15}$

True (False)

Is the equation true or false?

1. $13 - 9 \stackrel{?}{=} 11 - 7$ 13 − 9:   11 − 7:

   $\underline{} \stackrel{?}{=} \underline{}$

   True   False

2. $9 + 8 \stackrel{?}{=} 17 + 0$ True

   $\underline{} \stackrel{?}{=} \underline{}$ False

3. $12 - 4 \stackrel{?}{=} 15 - 6$ True

   $\underline{} \stackrel{?}{=} \underline{}$ False

4. $4 + 5 \stackrel{?}{=} 11 - 3$ True

   $\underline{} \stackrel{?}{=} \underline{}$ False

5. $15 - 7 \stackrel{?}{=} 4 + 4$ True

   $\underline{} \stackrel{?}{=} \underline{}$ False

Chapter 5 | Lesson 5   two hundred seventy-one   271

6. **Reasoning** Circle all of the equations that are false.

$7 + 2 \stackrel{?}{=} 11 - 2$ $3 \stackrel{?}{=} 12 - 8$ $4 + 1 + 4 \stackrel{?}{=} 14 - 6$

7. **Modeling Real Life** You have 9 badges. You earn 3 more. Your friend has 5 badges and earns 7 more. Do you each have the same number of badges?

Analyze a Problem What do you know? What do you need to find?

___ + ___ $\stackrel{?}{=}$ ___ + ___

___ $\stackrel{?}{=}$ ___

Yes   No

8. **DIG DEEPER!** Without solving, tell whether the equation is true or false. How do you know?

$10 + 1 \stackrel{?}{=} 10 - 1$

True   False

Review & Refresh

9. ___ + 2 = 6

10. ___ + 3 = 9

Name _____

Learning Target: Find the number that makes an equation true.

Make True Equations 5.6

Explore and Grow

Complete the equation.

14 − 5 = 3 + ___

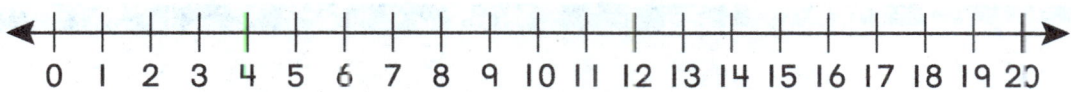

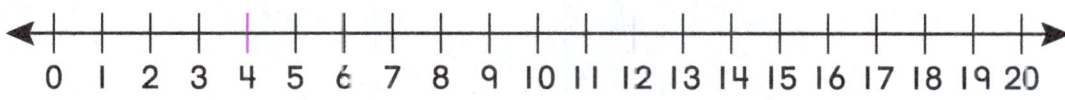

Chapter 5 | Lesson 6

two hundred seventy-three 273

Think and Grow

I know the value of the right side of the equation. $4 + 2 = 6$

$$13 - ? = 4 + 2$$

$$13 - ? = \underline{6}$$

The left side has to equal 6, and $13 - 7 = 6$.

$$13 - \underline{7} = \underline{6}$$

So, $13 - \underline{7} = 4 + 2$.

Show and Grow I can do it!

1. $? + 6 = 10 - 3$

   $? + 6 = \underline{}$

   $\underline{} + 6 = \underline{}$

   So, $\underline{} + 6 = 10 - 3$.

2. $12 - 9 = ? - 5$

   $\underline{} = ? - 5$

   $\underline{} = \underline{} - 5$

   So, $12 - 9 = \underline{} - 5$.

Name _____

Apply and Grow: Practice

3. ? + 8 = 9 + 6

    ? + 8 = ___

    ___ + 8 = ___

    So, ___ + 8 = 9 + 6.

4. 13 − 8 = ? − 6

    ___ = ? − 6

    ___ = ___ − 6

    So, 13 − 8 = ___ − 6.

5. 14 − 6 = ? + 2

    ___ = ? + 2

    ___ = ___ + 2

    So, 14 − 6 = ___ + 2.

6. 15 − ? = 3 + 3

    15 − ? = ___

    15 − ___ = ___

    So, 15 − ___ = 3 + 3.

7. ___ − 6 = 3 + 2 + 1

8. 6 + 4 + 4 = 6 + ___

9. **MP YOU BE THE TEACHER** Newton says 2 makes the equation true. Is Newton correct? Show how you know.

7 + 2 = 11 − ?

Chapter 5 | Lesson 6

Think and Grow: Modeling Real Life

You catch 11 butterflies. 4 fly away. Your friend catches 3 butterflies. How many more butterflies must your friend catch to have the same number as you?

Equation:

___ − ___ = ___ + ?

_____ butterflies

Show and Grow   I can think deeper!

10. You catch 15 leaves. 6 of them blow away. Your friend catches 12 leaves and some of them blow away. Now you each have the same number of leaves. How many of your friend's leaves blow away?

    Equation:

    ___ − ___ = ___ − ?

    _____ leaves

Name _____

Practice 5.6

Learning Target: Find the number that makes an equation true.

I know the value of the left side of the equation. 5 + 3 = 8

5 + 3 = ? − 4

_8_ = ? − 4

_8_ = _12_ − 4

So, 5 + 3 = _12_ − 4.

1. 12 − ? = 8 − 4

    12 − ? = ___

    12 − ___ = ___

    So, 12 − ___ = 8 − 4.

2. 7 + 9 = 8 + ?

    ___ = 8 + ?

    ___ = 8 + ___

    So, 7 + 9 = 8 + ___.

3. 4 + 3 = ___ − 7

4. 7 + ___ = 17 − 0

5. ___ + 20 = 8 + 10 + 2

6. 3 + 1 + 1 = 14 − ___

Chapter 5 | Lesson 6   two hundred seventy-seven 277

7. YOU BE THE TEACHER Descartes says 5 makes the equation true. Is Descartes correct? Show how you know.

$17 - 9 = ? - 2$

8. Modeling Real Life You catch 14 fireflies. You lose 8 of them. Your friend catches 11 fireflies and loses some of them. Now you each have the same number of fireflies. How many fireflies does your friend lose?

___ − ___ = ___ − ?

___ fireflies

9. DIG DEEPER! Use Newton's clue to complete the equation.

🔴 − ___ = 3 + 9

Review & Refresh

10. Color the squares.

 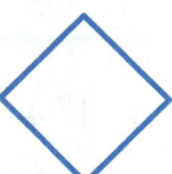  

Name _____

Learning Target: Solve subtraction word problems.

Problem Solving: Subtraction within 20

 **Explore and Grow**

Model the story.

There are 18 seagulls. Some of them fly away. There are 9 left. How many seagulls flew away?

_____ seagulls

Chapter 5 | **Lesson 7**

Think and Grow

There are 14 kids in a bounce house. Some of them get out. There are 5 kids left. How many kids got out of the bounce house?

Circle what you know.

Underline what you need to find.

Solve:

Start at 14. Count back to 5.

$$14 - 9 = 5$$

___9___ kids

Show and Grow — I can do it!

1. You have some stuffed animals. You give 3 away. You have 8 left. How many stuffed animals did you have to start?

   Circle what you know.   Underline what you need to find.

   Solve:

   ___ ◯ ___ = ___

   ____ stuffed animals

Name _____

✓ Apply and Grow: Practice

2. A group of students are at an arcade. 8 of them leave. There are 3 left. How many students were at the arcade to start?

Circle what you know.   Underline what you need to find.

Solve:

_____ ◯ _____ = _____

_____ students

3. You have 15 trucks. Your friend has 7. How many more trucks do you have?

_____ more trucks

4.  **Precision** You have 16 stickers. Your friend has 7 fewer than you. Which bar model shows how many stickers your friend has?

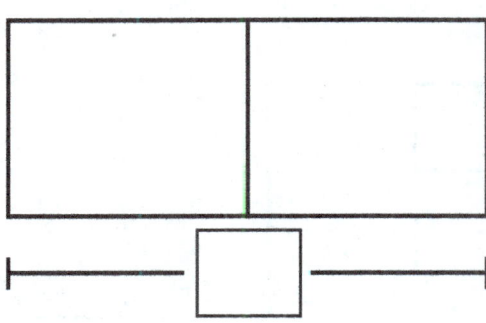

You: 16   You: 16
Friend: 7 | 9   Friend: 9 | 7

16 − 9 = 7   16 − 7 = 9

Chapter 5 | Lesson 7   two hundred eighty-one   281

Think and Grow: Modeling Real Life

Your friend's mask has 13 feathers. Your mask has 7 feathers. How many fewer feathers does your mask have?

Circle what you know.   Underline what you need to find.

Solve:

Friend:

You:

___ − ___ = ___

___ fewer feathers

Show and Grow   I can think deeper!

5. There are 12 party hats. There are 5 fewer noisemakers than party hats. How many noisemakers are there?

Circle what you know.   Underline what you need to find.

Solve:

___ − ___ = ___

___ noisemakers

Name _____   **Practice 5.7**

Learning Target: Solve subtraction word problems.

(You have 11 pebbles.) You toss some of them.
(You have 4 left.) How many pebbles did you toss?

Circle what you know.   Underline what you need to find.

Solve:

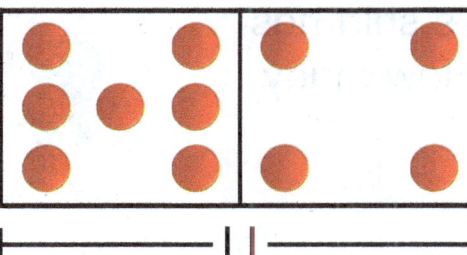   11 ⊖ 7 = 4

_7_ pebbles

1. You have 12 erasers. Your friend takes some of them. You have 5 left. How many erasers does your friend take?

   Circle what you know.   Underline what you need to find.

   Solve:
   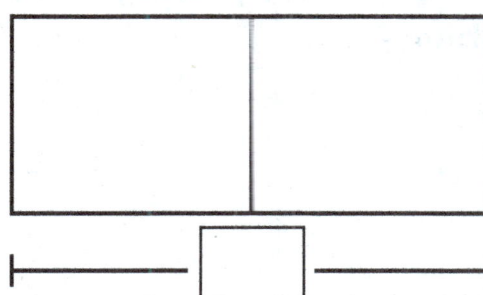   ___ ◯ ___ = ___

   ___ erasers

2. You have 17 glitter pens. Your friend has 9 fewer than you. How many does your friend have?

   ___ glitter pens

Chapter 5 | Lesson 7   two hundred eighty-three **283**

3. **Precision** A group of students are at a library. 6 of them leave. There are 7 left. Which part-part-whole model shows how many students were at the library to start?

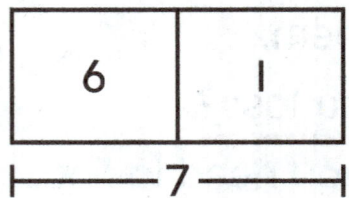
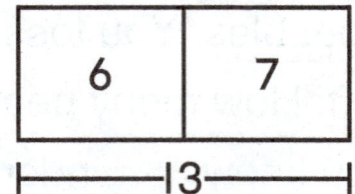

4. **Modeling Real Life** Your friend's shirt has 14 buttons. Your shirt has 7 fewer. How many buttons does your shirt have?

Friend: [   ]

You: [   ]

_____ buttons

5. **DIG DEEPER!** There are 7 bees near a beehive. 6 more bees fly to the beehive. Then 4 of them fly away. How many bees are left at the beehive?

_____ bees

Review & Refresh

6. There are 8 🦦.

   3 🦦 swim away.

   How many 🦦 are left?

   ___ − ___ = ___

   _____ 🦦

Name _____

Performance Task 5

1. You keep track of the number of honeybees and bumblebees you see.

Day	Honeybees
Monday	12
Tuesday	6
Wednesday	13

Day	Bumblebees
Monday	5
Tuesday	14
Wednesday	

a. How many more honeybees did you see on Monday than on Tuesday?

_____ more honeybees

b. How many fewer bees did you see on Monday than on Tuesday?

_____ fewer bees

c. How many bumblebees must you see on Wednesday so that the numbers of bees you see on Tuesday and Wednesday are the same?

_____ bumblebees

Three in a Row: Subtraction

To Play: Place the Three in a Row: Subtraction Game Cards in a pile. Players take turns. On your turn, flip over the top card and solve the problem. Place a counter on the answer. Your turn is over. Repeat this process until a player gets three in a row.

Name _____

Chapter 5 Practice

5.1 Count Back to Subtract within 20

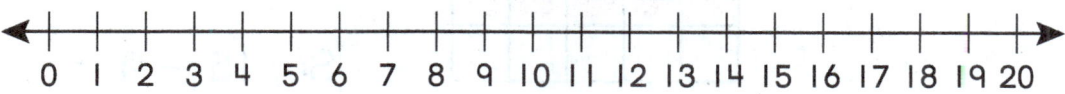

1. 11 − 3 = ___

2. 13 − 4 = ___

3. ___ = 15 − 3

4. ___ = 16 − 8

5.2 Use Addition to Subtract within 20

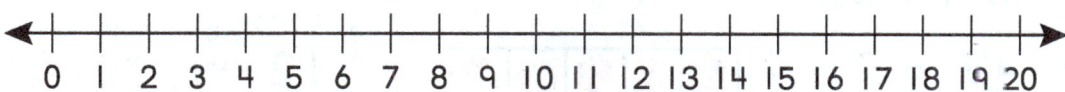

5. 11 − 9 = ?

   Think 9 + ___ = 11.

   So, 11 − 9 = ___.

6. 13 − 8 = ?

   Think 8 + ___ = 13.

   So, 13 − 8 = ___.

7. ___ = 20 − 7

8. ___ = 12 − 3

5.3 Subtract 9

Get to 10 to subtract.

9. 15 − 9 = ?

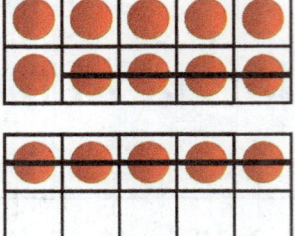

15 − ___ = 10

10 − ___ = ___

So, 15 − 9 = ___.

10. 17 − 9 = ?

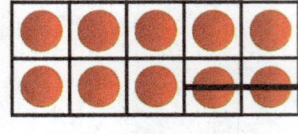

17 − ___ = 10

10 − ___ = ___

So, 17 − 9 = ___.

5.4 Get to 10 to Subtract

Get to 10 to subtract.

11. 12 − 7 = ?

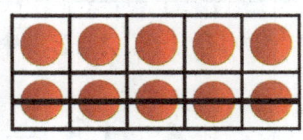

12 − ___ = 10

10 − ___ = ___

So, 12 − 7 = ___.

12. 17 − 8 = ?

17 − ___ = 10

10 − ___ = ___

So, 17 − 8 = ___.

5.5 More True or False Equations

Is the equation true or false?

13. $8 + 3 + 8 \stackrel{?}{=} 13 + 6$ $8 + 3 + 8:$ $13 + 6:$

$\underline{} \stackrel{?}{=} \underline{}$

True   False

---

14. $16 - 8 \stackrel{?}{=} 6 + 2$

$\underline{} \stackrel{?}{=} \underline{}$

True   False

15. $14 - 7 \stackrel{?}{=} 12 - 9$

$\underline{} \stackrel{?}{=} \underline{}$

True   False

5.6 Make True Equations

16. $11 - 7 = 10 - ?$

$\underline{} = 10 - ?$

$\underline{} = 10 - \underline{}$

So, $11 - 7 = 10 - \underline{}$.

17. $2 + 0 + 6 = ? - 5$

$\underline{} = ? - 5$

$\underline{} = \underline{} - 5$

So, $2 + 0 + 6 = \underline{} - 5$.

Chapter 5   two hundred eighty-nine   289

5.7 Problem Solving: Subtraction within 20

18. There are 13 people on a train. Some of them exit. There are 5 left. How many people exit the train?

Circle what you know.

Underline what you need to find.

Solve:

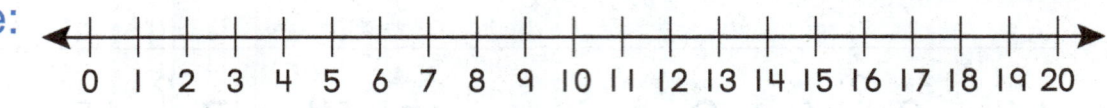

____ ◯ ____ = ____   ____ people

19. A group of students are at a museum. 8 of them leave. There are 7 left. How many students were there to start?

____ students

20. You and a friend play basketball. Your friend scores 17 points. You score 8 fewer. How many points do you score?

____ points

6 Count and Write Numbers to 120

- What are some ways people raise money?
- How many quarters are there in all?

Chapter Learning Target:
Understand counting.

Chapter Success Criteria:
- I can identify numbers on a chart.
- I can describe numbers on a chart.
- I can count or from a number.
- I can write numbers.

6 Vocabulary

Review Words
column
decade numbers
hundred chart
row

Organize It

Use the review words to complete the graphic organizer.

Define It

Use your vocabulary cards to identify the words.

23

Chapter 6 Vocabulary Cards

120 chart	column
decade numbers	digit
ones	ones place
row	tens

	1	2	3	4	5	6	7	8	9	10
	11	12	13	14	15	16	**17**	18	19	20
	21	22	23	24	25	26	**27**	28	29	30
	31	32	33	34	35	36	**37**	38	39	40
	41	42	43	44	45	46	**47**	48	49	50
	51	52	53	54	55	56	**57**	58	59	60
	61	62	63	64	65	66	**67**	68	69	70
	71	72	73	74	75	76	**77**	78	79	80
	81	82	83	84	85	86	**87**	88	89	90
	91	92	93	94	95	96	**97**	98	99	100
	101	102	103	104	105	106	**107**	108	109	110
	111	112	113	114	115	116	**117**	118	119	120

(blank hundreds chart 1–120)

The digits of 16 are 1 and 6.

16

	1	2	3	4	5	6	7	8	9	**10**
	11	12	13	14	15	16	17	18	19	**20**
	21	22	23	24	25	26	27	28	29	**30**
	31	32	33	34	35	36	37	38	39	**40**
	41	42	43	44	45	46	47	48	49	**50**
	51	52	53	54	55	56	57	58	59	**60**
	61	62	63	64	65	66	67	68	69	**70**
	71	72	73	74	75	76	77	78	79	**80**
	81	82	83	84	85	86	87	88	89	**90**
	91	92	93	94	95	96	97	98	99	**100**
	101	102	103	104	105	106	107	108	109	**110**
	111	112	113	114	115	116	117	118	119	**120**

2<u>3</u>

---

23 has 3 ones.

---

23 has 2 tens.

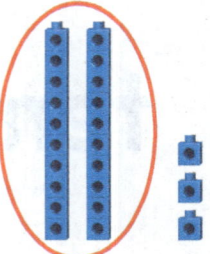

	1	2	3	4	5	6	7	8	9	10
	11	12	13	14	15	16	17	18	19	20
	21	22	23	24	25	26	27	28	29	30
	31	32	33	34	35	36	37	38	39	40
	41	**42**	**43**	**44**	**45**	**46**	**47**	**48**	**49**	**50**
	51	52	53	54	55	56	57	58	59	60
	61	62	63	64	65	66	67	68	69	70
	71	72	73	74	75	76	77	78	79	80
	81	82	83	84	85	86	87	88	89	90
	91	92	93	94	95	96	97	98	99	100
	101	102	103	104	105	106	107	108	109	110
	111	112	113	114	115	116	117	118	119	120

Chapter 6 Vocabulary Cards

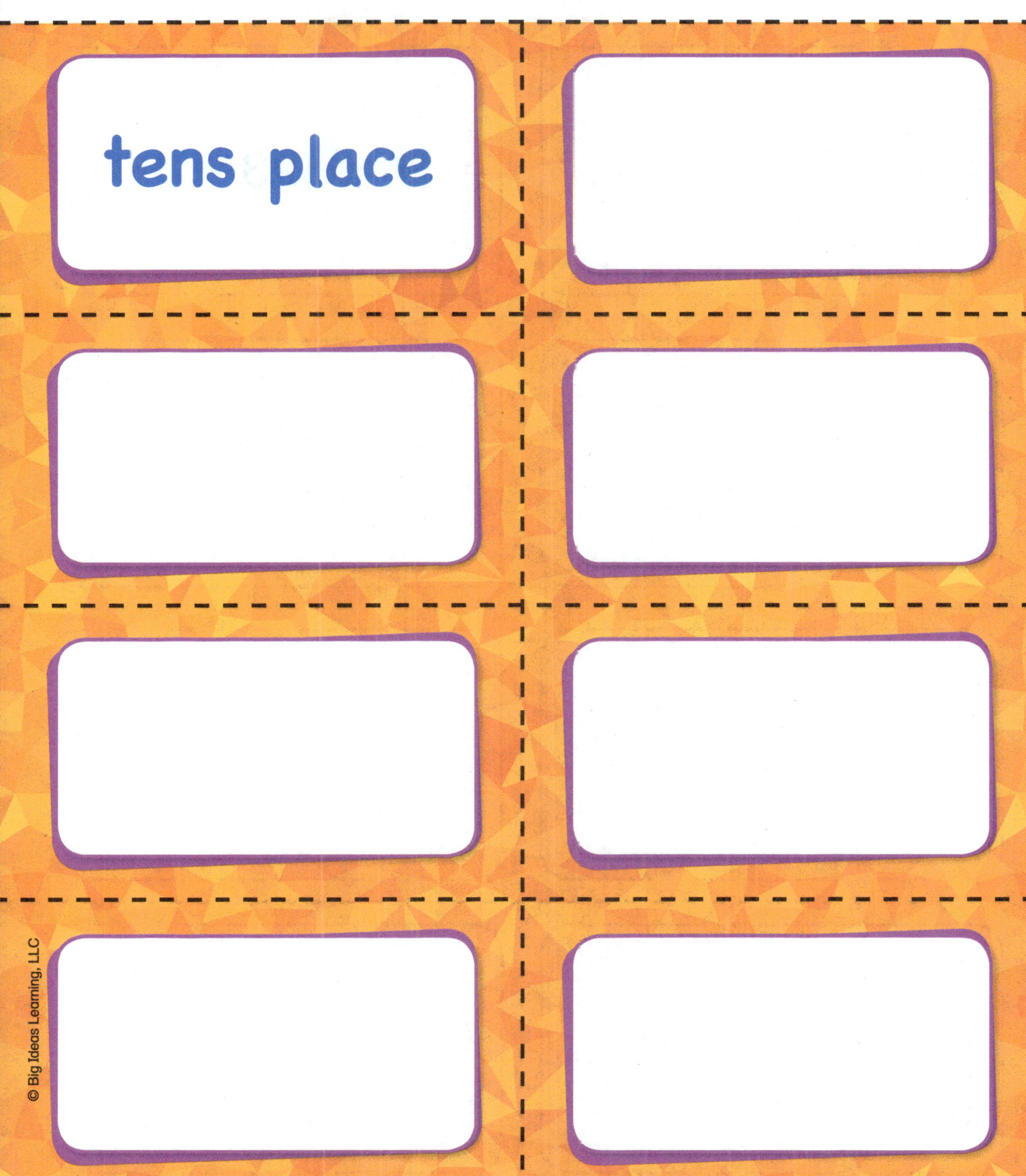

tens place

23

Name _____

Learning Target: Count to 120 by ones.

Count to 120 by Ones  **6.1**

Explore and Grow

Point to each number as you count to 120. Color the first two rows and the last two rows. How are the rows the same? How are they different?

1	2	3	4	5	6	7	8	9	10
11	12	13	14	15	16	17	18	19	20
21	22	23	24	25	26	27	28	29	30
31	32	33	34	35	36	37	38	39	40
41	42	43	44	45	46	47	48	49	50
51	52	53	54	55	56	57	58	59	60
61	62	63	64	65	66	67	68	69	70
71	72	73	74	75	76	77	78	79	80
81	82	83	84	85	86	87	88	89	90
91	92	93	94	95	96	97	98	99	100
101	102	103	104	105	106	107	108	109	110
111	112	113	114	115	116	117	118	119	120

Chapter 6 | **Lesson 1**

two hundred ninety-three

Think and Grow

> Count by ones: fourteen, fifteen, sixteen, seventeen, eighteen, nineteen

14, __15__, __16__, __17__, __18__, __19__

1	2	3	4	5	6	7	8	9	10
11	12	13	14	15	16	17	18	19	20
21	22	23	24	25	26	27	28	29	30
31	32	33	34	35	36	37	38	39	40
41	42	43	44	45	46	47	48	49	50
51	52	53	54	55	56	57	58	59	60
61	62	63	64	65	66	67	68	69	70
71	72	73	74	75	76	77	78	79	80
81	82	83	84	85	86	87	88	89	90
91	92	93	94	95	96	97	98	99	100
101	102	103	104	105	106	107	108	109	110
111	112	113	114	115	116	117	118	119	120

← **row** (row 51–60 highlighted)

120 chart

Show and Grow — I can do it!

Count by ones to write the missing numbers.

1. 82, _____, _____, _____, _____, _____

2. 103, _____, _____, _____, _____, _____

Name _____

 **Apply and Grow: Practice**

Count by ones to write the missing numbers.

3. 56, ____, ____, ____, ____, ____

4. 98, ____, ____, ____, ____, ____

5. 115, ____, ____, ____, ____, ____

6. ____, ____, 42, ____, ____, ____

Write the missing numbers in the chart.

7.
32		34	
	43		45

8.
	82		
91		93	

9. **Maintain Accuracy** Write a number between 95 and 105. Then count by ones to write the next 7 numbers.

____, ____, ____, ____, ____, ____, ____, ____

Chapter 6 | Lesson 1   two hundred ninety-five 295

Think and Grow: Modeling Real Life

You have 108 bouncy balls. You want 112. How many more bouncy balls do you need?

Draw more balls to show 112:

_____ more bouncy balls

Show and Grow   I can think deeper!

10. You have 66 rocks. You want 75. How many more rocks do you need?

    Draw more rocks to show 75:

    _____ more rocks

Name _____

Practice 6.1

Learning Target: Count to 120 by ones.

1	2	3	4	5	6	7	8	9	10
11	12	13	14	15	16	17	18	19	20
21	22	23	24	25	26	27	28	29	30
31	32	33	34	35	36	37	38	39	40
41	42	43	44	45	46	47	48	49	50
51	52	53	54	55	56	57	58	59	60
61	62	63	64	65	66	67	68	69	70
71	72	73	74	75	76	77	78	79	80
81	82	83	84	85	86	87	88	89	90
91	92	93	94	95	96	97	98	99	100
101	102	103	104	105	106	107	108	109	110
111	112	113	114	115	116	117	118	119	120

72, **73**, **74**, **75**, **76**, **77**

Count by ones to write the missing numbers.

1. 57, _____, _____, _____, _____, _____

2. 109, _____, _____, _____, _____, _____

3. 40, _____, _____, _____, _____, _____

4. _____, _____, _____, 100, _____, _____

Chapter 6 | Lesson 1

Write the missing numbers in the chart.

5.

20		22
	31	33

6.

	103	
112		114

7. **Maintain Accuracy** Write a number between 85 and 95. Then count by ones to write the next 7 numbers.

_____, _____, _____, _____, _____, _____, _____, _____

8. **Modeling Real Life** There are 110 tokens. You want 119. How many more tokens do you need?

_____ more tokens

9. **DIG DEEPER!** How is counting forward similar to addition?

Review & Refresh

10. ? − 6 = 4

6	4

[ ]

Think 6 + 4 = _____.

So, _____ − 6 = 4.

298 two hundred ninety-eight

Name _____

Count to 120 by Tens

Learning Target: Count to 120 by tens.

Explore and Grow

Count to 10. Circle the number. Count 10 more. Circle the number. Continue until you reach 120.

1	2	3	4	5	6	7	8	9	10
11	12	13	14	15	16	17	18	19	20
21	22	23	24	25	26	27	28	29	30
31	32	33	34	35	36	37	38	39	40
41	42	43	44	45	46	47	48	49	50
51	52	53	54	55	56	57	58	59	60
61	62	63	64	65	66	67	68	69	70
71	72	73	74	75	76	77	78	79	80
81	82	83	84	85	86	87	88	89	90
91	92	93	94	95	96	97	98	99	100
101	102	103	104	105	106	107	108	109	110
111	112	113	114	115	116	117	118	119	120

Chapter 6 | Lesson 2   two hundred ninety-nine

Think and Grow

40, 50, 60, 70, 80, 90

Count by tens: forty, fifty, sixty, seventy, eighty, ninety

1	2	3	4	5	6	7	8	9	10
11	12	13	14	15	16	17	18	19	20
21	22	23	24	25	26	27	28	29	30
31	32	33	34	35	36	37	38	39	40
41	42	43	44	45	46	47	48	49	50
51	52	53	54	55	56	57	58	59	60
61	62	63	64	65	66	67	68	69	70
71	72	73	74	75	76	77	78	79	80
81	82	83	84	85	86	87	88	89	90
91	92	93	94	95	96	97	98	99	100
101	102	103	104	105	106	107	108	109	110
111	112	113	114	115	116	117	118	119	120

↑ column

↑ decade numbers

Show and Grow   I can do it!

Count by tens to write the missing numbers.

1. 70, _____, _____, _____, _____, _____

2. 31, _____, _____, _____, _____, _____

Apply and Grow: Practice

Count by tens to write the missing numbers.

3. 62, ____, ____, ____, ____, ____

4. 43, ____, ____, ____, ____, ____

5. ____, ____, 30, ____, ____, ____

6. **Patterns** Write the missing numbers from the chart. Then count on by tens to write the next three numbers.

| ? | 72 | 73 | 74 | 75 | 76 | 77 | 78 | 79 | 80 |
| ? | 82 | 83 | 84 | 85 | 86 | 87 | 88 | 89 | 90 |

____, ____, ____, ____, ____

7. **YOU BE THE TEACHER** Your friend counts by tens starting with 27. Is your friend correct? Show how you know.

27, 37, 47, 67, 77, 87

Chapter 6 | Lesson 2

Think and Grow: Modeling Real Life

You have 50 points. On your next turn, you knock over 6 cans. How many points do you have now?

Write the numbers:

_____ points

Show and Grow   I can think deeper!

8. You have 21 points. On your next turn, 3 beanbags land in the circle. How many points do you have now?

Write the numbers:

_____ points

302   three hundred two

Practice 6.2

Learning Target: Count to 120 by tens.

45, __55__, __65__, __75__, __85__, __95__

Count by tens to write the missing numbers.

1. 69, ____, ____, ____, ____, ____

2. 41, ____, ____, ____, ____, ____

3. 16, ____, ____, ____, ____, ____

4. ____, ____, ____, 94, ____, ____

5. **Patterns** Write the missing numbers from the chart. Then count on by tens to write the next three numbers.

1	2	3	4	5		7	8	9	10
11	12	13	14	15		17	18	19	20

6. **DIG DEEPER!** You count to 50. You only count 5 numbers. Did you count by ones or by tens? Show how you know.

7. **Modeling Real Life** You have 30 points. On your next turn, 4 balls stick to the wall. How many points do you have now?

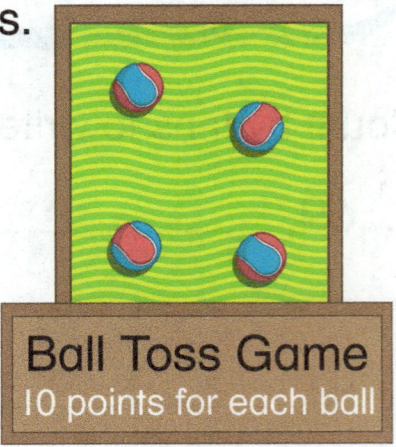

Ball Toss Game
10 points for each ball

_____ points

Review & Refresh

8. $3 + 1 =$ _____

9. $5 - 1 =$ _____

Name _____

Learning Target: Understand and write numbers from 11 to 19.

Compose Numbers 11 to 19

Explore and Grow

Color to show 13 and 17. What is the same about the numbers? What is different?

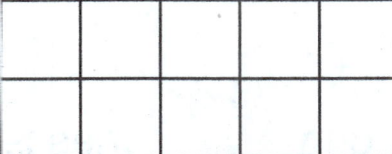

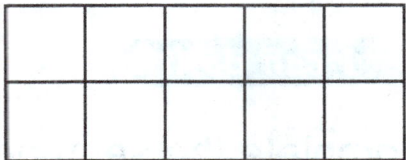

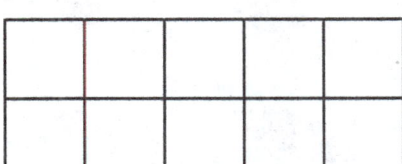

Analyze a Problem
What is the best way to color in the ten frames to answer the questions?

Chapter 6 | **Lesson 3**

three hundred five 305

Think and Grow

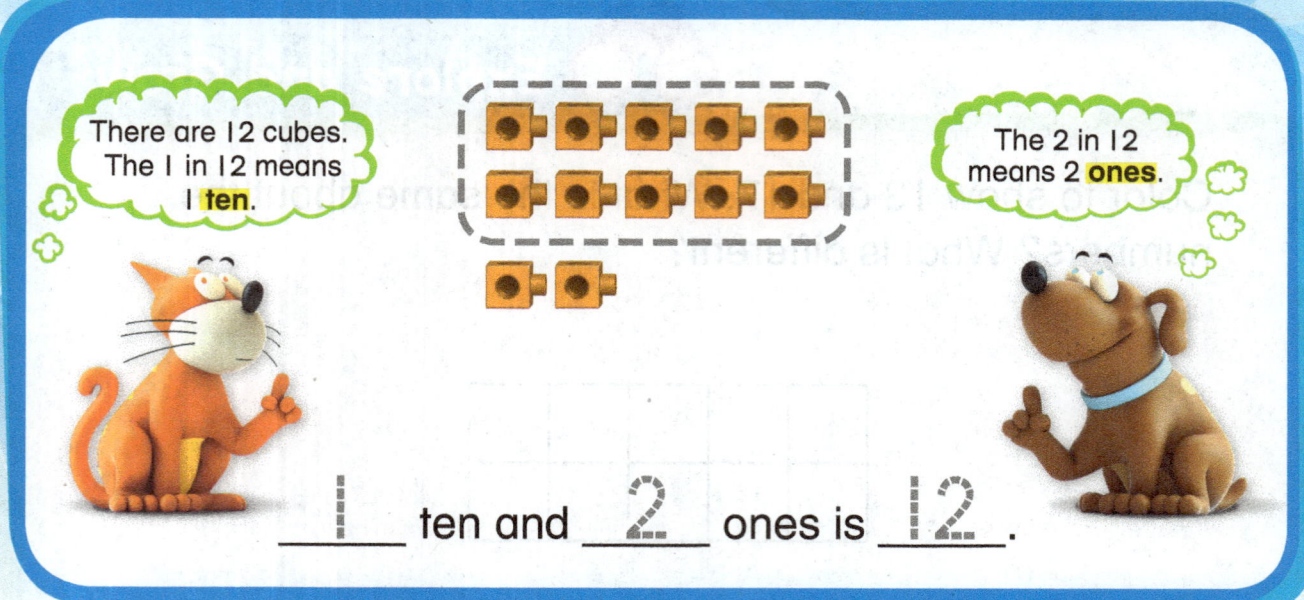

___1___ ten and ___2___ ones is ___12___.

Show and Grow — I can do it!

1. Circle 10 feathers. Complete the sentence.

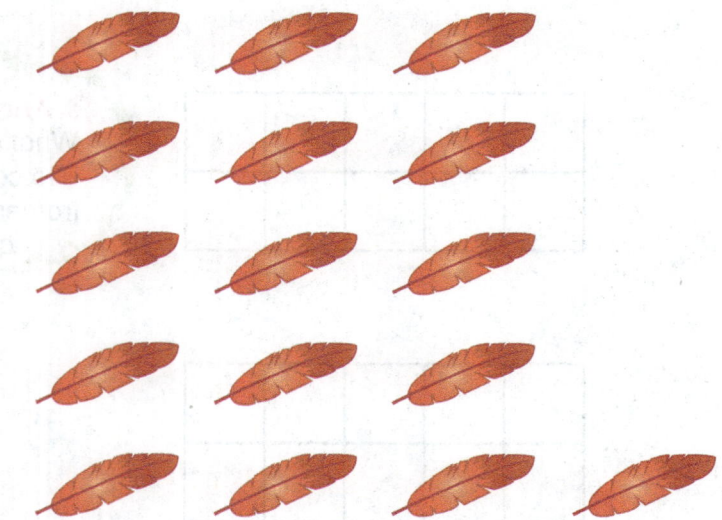

_____ ten and _____ ones is _____.

Name _____

✓ Apply and Grow: Practice

Circle 10 objects. Complete the sentence.

2.

_____ ten and _____ ones is _____.

3.

_____ ten and _____ ones is _____.

4.

_____ ten and _____ ones is _____.

5. **Number Sense** Color to show the number. Complete the sentence.

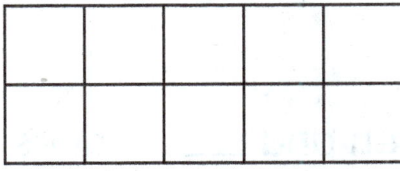
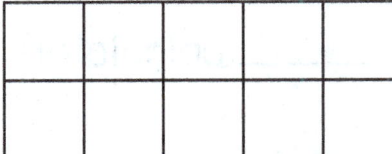

(16)

_____ ten and _____ ones is _____.

Chapter 6 | Lesson 3

Think and Grow: Modeling Real Life

You have 15 footballs. A bag can hold 10. You fill a bag. How many footballs are *not* in the bag?

Draw a picture:

Write the missing numbers: _____ ten and _____ ones

_____ footballs

Show and Grow   I can think deeper!

6. Your teacher has 18 calculators. A case can hold 10. Your teacher fills a case. How many calculators are *not* in the case?

Draw a picture:

Write the missing numbers: _____ ten and _____ ones

_____ calculators

Name _____

Practice 6.3

Learning Target: Understand and write numbers from 11 to 19.

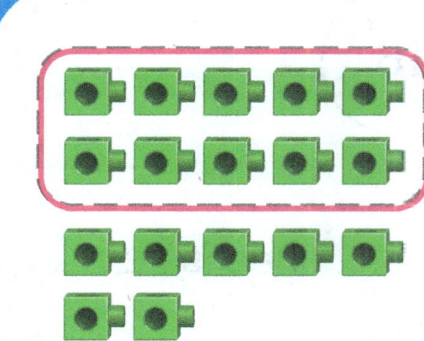

__1__ ten and __7__ ones s __17__.

Circle 10 objects. Complete the sentence.

1.

_____ ten and _____ one is _____.

2.

_____ ten and _____ ones is _____.

3.

_____ ten and _____ ones is _____.

Chapter 6 | Lesson 3

4. **Number Sense** Color to show the number. Complete the sentence.

_____ ten and _____ ones is _____.

5. **Number Sense** Match.

1 ten and 3 ones	1 ten and 8 ones	12 ones
13	12	18

6. **Modeling Real Life** You have 16 books. A backpack can hold 10. You fill a backpack. How many books are *not* in the backpack?

_____ books

7. **Modeling Real Life** In Exercise 6, how many backpacks do you need to hold all your books?

_____ backpacks

Review & Refresh

8. 10 + 0 = _____

9. 10 + 10 = _____

Name _____

Learning Target: Understand and write decade numbers.

Tens  6.4

Explore and Grow

Circle groups of 10. Write the number of groups.

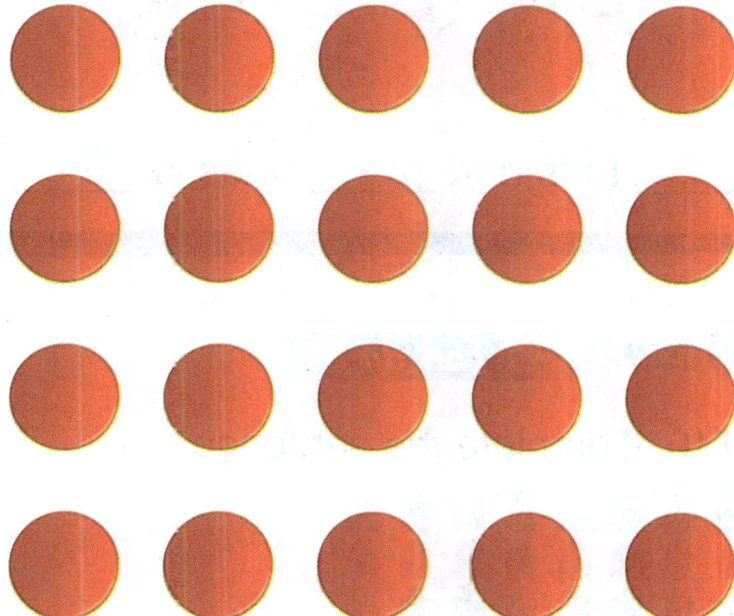

_____ groups

How many counters are there in all?

_____ counters

Repeated Reasoning
What do you notice about the number of groups and the decade number?

Chapter 6 | Lesson 4

three hundred eleven 311

Think and Grow

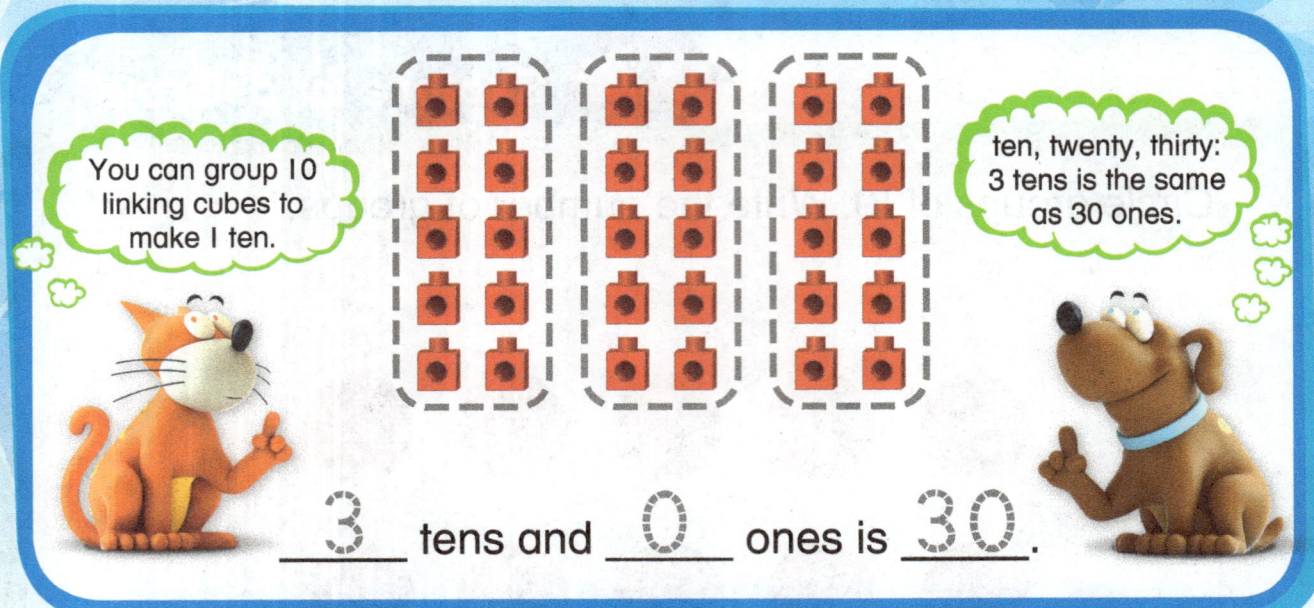

___3___ tens and ___0___ ones is ___30___.

Show and Grow   I can do it!

Circle groups of 10. Complete the sentence.

1. _____ tens and _____ ones is _____.

2. _____ tens and _____ ones is _____.

Name _____

✓ Apply and Grow: Practice

Circle groups of 10. Complete the sentence.

3.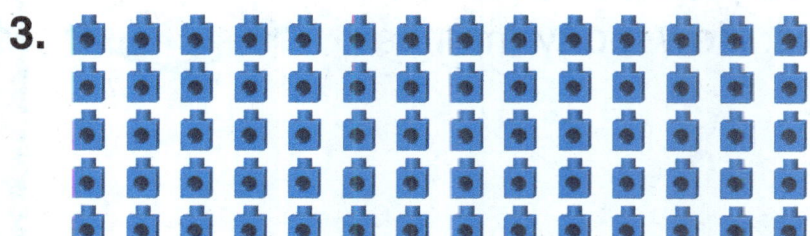

_____ tens and _____ ones is _____.

4.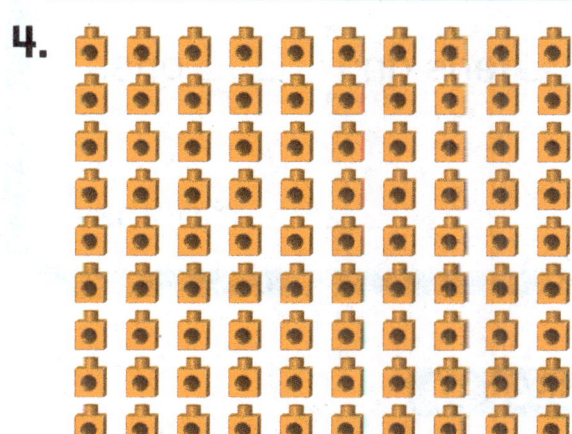

_____ tens and _____ ones is _____.

5.

_____ ten and _____ ones is _____.

6. **Number Sense** You have 4 groups of 10 linking cubes. How many linking cubes do you have?

_____ linking cubes

Chapter 6 | Lesson 4

Think and Grow: Modeling Real Life

You read 10 books every month. You want to read 40 books. How many months does it take?

Draw a picture:

Write the missing numbers: _____ tens and _____ ones

_____ months

Show and Grow   I can think deeper!

7. There are 10 dog bones in each box. You need 20 bones. How many boxes do you need?

Draw a picture:

Write the missing numbers: _____ tens and _____ ones

_____ boxes

Name _____

Practice 6.4

Learning Target: Understand and write decade numbers.

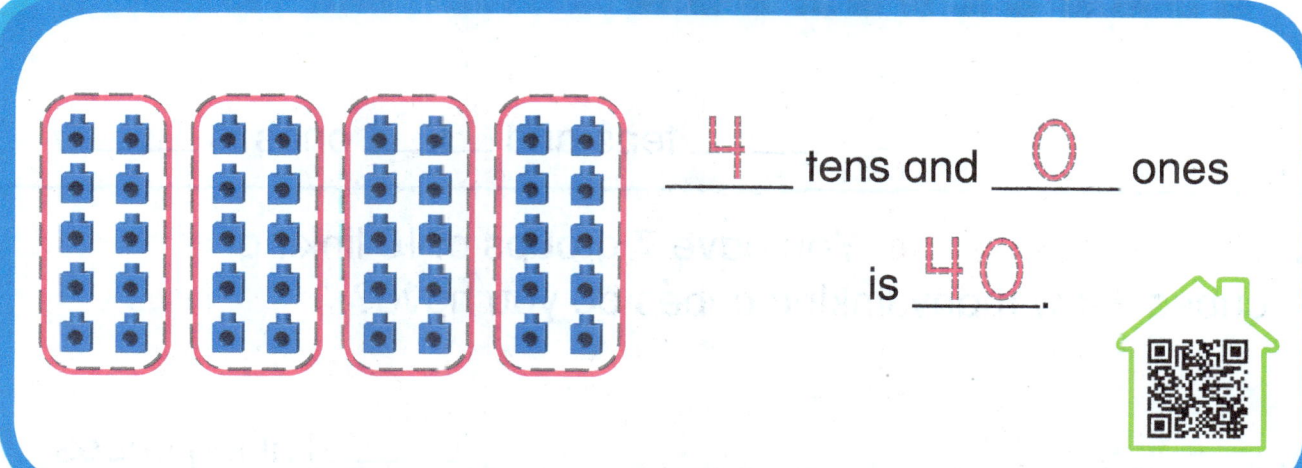

__4__ tens and __0__ ones

is __40__.

Circle groups of 10. Complete the sentence.

1.

_____ tens and _____ ones is _____.

2.

_____ tens and _____ ones is _____.

3.

_____ tens and _____ ones is _____.

Chapter 6 | Lesson 4   three hundred fifteen   315

Circle groups of 10. Complete the sentence.

4.

_____ tens and _____ ones is _____.

5. **Number Sense** You have 7 groups of 10 linking cubes. How many linking cubes do you have?

_____ linking cubes

6. **Modeling Real Life** You swim 10 laps at every practice. You want to swim 50 laps. How many practices will it take?

_____ practices

7. **DIG DEEPER!** How many tens is 500?

1 ten is 10. 10 tens is 100.

Review & Refresh

8. $4 + 3 + 4 =$ _____

9. $1 + 5 + 9 =$ _____

10. $2 + 2 + 1 =$ _____

11. $7 + 3 + 6 =$ _____

Name _____

Learning Target: Count tens and ones to write numbers.

 Tens and Ones 6.5

Explore and Grow

Model 2 tens and 3 ones. Write the number.

Tens	Ones

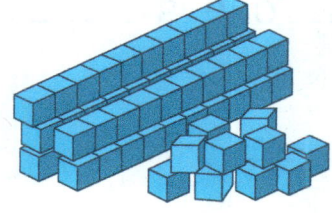

_____

Chapter 6 | Lesson 5

three hundred seventeen 317

# Think and Grow

Tens	Ones
(4 tens rods)	(5 ones cubes)

→

Tens	Ones
4	5

__4__ tens and __5__ ones is __45__.

> The 4 in 45 is in the **tens place**. The 5 in 45 is in the **ones place**.

Show and Grow I can do it!

1.

Tens	Ones
(2 tens rods)	(1 one cube)

→

Tens	Ones

_____ tens and _____ one is _____.

✓ Apply and Grow: Practice

2.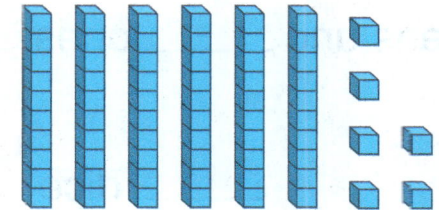

_____ tens and _____ ones is _____.

3.

_____ tens and _____ ones is _____.

4.

_____ tens and _____ ones is _____.

5. 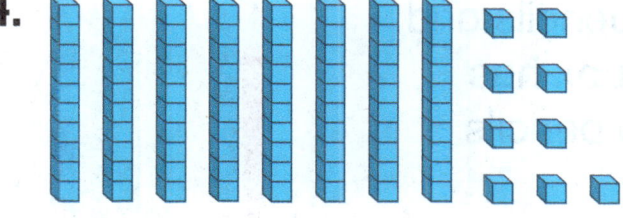 **YOU BE THE TEACHER** You have 92 linking cubes. Your friend says that there are 2 tens and 9 ones. Is your friend correct? Show how you know.

Think and Grow: Modeling Real Life

Your teacher has 2 packages of dice and 3 extra dice. Each package has 10 dice. How many dice are there in all?

Draw a picture:

Write the missing numbers: _____ tens and _____ ones

_____ dice

Show and Grow   I can think deeper!

6. You have 3 boxes of colored pencils and 4 extra colored pencils. Each box has 10 pencils. How many colored pencils are there in all?

Draw a picture:

Write the missing numbers: _____ tens and _____ ones

_____ colored pencils

Name _____

Learning Target: Count tens and ones to write numbers.

Practice 6.5

Tens	Ones
(5 rods)	(3 cubes)

→

Tens	Ones
5	3

__5__ tens and __3__ ones is __53__.

1.

Tens	Ones
(6 rods)	(9 cubes)

→

Tens	Ones

_____ tens and _____ ones is _____.

2.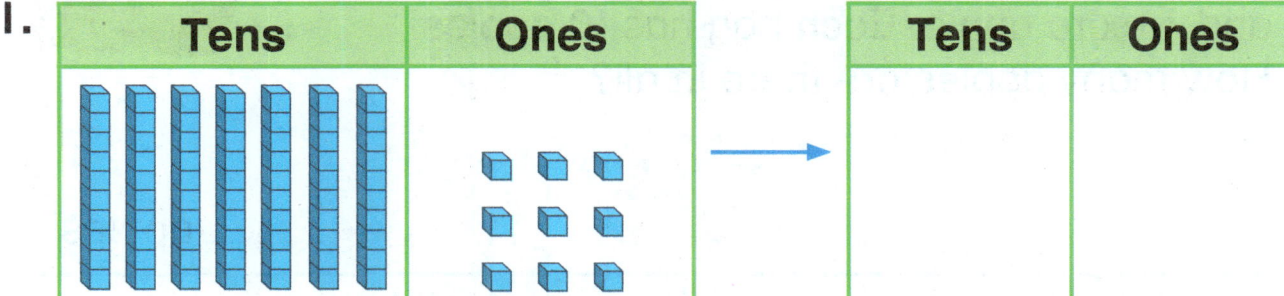

Tens	Ones

_____ tens and _____ one is _____.

Chapter 6 | Lesson 5   three hundred twenty-one 321

3.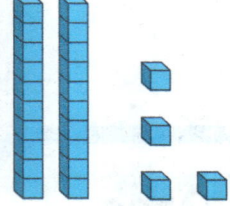

Tens	Ones

_____ tens and _____ ones is _____.

4. **YOU BE THE TEACHER** You have 17 linking cubes. Your friend says that there is 1 ten and 7 ones. Is your friend correct? Show how you know.

5. **Modeling Real Life** You have 5 bags of apples and 1 extra apple. Each bag has 10 apples. How many apples are there in all?

_____ apples

6. **DIG DEEPER!** Are Newton and Descartes modeling the same number? Show how you know.

Yes   No

Review & Refresh

7. _____ + 6 = 10

8. _____ + 2 = 8

Name _____

Learning Target: Use quick sketches to model numbers as tens and ones.

Explore and Grow

Model the number 26.

Tens	Ones

Chapter 6 | Lesson 6

three hundred twenty-three 323

Think and Grow

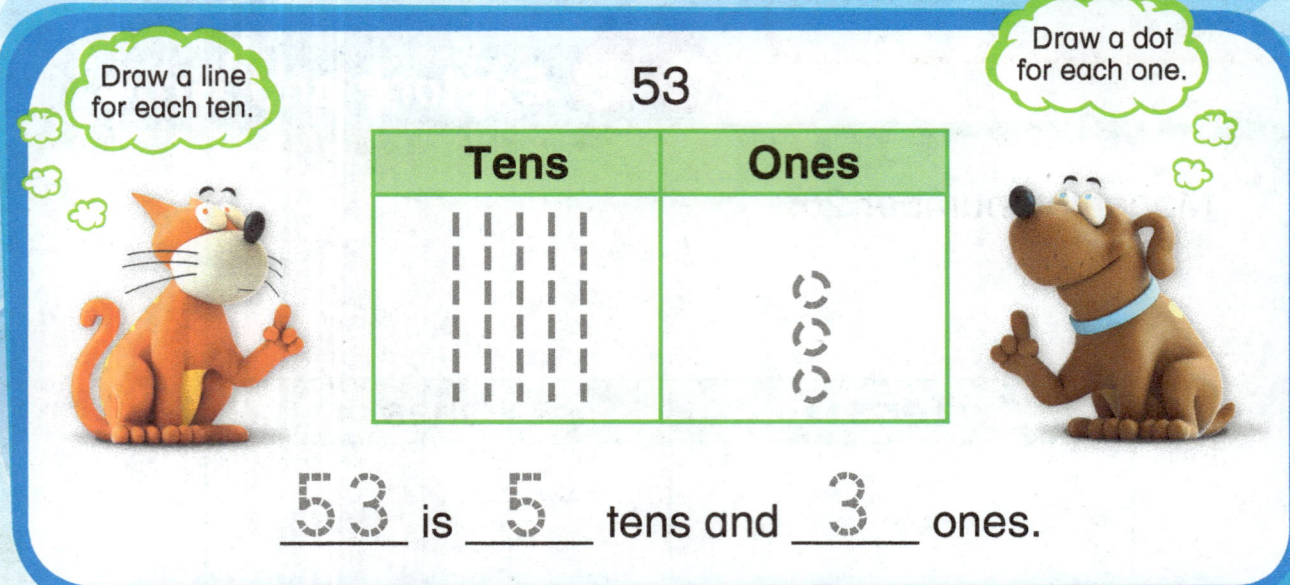

Show and Grow   I can do it!

Make a quick sketch. Complete the sentence.

1. 72

Tens	Ones

_____ is _____ tens and _____ ones.

2. 36

Tens	Ones

_____ is _____ tens and _____ ones.

Name _____

Apply and Grow: Practice

Make a quick sketch. Complete the sentence.

3. 45

Tens	Ones

_____ is _____ tens and _____ ones.

4. 87

Tens	Ones

_____ is _____ tens and _____ ones.

5. 64

Tens	Ones

_____ is _____ tens and _____ ones.

6. **DIG DEEPER!** Find the sum of the numbers shown by the quick sketches.

_____ tens and _____ ones is _____.

Think and Grow: Modeling Real Life

You need 58 plates for a party. You have 51. How many more plates do you need?

Complete the model:

_____ more plates

Show and Grow   I can think deeper!

7. You need 80 tickets for a prize. You have 73. How many more tickets do you need?

   Complete the model:

   _____ more tickets

Name _____   **Practice 6.6**

Learning Target: Use quick sketches to model numbers as tens and ones.

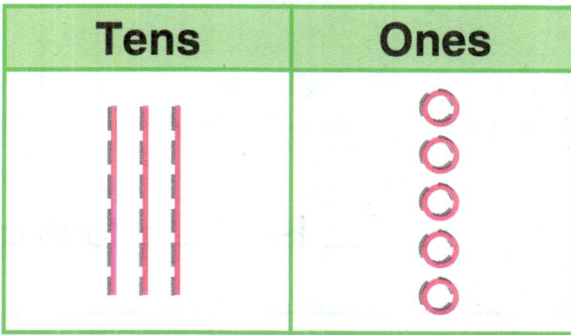

35

__35__ is __3__ tens and __5__ ones.

Make a quick sketch. Complete the sentence.

1. 27

Tens	Ones

_____ is _____ tens and _____ ones.

2. 61

Tens	Ones

_____ is _____ tens and _____ one.

Chapter 6 | Lesson 6   three hundred twenty-seven   **327**

Make a quick sketch. Complete the sentence.

3. 92

Tens	Ones

_____ is _____ tens and _____ ones.

4. **DIG DEEPER!** Find the sum of the numbers shown by the quick sketches.

_____ tens and _____ ones is _____.

5. **Modeling Real Life** You need 55 beads to make a necklace. You have 48. How many more beads do you need?

_____ more beads

Review & Refresh

6. Color the shapes that have only 4 sides.

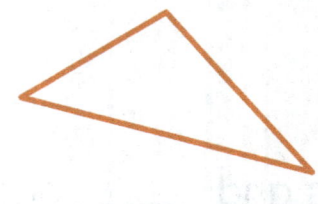 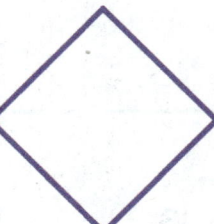 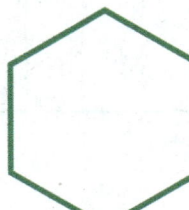 

Understand Place Value

6.7

Learning Target: Understand the value of each digit in a two-digit number.

Explore and Grow

Newton has 2 rods. Make a quick sketch. Write the number.

_____

Descartes has 2 cubes. Make a quick sketch. Write the number.

_____

How are the models alike? How are they different?

Chapter 6 | Lesson 7

Think and Grow

36 has 2 **digits**.

36

Tens	Ones
|||	ooooo o

___3___ tens is ___30___.

___6___ ones is ___6___.

I ten is equal to 10 ones. So, 3 tens is equal to 30 ones.

___3___ tens and ___6___ ones is ___36___.

Show and Grow   I can do it!

1. Make a quick sketch. Complete the sentences.

64

Tens	Ones

_____ tens is _____.

_____ ones is _____.

_____ tens and _____ ones is _____.

Name _____

Apply and Grow: Practice

Make a quick sketch. Complete the sentences.

2. 72

Tens	Ones

_____ tens is _____.

_____ ones is _____.

_____ tens and _____ ones is _____.

3. 98

Tens	Ones

_____ tens is _____.

_____ ones is _____.

_____ tens and _____ ones is _____.

4. 57

_____ tens is _____.

_____ ones is _____.

_____ tens and _____ ones is _____.

Chapter 6 | Lesson 7

Think and Grow: Modeling Real Life

You have 94 charms to make bracelets. There are 10 charms on each bracelet. How many bracelets can you make?

Model:

Write the missing numbers: _____ tens and _____ ones

_____ bracelets

Show and Grow   I can think deeper!

5. You have 67 seeds. You plant 10 seeds in a row. How many rows can you plant?

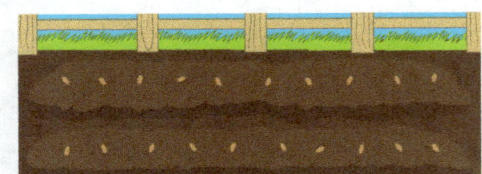

Model:

Write the missing numbers: _____ tens and _____ ones

_____ rows

Name _____

Practice 6.7

Learning Target: Understand the value of each digit in a two-digit number.

25

Tens	Ones
||	ooooo

__2__ tens is __20__.

__5__ ones is __5__.

__2__ tens and __5__ ones is __25__.

Make a quick sketch. Complete the sentences.

1. 81

Tens	Ones

_____ tens is _____.

_____ one is _____.

_____ tens and _____ one is _____.

2. 53

Tens	Ones

_____ tens is _____.

_____ ones is _____.

_____ tens and _____ ones is _____.

Chapter 6 | Lesson 7

three hundred thirty-three 333

3. 49

_____ tens is _____.

_____ ones is _____.

_____ tens and _____ ones is _____.

4. **Modeling Real Life** You have 77 crayons. A box can hold 10 crayons. How many boxes can you fill?

_____ boxes

5. **DIG DEEPER!** In Exercise 4, how many crayons are *not* in boxes? How do you know?

Use Math Tools
How can you use [blocks] to help?

_____ crayons

Review & Refresh

Is the equation true or false?

6. $4 + 9 \stackrel{?}{=} 2 + 3 + 5$

True   False

7. $5 + 3 \stackrel{?}{=} 4 + 4$

True   False

334   three hundred thirty-four

Name _____

Learning Target: Show different ways to write numbers.

Write Numbers in Different Ways 6.8

Explore and Grow

Model 27 two ways.

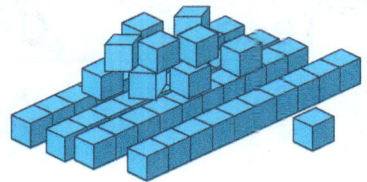

Tens	Ones

Construct an Argument
Can you model 27 using only tens? Why or why not?

_____ tens and _____ ones is _____.

_____ tens and _____ ones is _____.

Chapter 6 | Lesson 8 three hundred thirty-five 335

Think and Grow

Model 46 two ways.

Tens	Ones
IIII	OOOOOO

__4__ tens and
__6__ ones is 46.

Tens	Ones
III	OOOOOOOOOOOOOOOO

__3__ tens and
__16__ ones is 46.

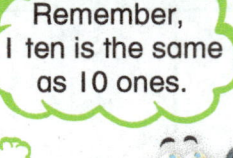

Remember, 1 ten is the same as 10 ones.

Show and Grow   I can do it!

1. Model 25 two ways.

Tens	Ones

____ tens and ____ ones is 25.

Tens	Ones

____ tens and ____ ones is 25.

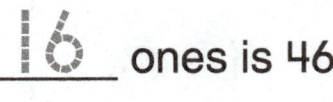

Name _____

 **Apply and Grow: Practice**

2. Model 52 two ways.

Tens	Ones

_____ tens and _____ ones is 52.

Tens	Ones

_____ tens and _____ ones is 52.

3. Model 14 two ways.

Tens	Ones

_____ ten and _____ ones is 14.

Tens	Ones

_____ ten and _____ ones is 14.

4. **DIG DEEPER!** Circle all of the ways that show 39.

3 + 9   2 tens and 19 ones   9 tens and 3 ones

10 + 29   3 tens and 19 ones   39 ones

Chapter 6 | Lesson 8   three hundred thirty-seven   337

Think and Grow: Modeling Real Life

The models show how many seashells you and your friend have. Does your friend have the same number of seashells as you?

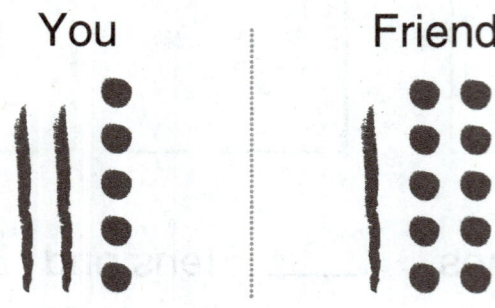

Circle: Yes   No

Show how you know:

Show and Grow — I can think deeper!

5. The models show how many erasers you and your friend have. Does your friend have the same number of erasers as you?

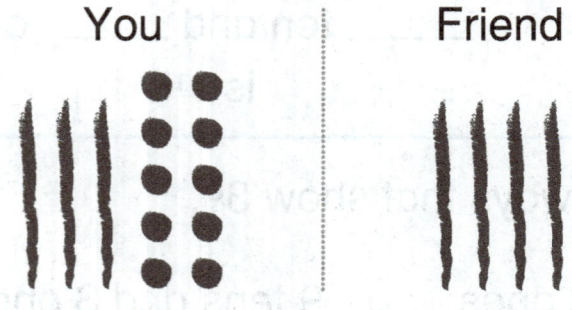

Circle: Yes   No

Show how you know:

Practice 6.8

Learning Target: Show different ways to write numbers.

Model 18 two ways.

Tens	Ones
|	ooooo ooo

__1__ ten and
__8__ ones is 18.

Tens	Ones
	oooo oooo oooo oooo oo

__0__ tens and
__18__ ones is 18.

1. Model 49 two ways.

Tens	Ones

_____ tens and
_____ ones
is 49.

Tens	Ones

_____ tens and
_____ ones
is 49.

Chapter 6 | Lesson 8   three hundred thirty-nine

2. **DIG DEEPER!** Circle all of the ways that show 45.

   40 + 5   45 tens and 0 ones   4 tens and 5 ones

   20 + 15   2 tens and 25 ones   54 ones

3. **Modeling Real Life** The models show the number of toy cars you and your friend have. Does your friend have the same number of toy cars as you?

   You    Friend

   Circle: Yes   No

   Show how you know:

Review & Refresh

Circle the heavier object.

4.

5.

Name _____

Learning Target: Count and write numbers to 120.

Count and Write Numbers to 120

Explore and Grow

How many balls are there? How did you count?

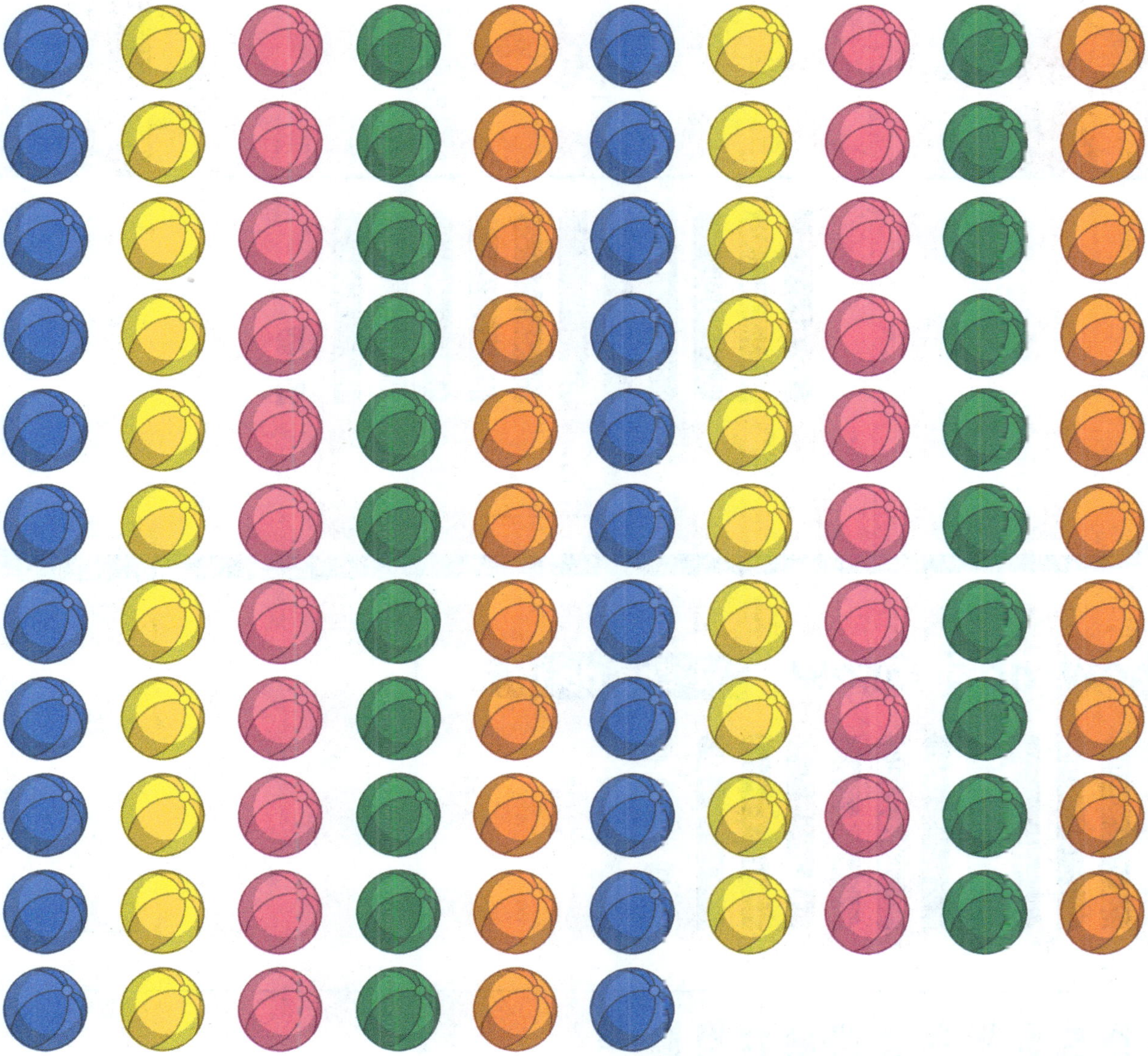

_____ balls

Chapter 6 | Lesson 9   three hundred forty-one   **341**

Think and Grow

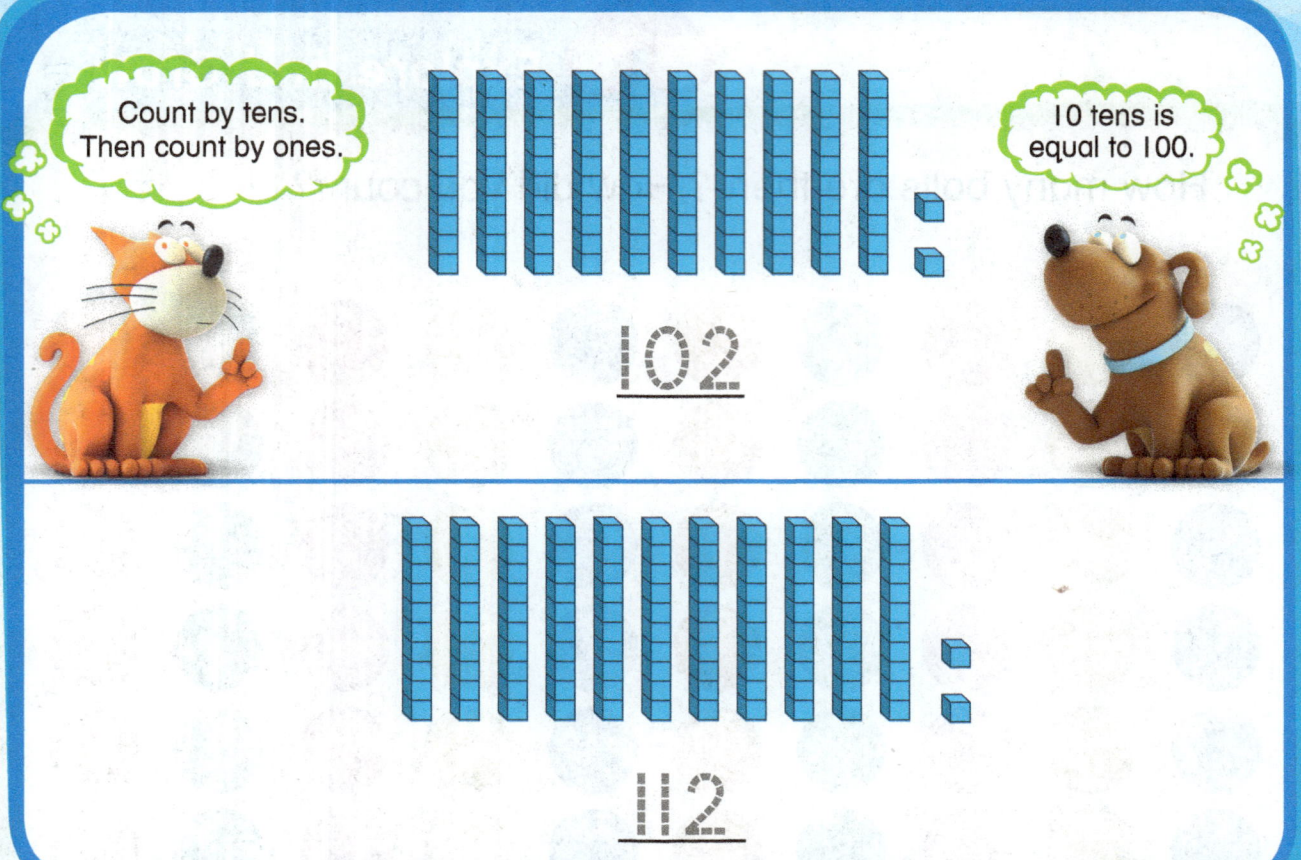

Count by tens. Then count by ones.

10 tens is equal to 100.

102

112

Show and Grow — I can do it!

1.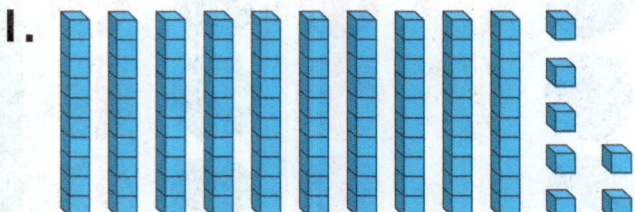

_____

2.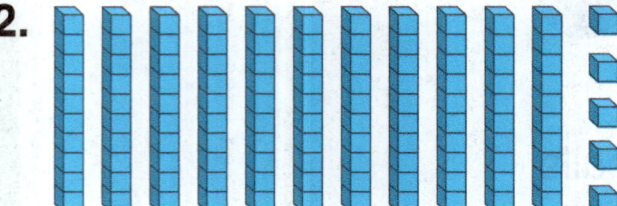

_____

Name _____

✓ Apply and Grow: Practice

3.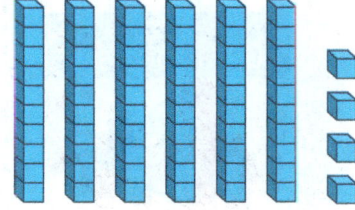

   _____

4.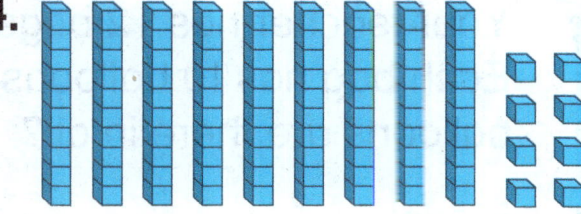

   _____

5.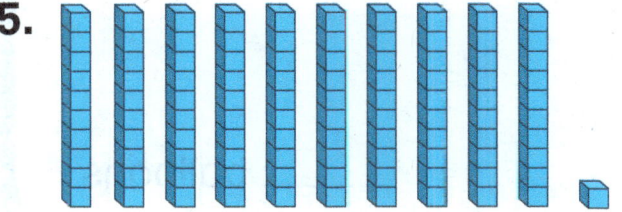

   _____

6.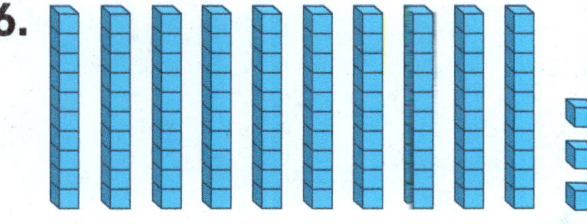

   _____

7.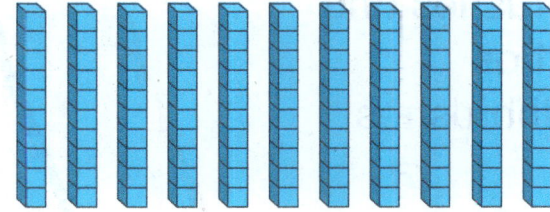

   _____

8. **DIG DEEPER!** What number is equal to 10 tens and 8 ones? Show how you know.

Think and Grow: Modeling Real Life

Your teacher has 12 bags of balloons. Each bag has 10 balloons. How many balloons are there in all?

Model:

_____ balloons

Show and Grow   I can think deeper!

9. A dentist has 10 boxes of toothbrushes and 9 extra toothbrushes. Each box has 10 toothbrushes. How many toothbrushes are there in all?

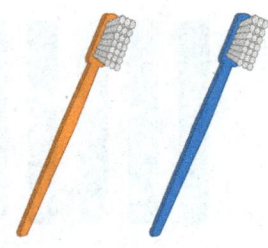

Model:

_____ toothbrushes

Name _____

Learning Target: Count and write numbers to 120.

Practice 6.9

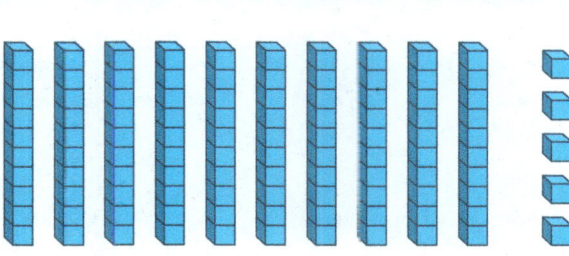

105

1. [blocks image]

    _____

2. [blocks image]

    _____

3.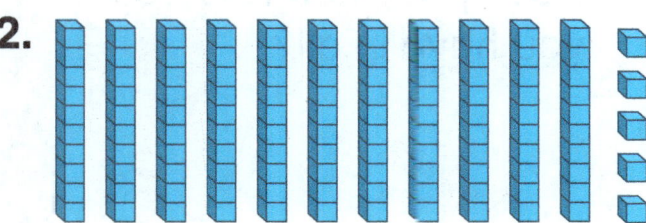

    _____

4.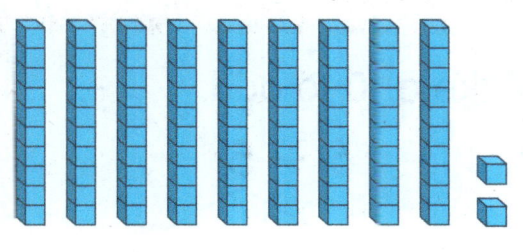

    _____

Chapter 6 | Lesson 9   three hundred forty-five   345

5. DIG DEEPER! What number is equal to 11 tens and 2 ones? Show how you know.

6. Modeling Real Life You have 4 packs of baseball cards and 6 packs of football cards. Each pack has 10 cards. How many cards do you have in all?

_____ cards

Review & Refresh

Make a 10 to add.

7. 6 + 5

    6 + ___ + ___

    10 + ___ = ___

    So, 6 + 5 = ___.

8. 7 + 8

    7 + ___ + ___

    10 + ___ = ___

    So, 7 + 8 = ___.

Name _____

Performance Task 6

1. Your class sells candles for a fundraiser. You earn 10 dollars for every large candle you sell and 1 dollar for every small candle.

   a. You sell 6 large candles. How much money do you raise?

   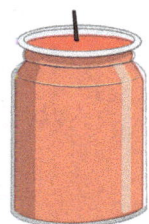

   _____ dollars

   b. You want to raise 72 dollars. How much more money do you need to raise?

   _____ more dollars

   c. You also sell 12 small candles. Do you reach your goal?

   Yes   No

2. Your friend wants to raise 54 dollars. What are two ways your friend can sell large and small candles to reach her goal?

   Analyze a Problem
   What information do you need to solve the problem?

   _____ large candles and _____ small candles

   _____ large candles and _____ small candles

Chapter 6   three hundred forty-seven   347

Drop and Build

To Play: Take turns. On your turn, toss a cube onto a 120 chart so that your partner cannot see. Build the number you land on with base ten blocks. Have your partner say and write the number. Use the 120 chart to check the answer. Play until each partner builds three numbers.

Tens	Ones

Name _____

Chapter Practice 6

6.1 Count to 120 by Ones

1. Count by ones to write the missing numbers.

   99, _____, _____, _____, _____, _____

Write the missing numbers.

2.
68		70	
	79		81

3.
100		102	
	111		

6.2 Count to 120 by Tens

4. **Patterns** Write the missing numbers from the chart. Then count on by tens to write the next two numbers.

81	82	83	?	85	86	87	88	89	90
91	92	93	?	95	96	97	98	99	100

5. **YOU BE THE TEACHER** Your friend counts by tens starting with 53. Is your friend correct? Show how you know.

53, 63, 73, 83, 103

Chapter 6   three hundred forty-nine 349

6.3 Compose Numbers 11 to 19

6. Circle 10 ducks. Complete the sentence.

_____ ten and _____ ones is _____.

7.  **Modeling Real Life** You have 19 tennis balls. A bag can hold 10. You fill a bag. How many tennis balls are *not* in the bag?

_____ tennis balls

6.4 Tens

8. Circle groups of 10. Complete the sentence.

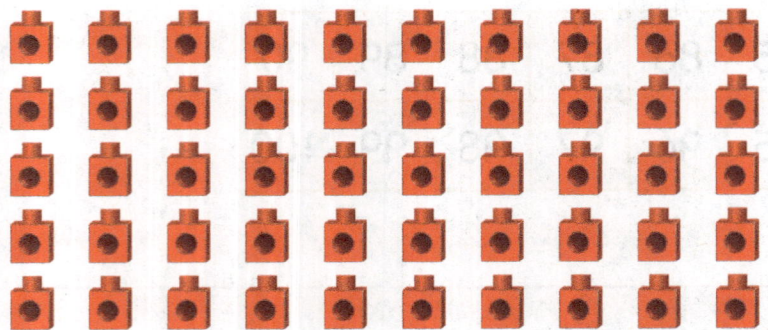

_____ tens and _____ ones is _____.

350 three hundred fifty

6.5 Tens and Ones

9.

Tens	Ones
(8 tens rods)	(8 ones cubes)

→

Tens	Ones

_____ tens and _____ ones is _____.

10. **Modeling Real Life** You have 6 boxes of plastic cups and 3 extra cups. Each box has 10 cups. How many cups are there in all?

_____ plastic cups

6.6 Make Quick Sketches

Make a quick sketch. Complete the sentence.

11. 17

_____ is _____ ten and _____ ones.

12. 84

_____ is _____ tens and _____ ones.

Chapter 6   three hundred fifty-one   351

 **Understand Place Value**

13. 39

_____ tens is _____.

_____ ones is _____.

_____ tens and _____ ones is _____.

6.8 Write Numbers in Different Ways

14. Model 59 two ways.

Tens	Ones

Tens	Ones

_____ tens and _____ ones is 59.

_____ tens and _____ ones is 59.

 **Count and Write Numbers to 120**

15.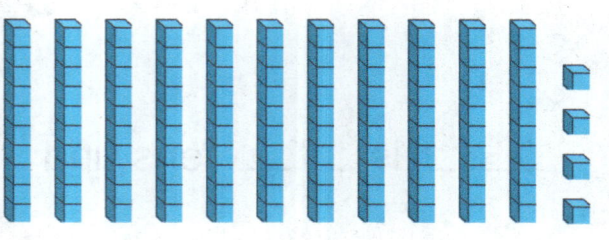

_____

16.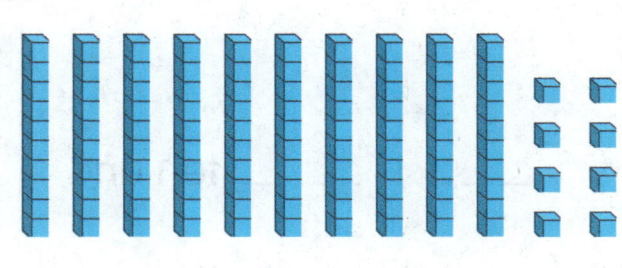

_____

352 three hundred fifty-two

7 Compare Two-Digit Numbers

- What are your favorite toys?
- How many red blocks are there? How many blue blocks are there? Are there more red blocks or blue blocks?

Chapter Learning Target:
Understand two-digit numbers.

Chapter Success Criteria:
- I can identify two-digit numbers.
- I can describe two-digit numbers.
- I can locate two-digit numbers on a number line.
- I can compare two-digit numbers.

7 Vocabulary

Name _____

Review Words
fewer
more

Organize It

Use the review words to complete the graphic organizer.

Define It

Use your vocabulary cards to complete the puzzle.

Across

1. 26 > 23

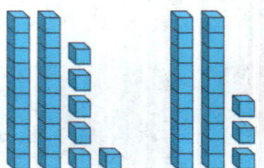

Down

2. 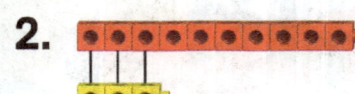   3. 22 < 38

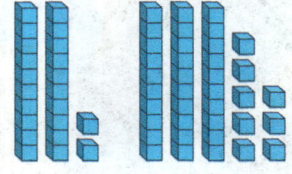

354   three hundred fifty-four

Chapter 7 Vocabulary Cards

| compare | greater than |

| less than | |

Name _____

Learning Target: Compare two numbers between 11 and 19.

Compare Numbers 11 to 19 — 7.1

 **Explore and Grow**

Model each number. Circle the greater number.

15

17

 **Justify a Result**
How do you know which number is greater?

Chapter 7 | Lesson 1

Think and Grow

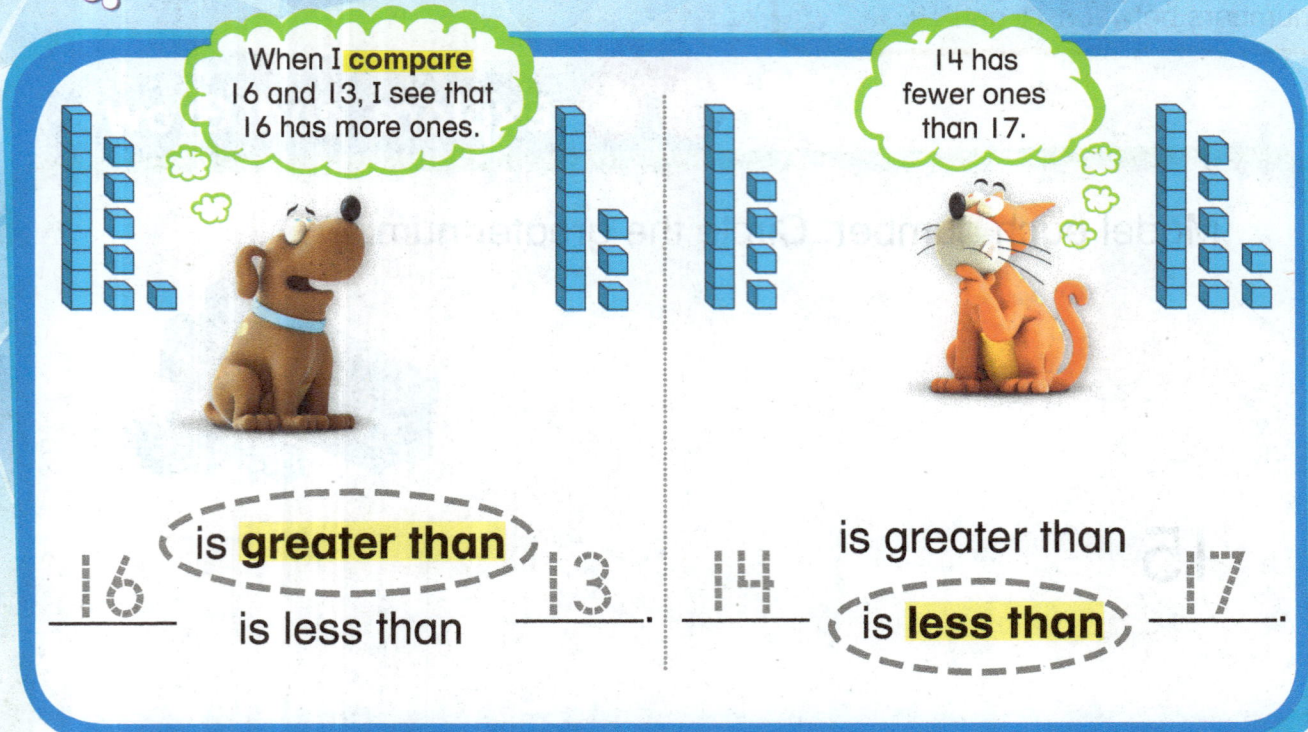

Show and Grow I can do it!

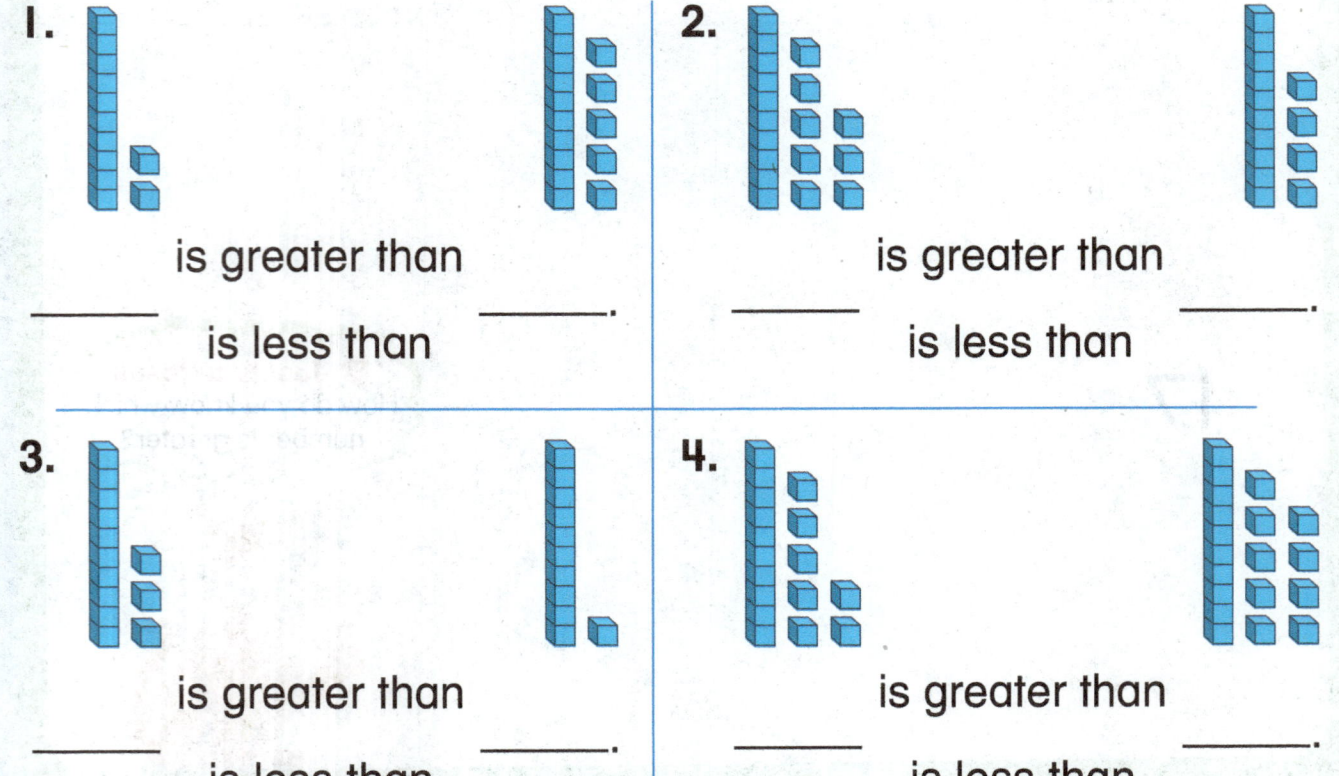

Name _____

 **Apply and Grow: Practice**

5.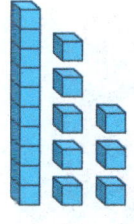

_____ is greater than _____.

_____ is less than _____.

6.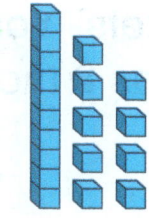

_____ is greater than _____.

_____ is less than _____.

Make quick sketches to compare the numbers.

7.

_____ is greater than _____.

11   12.

_____ is less than _____.

8.

_____ is greater than _____.

15   13.

_____ is less than _____.

9. **DIG DEEPER!** Choose two numbers to complete the sentences.

 12   18
 15
 13    16   19

Use Math Tools
How can you use base ten blocks to check your answers?

_____ is greater than _____.

_____ is less than _____.

Chapter 7 | Lesson 1

three hundred fifty-seven 357

Think and Grow: Modeling Real Life

You have 16 tickets. Your friend has 11 tickets and wins 8 more. Who has more tickets?

                       <u>You</u>   <u>Friend</u>

Number of tickets:

Models:

Compare: _____ is greater than _____.

Who has more tickets?   You   Friend

Show and Grow   I can think deeper!

10. You have 7 feathers and find 6 more. Your friend has 12 feathers. Who has more feathers?

                       <u>You</u>   <u>Friend</u>

Number of feathers:

Models:

Compare: _____ is greater than _____.

Who has more feathers?   You   Friend

Name _____

Practice 7.1

Learning Target: Compare two numbers between 11 and 19.

> 14 has more ones than 11.

> 17 has fewer ones than 19.

14 (is greater than) 11.
___ is less than ___.

17 ___ is greater than ___.
(is less than) 19.

1.

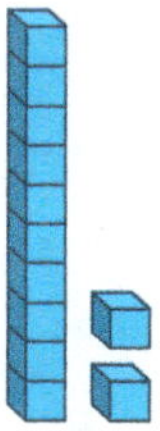

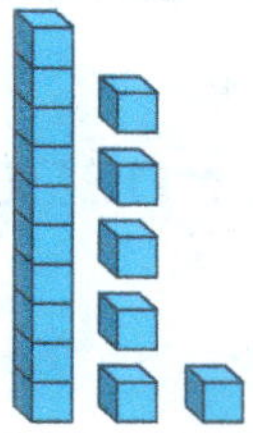

___ is greater than ___.
___ is less than ___.

2.

___ is greater than ___.
___ is less than ___.

Make quick sketches to compare the numbers.

3.

___ is greater than ___.
19 is less than 12.

4.

___ is greater than ___.
11 is less than 17.

Chapter 7 | Lesson 1   three hundred fifty-nine   **359**

5. ___ is greater than ___.
17   is less than   13.

6. ___ is greater than ___.
12   is less than   14.

7. **DIG DEEPER!** Choose two numbers to complete the sentences.

11   17
14
12   18
   15

_____ is greater than _____.

_____ is less than _____.

8. **Modeling Real Life** Your tower has 16 red blocks. Your friend's tower has 10 red blocks and 4 blue blocks. Who uses more blocks?

_____ is greater than _____.

Who has more?   You   Friend

Review & Refresh

9. Make a quick sketch to complete the sentence.

59

Tens	Ones

_____ is _____ tens and _____ ones.

Name _____

Learning Target: Compare two numbers within 100.

Compare Numbers 7.2

Explore and Grow

Model each number. Circle the greater number.

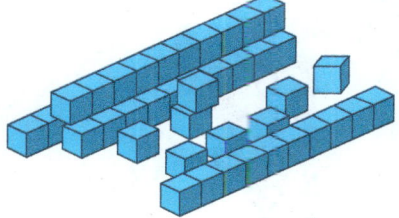

34

26

Use Math Tools
How can you use a 120 chart to compare the numbers?

Chapter 7 | Lesson 2

three hundred sixty-one 361

Think and Grow

First, compare the tens. 3 tens are fewer than 4 tens.

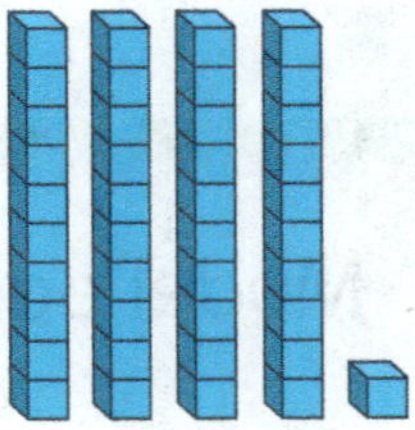

36 is greater than / (is less than) 41.

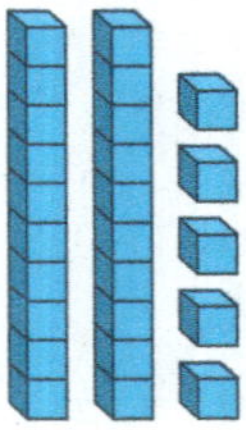

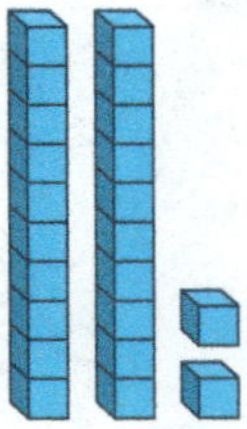

25 (is greater than) / is less than 22.

The tens are the same. Compare the ones. 5 ones are more than 2 ones.

Show and Grow — I can do it!

1. 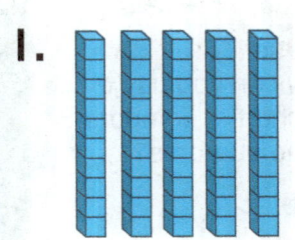 ____ is greater than / is less than ____.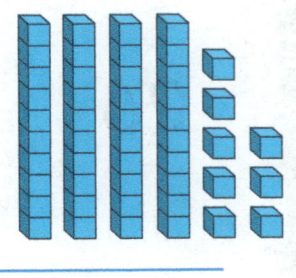

2. 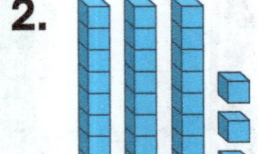 ____ is greater than / is less than ____.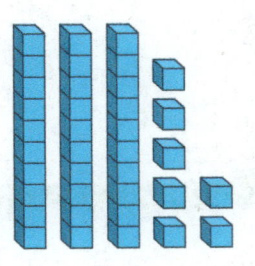

Name _____

 **Apply and Grow: Practice**

3. 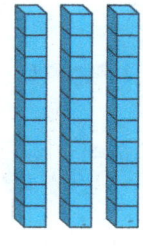   ____ is greater than ____.
   ____ is less than ____.
   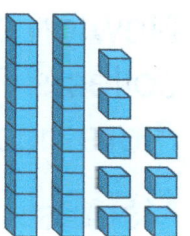

4. 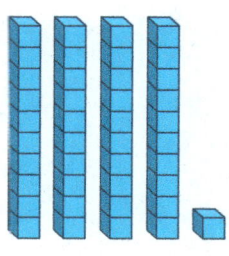   ____ is greater than ____.
   ____ is less than ____.
   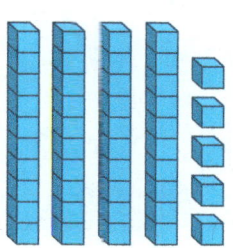

5. Make quick sketches to compare the numbers.

   63   is greater than   80.
        is less than

6. **DIG DEEPER!** Write a number that is greater than 90 but less than 94. Show how you know.

   ____

Chapter 7 | Lesson 2

Think and Grow: Modeling Real Life

Newton collects 61 acorns. Descartes collects 75 acorns. Who collects more acorns?

Models: Newton   Descartes

Compare: _____ is greater than _____.

Who collects more acorns?   Newton   Descartes

Show and Grow   I can think deeper!

7. You pick 57 blueberries. Your friend picks 53 blueberries. Who picks more blueberries?

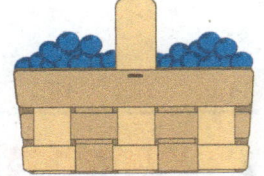

Models: You   Friend

Compare: _____ is greater than _____.

Who picks more blueberries?   You   Friend

Name _____

Practice 7.2

Learning Target: Compare two numbers within 100.

First, compare the tens. 4 tens are more than 2 tens.

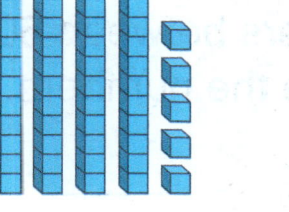

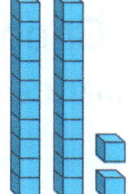

_45_ is greater than / is less than _22_.

1. 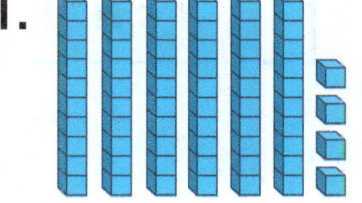 ___ is greater than / is less than ___.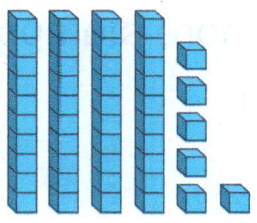

2. 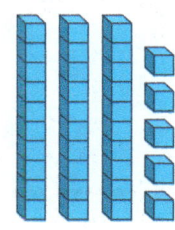 ___ is greater than / is less than ___.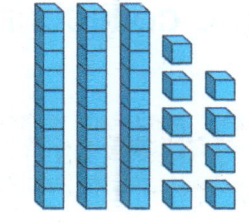

3. Make quick sketches to compare the numbers.

   91 is greater than / is less than 70.

Chapter 7 | Lesson 2   three hundred sixty-five

4. 68 is greater than ____.
____ is less than 86.

5. DIG DEEPER! Choose 2 numbers between 50 and 99. Write a sentence to compare the numbers.

____ ____

6. Modeling Real Life You collect 37 stamps. Your friend collects 27 stamps. Who collects more stamps?

Who collects more stamps?   You   Friend

Review & Refresh

Circle the taller object.

7.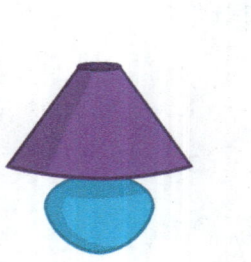

8.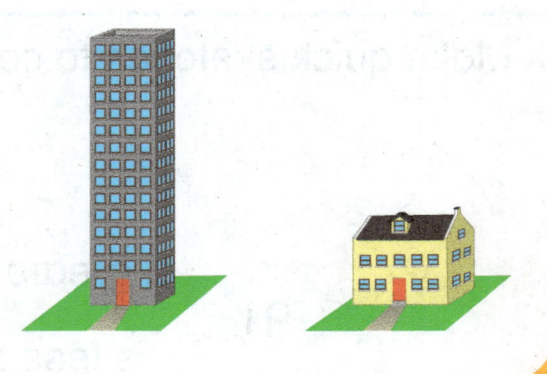

Compare Numbers Using Place Value — 7.3

Learning Target: Use place value to compare two numbers within 100.

Explore and Grow

Model each number. What is the same about the models? What is different? Circle the greater number.

32

Tens	Ones

23

Tens	Ones

Chapter 7 | Lesson 3

Think and Grow

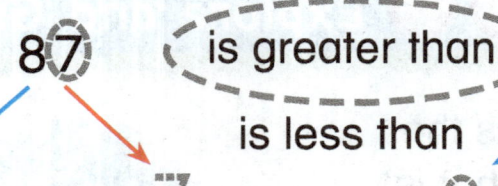

87 is greater than / is less than 83.

The tens digits are the same. The ones digits help me decide.

__8__ tens __7__ ones   __8__ tens __3__ ones

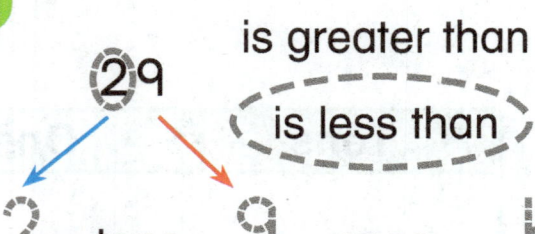

2 tens are less than 4 tens. The tens digits help me decide.

29 is greater than / is less than 42.

__2__ tens __9__ ones   __4__ tens __2__ ones

Show and Grow — I can do it!

Compare. Which digits help you decide?

1. 61 is greater than / is less than 53.

   ____ tens ____ one   ____ tens ____ ones

2. 70 is greater than / is less than 74.

   ____ tens ____ ones   ____ tens ____ ones

Name _____

Apply and Grow: Practice

Compare. Which digits help you decide?

3.   39   is greater than
          is less than   48.

_____ tens _____ ones   _____ tens _____ ones

4.   80   is greater than
          is less than   62.

_____ tens _____ ones   _____ tens _____ ones

5.   26   is greater than   6.   51   is greater than
          is less than   23.   is less than   86.

7.   17   is greater than   8.   97   is greater than
          is less than   71.   is less than   92.

9. **Precision** Match each ball with its bucket.

Less than 65

58 67 62

64 73 68

Greater than 65

Chapter 7 | Lesson 3   three hundred sixty-nine   369

Think and Grow: Modeling Real Life

Who has more points?

Newton's points: _____   Descartes's points: _____

Compare: _____ is greater than _____.

_____ has more points.

Show and Grow I can think deeper!

10. Who has more points?

Newton's points: _____   Descartes's points: _____

Compare: _____ is greater than _____.

_____ has more points.

Name _____

Practice 7.3

Learning Target: Use place value to compare two numbers within 100.

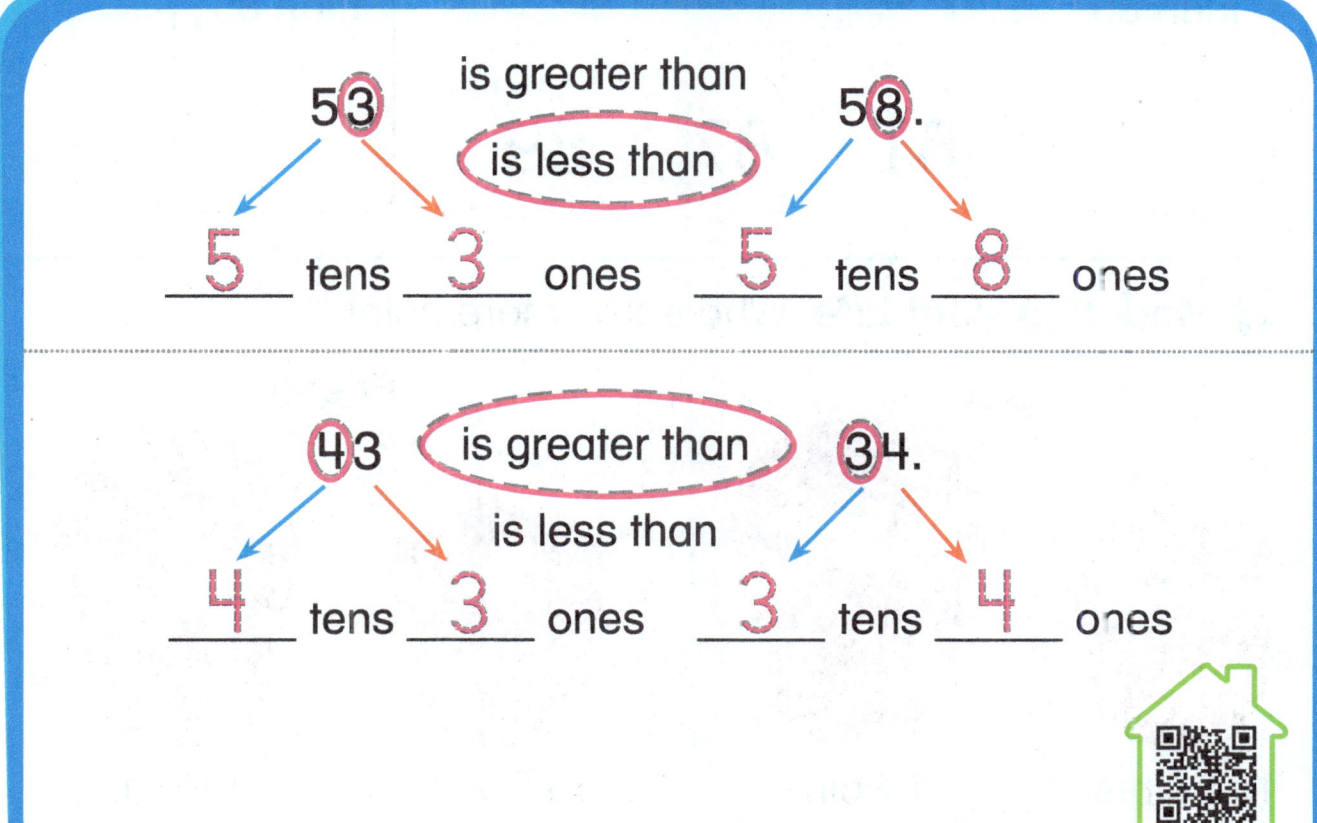

Compare. Which digits help you decide?

1. 16 is greater than / is less than 12.

   ____ ten ____ ones   ____ ten ____ ones

2. 32 is greater than / is less than 38.

3. 7 is greater than / is less than 25.

Chapter 7 | Lesson 3   three hundred seventy-one **371**

4. **Precision** Match each card with its pile.

Less than 85	93 79 84	Greater than 85
	81 87 89	

5. **Modeling Real Life** Who earns more points?

You
 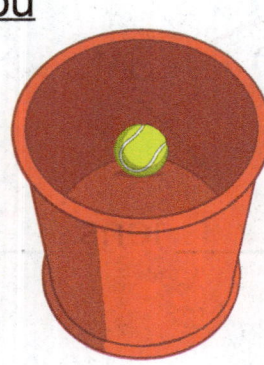
10 Points   1 Point

Friend
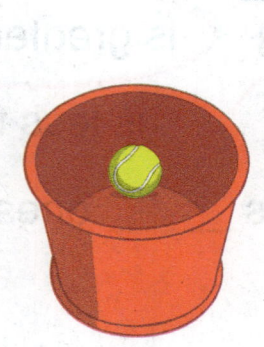 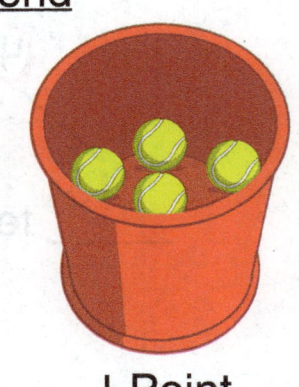
10 Points   1 Point

_____ is greater than _____.

Who earns more points?   You   Friend

Review & Refresh

Is the equation true or false?

6. $15 - 9 \stackrel{?}{=} 11 - 5$

   $\_\_\_ \stackrel{?}{=} \_\_\_$

   True   False

7. $4 + 7 \stackrel{?}{=} 16 - 4$

   $\_\_\_ \stackrel{?}{=} \_\_\_$

   True   False

Compare Numbers Using Symbols

7.4

Name _____

Learning Target: Use symbols to compare two numbers within 100.

 **Explore and Grow**

Make quick sketches. Complete the sentences.

27

Less than 27	Equal to 27	Greater than 27
____ < 27	____ = 27	____ > 27

Chapter 7 | Lesson 4

three hundred seventy-three 373

Think and Grow

< means *is less than*.
> means *is greater than*.
= means *is equal to*.

25 ___is equal to___ 25.

25 ⬯=⬯ 25

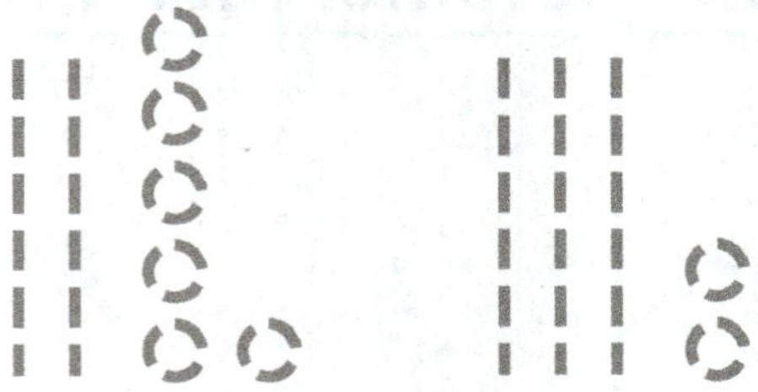

26 ___is less than___ 32.

26 ⬯<⬯ 32

41 ___is greater than___ 14.

41 ⬯>⬯ 14

Remember: Compare tens first. Then compare ones.

Show and Grow — I can do it!

Make quick sketches to model each number. Compare.

1. 53 _____ 39.

    53 ◯ 39

2. 28 _____ 34.

    28 ◯ 34

Name _____

 Apply and Grow: Practice

Make quick sketches to model each number. Compare.

3.

61 _____ 72.

61 ◯ 72

4.

47 _____ 47.

47 ◯ 47

Compare.

5.

83 _____ 49.

83 ◯ 49

6.

75 _____ 99.

75 ◯ 99

7.

54 ◯ 70

8.

17 ◯ 9

9.

86 ◯ 86

10. **DIG DEEPER!** Choose 2 cards for each problem. Compare the numbers. Use each card once.

| 31 | 24 | 89 | 13 | 24 | 63 |

____ < ____   ____ > ____   ____ = ____

Chapter 7 | Lesson 4

 Think and Grow: Modeling Real Life

You have 90 beads. Your friend has 75 beads. Who has more beads?

Models:

Compare: _____ ◯ _____

Who has more beads?   You   Friend

Show and Grow   I can think deeper!

11. You have 48 toy figures. Your friend has 54 toy figures. Who has fewer toy figures?

Models:

Compare: _____ ◯ _____

Who has fewer toy figures?   You   Friend

Name _____   Practice **7.4**

Learning Target: Use symbols to compare two numbers within 100.

< means *is less than*.
> means *is greater than*.
= means *is equal to*.

44 ___is less than___ 60.

44 < 60

Make quick sketches to model each number. Compare.

1.

37 _____ 15.

37 ◯ 15

2.

22 _____ 22.

22 ◯ 22

Compare.

3. 97 ◯ 79

4. 51 ◯ 83

5. 39 ◯ 62

Chapter 7 | Lesson 4   three hundred seventy-seven   377

Compare.

6. 19 ◯ 91

7. 73 ◯ 68

8. 32 ◯ 32

9. **DIG DEEPER!** Use each of the numbers once to complete the puzzle.

74   45   21

81 > _____   56 < _____   21 = _____

10. **Modeling Real Life** Who has more points?

_____ ◯ _____

_____ has more points.

Review & Refresh

11. $6 + 8 =$ _____

12. $12 + 5 =$ _____

13. _____ $= 0 + 11$

14. _____ $= 4 + 9$

Name _____

Compare Numbers Using a Number Line — 7.5

Learning Target: Use a number line to compare two numbers within 100.

Explore and Grow

Circle a number that is less than 45. Underline a number that is greater than 45. How do you know you are correct?

_____ < 45

_____ > 45

Find a Rule
What do you notice about the numbers to the right of 45 on the number line? to the left of 45?

Chapter 7 | Lesson 5

 **Think and Grow**

Numbers to the left of 65 on a number line are less than 65.

Numbers to the right of 65 on a number line are greater than 65.

less than 65 | greater than 65

56 57 58 59 60 61 62 63 64 **65** 66 67 68 69 70 71 72 73 74

60  65   65 65   70 65

Show and Grow   I can do it!

Compare.

30 31 32 33 34 35 36 37 38 39 40 41 42 43 44 45 46 47 48 49 50

1. 43 ◯ 48

2. 44 ◯ 36

3. 39 ◯ 39

4. 31 ◯ 50

5. 37 ◯ 33

6. 38 ◯ 42

Name _____

 **Apply and Grow: Practice**

Compare.

65 66 67 68 69 70 71 72 73 74 75 76 77 78 79 80 81 82 83 84 85

7. 65 ◯ 66

8. 71 ◯ 81

9. 83 ◯ 85

10. 74 ◯ 69

11. 78 ◯ 77

12. 72 ◯ 72

Write a number that makes the statement true.

13. ____ > 47

14. ____ < 76

15. 81 = ____

16. **DIG DEEPER!** Newton is thinking of a number that is less than 83 and greater than 74. His number has 6 ones. What is Newton's number?

____

Chapter 7 | Lesson 5   three hundred eighty-one   381

Think and Grow: Modeling Real Life

The number on your bus is less than 91. Which buses can be yours?

88

90

92

Show how you know:

Show and Grow I can think deeper!

17. The number on your plane is greater than 58. Which planes can be yours?

63

49

60

Show how you know:

Name _____

Practice 7.5

Learning Target: Use a number line to compare two numbers within 100.

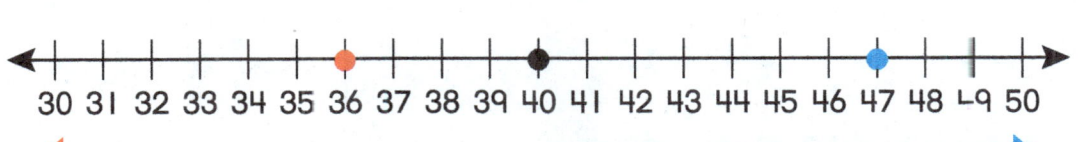

36 < 40   40 = 40   47 > 40

Compare.

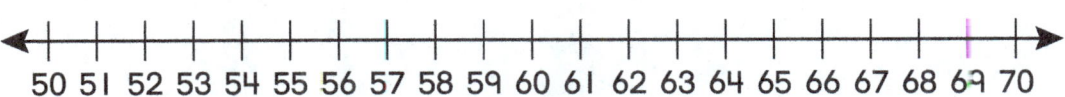

1. 53 ◯ 56

2. 70 ◯ 60

3. 63 ◯ 67

4. 68 ◯ 55

Write a number that makes the statement true.

5. 55 < _____

6. 62 = _____

7. 75 > _____

Chapter 7 | Lesson 5   three hundred eighty-three   383

8. **Communicate Clearly** How can you use a number line to tell whether 68 is greater than or less than 42?

9. **Modeling Real Life** The number on your taxi is greater than 40. Which taxis can be yours?

39   46   51

Show how you know:

10. **DIG DEEPER!** Newton's taxi number is greater than 30 and less than 45. Draw a line under his taxi.

Review & Refresh

11. You have 9 pencils. 7 are blue. The rest are orange. How many orange pencils do you have?

_____ orange pencils

Name _____

I More, I Less; 10 More, 10 Less 7.6

Learning Target: Identify numbers that are 1 more, 1 less, 10 more, and 10 less than a number.

Explore and Grow

Model 43. Use your model to complete the sentences.

1 more than 43 is _____.

1 less than 43 is _____.

10 more than 43 is _____.

10 less than 43 is _____.

MP Patterns
Which digit changes when you find 1 more or 1 less? when you find 10 more or 10 less?

 **Think and Grow**

24

1 more than 24 is 25.

1 less than 24 is 23.

10 more than 24 is 34.

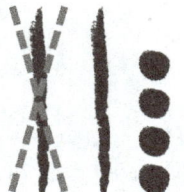

10 less than 24 is 14.

Show and Grow I can do it!

1.

1 more than 47 is _____.

1 less than 47 is _____.

10 more than 47 is _____.

10 less than 47 is _____.

2.

1 more than 61 is _____.

1 less than 61 is _____.

10 more than 61 is _____.

10 less than 61 is _____.

Name _____

✓ Apply and Grow: Practice

3.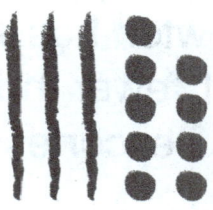

1 more than 39 is ____.   10 more than 39 is ____.

1 less than 39 is ____.   10 less than 39 is ____.

		1 more	1 less	10 more	10 less
4.	56				
5.	75				
6.	33				
7.	80				
8.	12				

9. **Number Sense** Make a quick sketch for the number that is 10 less than the model. What is the new number?

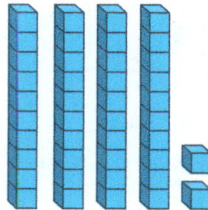

____

Chapter 7 | Lesson 6   three hundred eighty-seven 387

Think and Grow: Modeling Real Life

You have 25 markers. Newton has 10 more than you. Descartes has 1 fewer than Newton. How many markers does Descartes have?

Models:

Make a Plan
Describe the steps you will take to solve.

_____ markers

Show and Grow I can think deeper!

10. You have 42 party blowers. Descartes has 10 fewer than you. Newton has 1 more than Descartes. How many party blowers does Newton have?

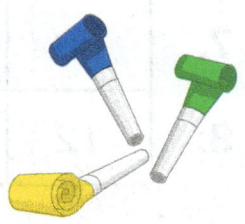

Models:

_____ party blowers

Name _____

Practice  7.6

Learning Target: Identify numbers that are 1 more, 1 less, 10 more, and 10 less than a number.

18

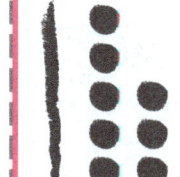

1 more than 18 is __19__.

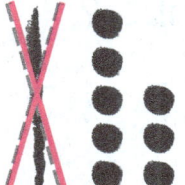

1 less than 18 is __17__.

10 more than 18 is __28__.

10 less than 18 is __8__.

1.

   1 more than 63 is _____.

   1 less than 63 is _____.

   10 more than 63 is _____.

   10 less than 63 is _____.

2.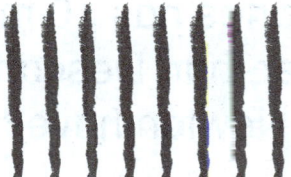

   1 more than 80 is _____.

   1 less than 80 is _____.

   10 more than 80 is _____.

   10 less than 80 is _____.

Chapter 7 | Lesson 6 — three hundred eighty-nine 389

	1 more	1 less	10 more	10 less
3. 82				
4. 16				
5. 68				

6. **Number Sense** Make a quick sketch for the number that is 1 more than the model. What is the new number?

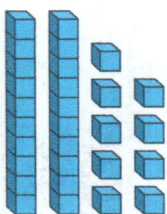

_____

7. **Modeling Real Life** You have 75 party cups. Descartes has 10 more than you. Newton has 1 fewer than Descartes. How many party cups does Newton have?

_____ party cups

Review & Refresh

8. You have 17 erasers. Your friend takes some of them. You have 9 left. How many erasers did your friend take?

_____ erasers

390 three hundred ninety

Name _____

Performance Task 7

1. Your school is having a toy drive. Each class wants to collect more than 100 toys.

    a. Your friend's class collects 89 toys. Your cousin's class collects 72 toys. Whose class collects more toys?

    Your _____'s class collects more toys.

    b. Your class collects 10 more toys than your friend's class. Does your class reach the goal?

    Analyze a Problem
    What must happen in order for your class to reach the goal?

    Yes   No

2. Use the clues to match each class with the number of toys it collects.

    • Class A collects 10 fewer toys than Class C.
    • Class B collects the fewest number of toys.

    Class A   Class B   Class C
      68   78   88

Chapter 7   three hundred ninety-one   391

Number Boss

To Play: Place Number Cards 0–9 in a pile. Each player flips two cards and makes a two-digit number. Compare the numbers. The player with the greater number takes both sets of cards. If the numbers are equal, flip cards again. The player with the greater number takes all of the cards. Repeat until all of the cards have been used.

Name _____

Chapter Practice 7

7.1 Compare Numbers 11 to 19

1. _____ is greater than _____.
   _____ is less than _____.

2.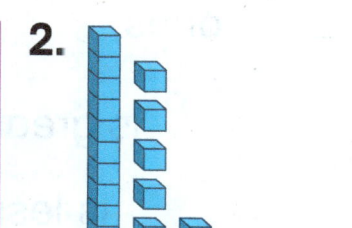
   _____ is greater than _____.
   _____ is less than _____.

7.2 Compare Numbers

3. 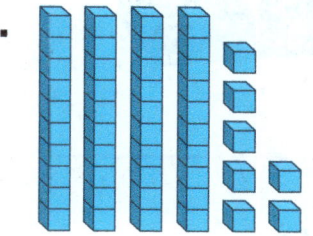 _____ is greater than _____.
   _____ is less than _____.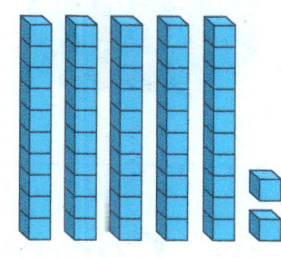

4. 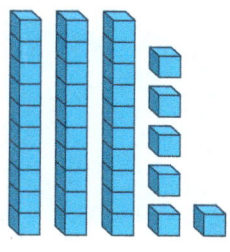 _____ is greater than _____.
   _____ is less than _____.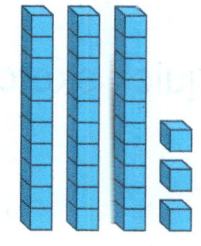

5. **MP Structure** Write a number that is greater than 78 but less than 82. Show how you know.

_____

Chapter 7   three hundred ninety-three   393

7.3 Compare Numbers Using Place Value

Compare. Which digits help you decide?

6.   46   is greater than / is less than   55.

_____ tens _____ ones   _____ tens _____ ones

7.   89   is greater than / is less than   98.

_____ tens _____ ones   _____ tens _____ ones

8. **MP Precision** Match each chip with its box.

 43   54   40

50   37   49

7.4 Compare Numbers Using Symbols

Make quick sketches to model each number. Compare.

9.   84 _____ 68.

84 ◯ 68

10.   29 _____ 42.

29 ◯ 42

394   three hundred ninety-four

7.5 Compare Numbers Using a Number Line

Compare.

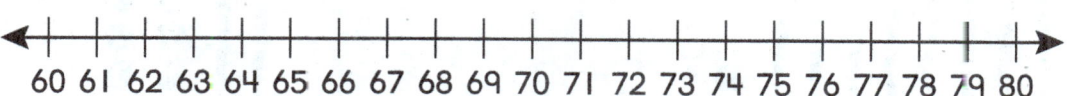

11. 62 ◯ 70

12. 78 ◯ 69

13. 75 ◯ 68

14. 64 ◯ 73

Write a number that makes the statement true.

15. _____ < 36

16. 28 = _____

17. _____ > 9

18. **Modeling Real Life** The number on your train is less than 34. Which trains can be yours?

29

42

30

Show how you know:

Chapter 7   three hundred ninety-five   395

7.6 I More, I Less; 10 More, 10 Less

19.

I more than 82 is _____.

I less than 82 is _____.

10 more than 82 is _____.

10 less than 82 is _____.

20.

I more than 29 is _____.

I less than 29 is _____.

10 more than 29 is _____.

10 less than 29 is _____.

21. **Modeling Real Life** You have 34 oranges. Newton has 1 fewer than you. Descartes has 10 fewer than Newton. How many oranges does Descartes have?

_____ oranges

396　three hundred ninety-six

Cumulative Practice 1-7

1. 6 people play basketball. Shade the circle next to the picture that shows how many more people need to join the group so there are 10 in all.

2. Shade the circles next to the choices that match the model.

   ◯ 6 tens and 3 ones   ◯ 63

   ◯ 3 tens and 6 ones   ◯ 36

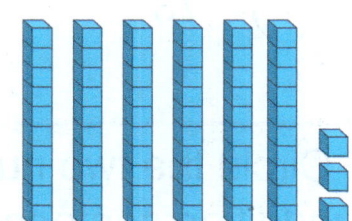

3. Newton has 8 toys. Shade the circle next to the picture that does *not* show a way he could share his toys with Descartes.

   ◯  : 4  : 4   ◯ : 7  : 1

   ◯ : 2   : 7   ◯ : 3   : 5

Chapter 7   three hundred ninety-seven

4. A group of students are at a carnival. 4 of them leave. There are 8 left. How many students were at the carnival to start?

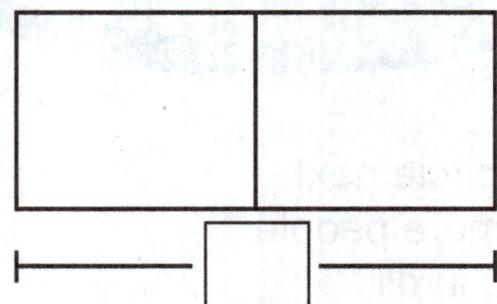

____ ◯ ____ = ____

____ students

5. Shade the circle next to the number that completes the puzzle.

○ 70

○ 62

○ 64

○ 73

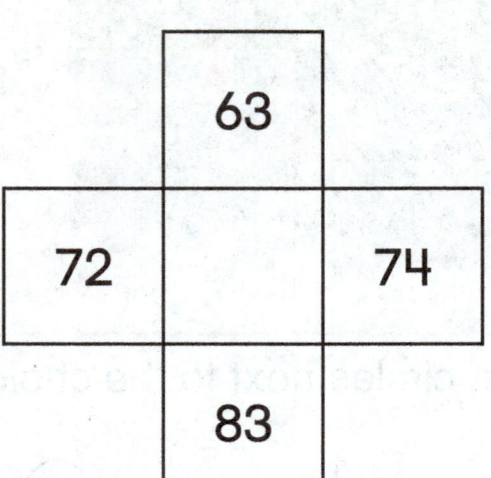

6. Circle the two numbers that complete the addition sentence.

2   3   8   9

____ + ____ + 9 = 19
         \ /
          10

7. Shade the circle next to the number that tells how many ferrets are outside the cage.

○ 5

○ 4

○ 0

○ 1

8. Use the picture to complete the sentence.

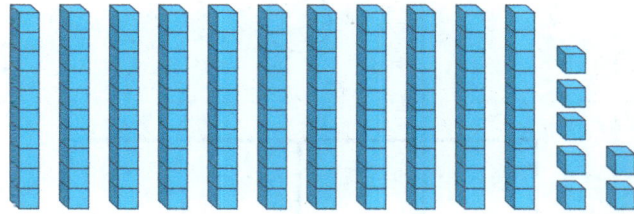

_____ tens and _____ ones is _____.

9. Is each equation true or false?

$0 + 1 \stackrel{?}{=} 0 + 8 + 1$ True   False

$2 + 2 \stackrel{?}{=} 9 - 5$ True   False

$9 - 2 \stackrel{?}{=} 7 - 5$ True   False

$10 - 3 \stackrel{?}{=} 4 + 3$ True   False

Chapter 7   three hundred ninety-nine

10. Write <, >, or = to compare the numbers.

    21 ◯ 45   98 ◯ 97

    67 ◯ 60   36 ◯ 36

11. 4 boats are docked. Some more join them. Now there are 6. Shade the circle next to the models that show how many more boats joined the first group.

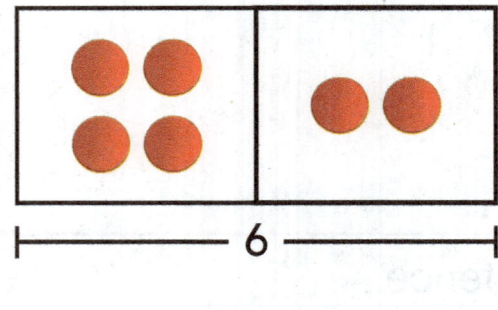

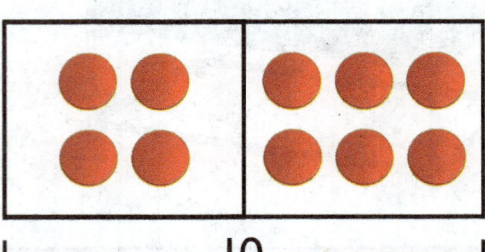

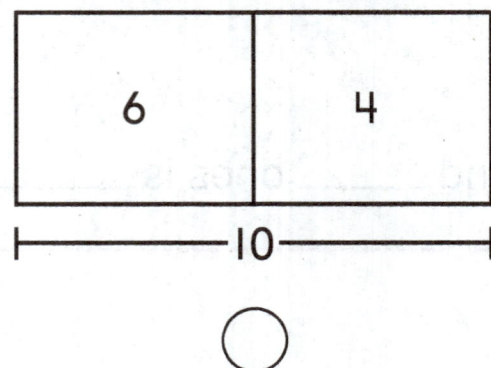

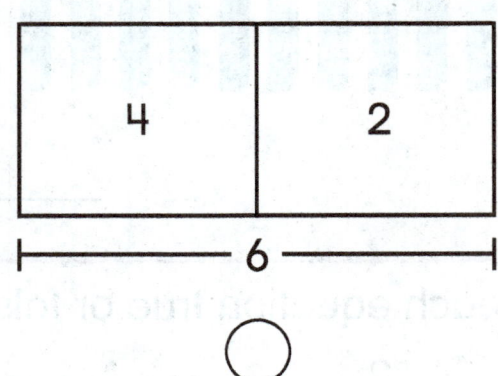

12. Write two addition equations that can be solved using the double 7 + 7.

    7 + ___ = ___   7 + ___ = ___

400   four hundred

Glossary

A

add [sumar]

2 + 4 = 6

addend [sumando]

4 + 3 = 7

addition equation [ecuación de adición]

4 + 5 = 9

analog clock [reloj analogo]

B

bar graph [gráfica de barras]

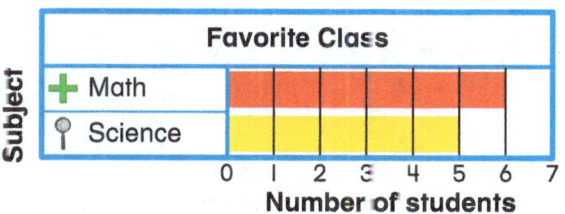

bar model [modelo de barra]

You:	5	
Friend:	2	3

C

column [columna]

1	2	3	4	5	6	7	8	9	10
11	12	13	14	15	16	17	18	19	20
21	22	23	24	25	26	27	28	29	30
31	32	33	34	35	36	37	38	39	40
41	42	43	44	45	46	47	48	49	50
51	52	53	54	55	56	57	58	59	60
61	62	63	64	65	66	67	68	69	70
71	72	73	74	75	76	77	78	79	80
81	82	83	84	85	86	87	88	89	90
91	92	93	94	95	96	97	98	99	100
101	102	103	104	105	106	107	108	109	110
111	112	113	114	115	116	117	118	119	120

A1

compare [comparar]

There are more red cubes than yellow cubes.

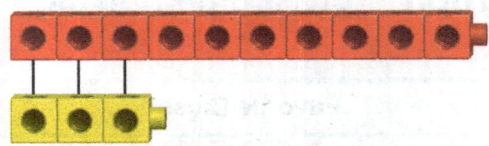

count back [contar hacia atrás]

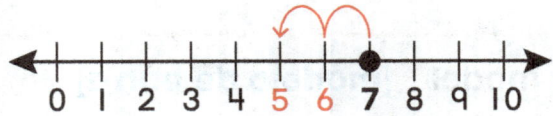

count on [contar hacia delante]

curved surface [superficie curva]

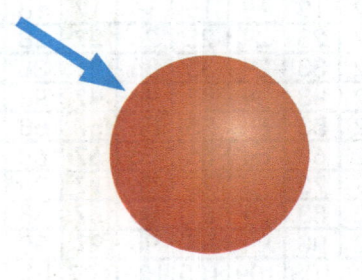

data [datos]

Favorite Class
math   science
science   math
science   math
math   science
math   science
math

decade numbers
[números de la década]

1	2	3	4	5	6	7	8	9	10
11	12	13	14	15	16	17	18	19	20
21	22	23	24	25	26	27	28	29	30
31	32	33	34	35	36	37	38	39	40
41	42	43	44	45	46	47	48	49	50
51	52	53	54	55	56	57	58	59	60
61	62	63	64	65	66	67	68	69	70
71	72	73	74	75	76	77	78	79	80
81	82	83	84	85	86	87	88	89	90
91	92	93	94	95	96	97	98	99	100
101	102	103	104	105	106	107	108	109	110
111	112	113	114	115	116	117	118	119	120

difference [diferencia]

$$8 - 3 = 5$$

digit [dígito]

The digits of 16 are 1 and 6.

16

digital clock [reloj digital]

doubles [dobles]

4 + 4 = 8

doubles minus 1
[dobles menos 1]

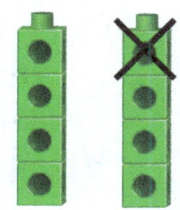

4 + 4 = 8, so 4 + 3 = 7

doubles plus 1
[dobles más 1]

4 + 4 = 8, so 4 + 5 = 9

E

edge [arista]

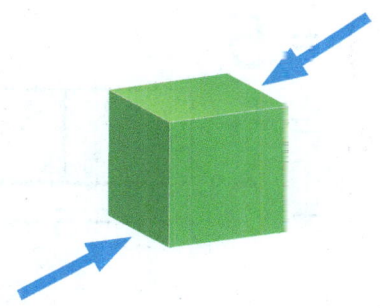

equal shares [partes iguales]

The squares show **equal shares**.

equals [igual]

8 + 2 = 10

8 plus 2 equals 10

A3

fact family [hecho de la familia]

2 + 3 = 5
3 + 2 = 5
5 − 2 = 3
5 − 3 = 2

fewer [menos]

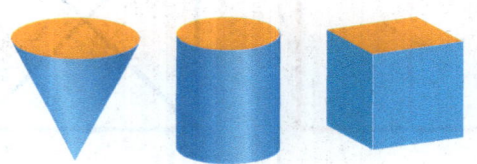

flat surface [superficie plana]

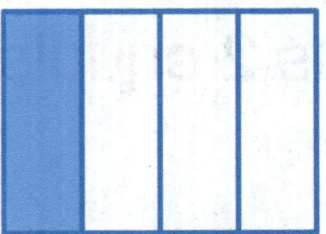

fourth of [cuarto de]

A **fourth of** the rectangle is shaded.

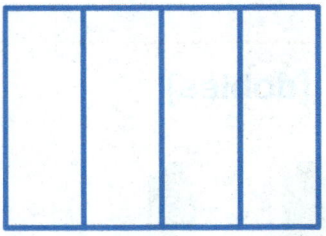

fourths [cuartos]

The rectangle is divided into **fourths**.

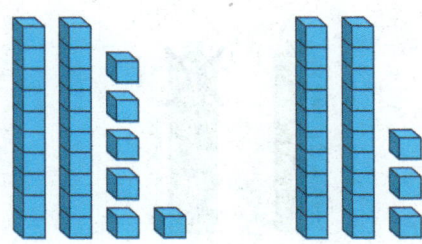

G

greater than [mayor que]

26 is greater than 23.
26 > 23

H

half hour [media hora]

A **half hour** is 30 minutes.

half of [mitad de]

Half of the circle is shaded.

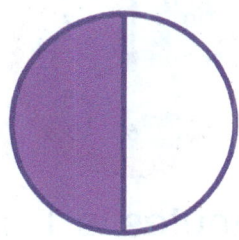

half past [y media]

half past 3

halves [mitades]

This circle is divided into **halves**.

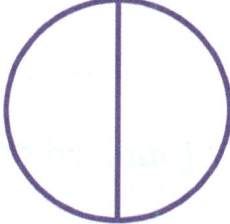

hour [hora]

An hour is 60 minutes.

hour hand [horario]

L

length [longitud]

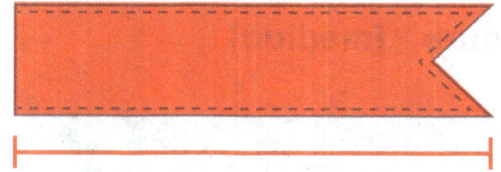

length unit [unidad de longitud]

A5

less than [menor que]

22 is less than 38.
22 < 38

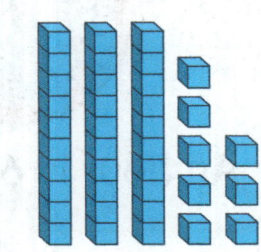

longest [más largo]

measure [medida]

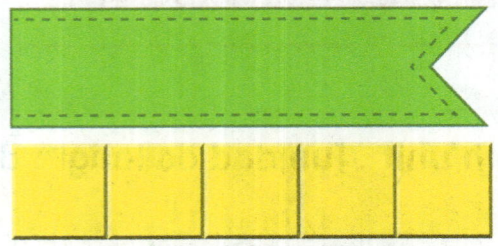

minus [menos]

3 − 1
3 minus 1

minute [minuto]

60 minutes is 1 hour.

minute hand [minutero]

more [más]

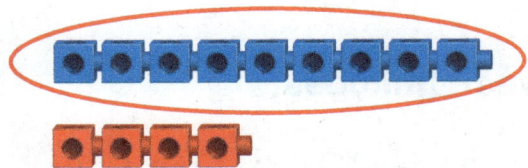

N

number line [numero de linea]

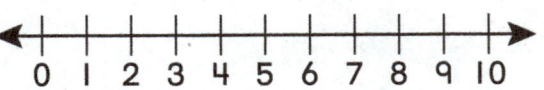

O

o'clock [en punto]

3 o'clock

---

120 chart [120 gráfico]

1	2	3	4	5	6	7	8	9	10
11	12	13	14	15	16	17	18	19	20
21	22	23	24	25	26	27	28	29	30
31	32	33	34	35	36	37	38	39	40
41	42	43	44	45	46	47	48	49	50
51	52	53	54	55	56	57	58	59	60
61	62	63	64	65	66	67	68	69	70
71	72	73	74	75	76	77	78	79	80
81	82	83	84	85	86	87	88	89	90
91	92	93	94	95	96	97	98	99	100
101	102	103	104	105	106	107	108	109	110
111	112	113	114	115	116	117	118	119	120

---

ones [unidades]

23 has 3 ones.

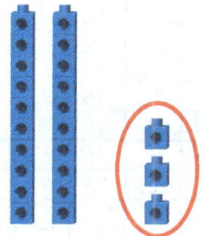

---

ones place [un lugar]

23

---

open number line
[abrir la línea numérica]

P

part [parte]

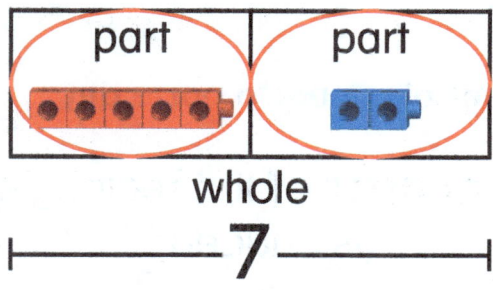

whole
7

---

part-part-whole model
[modelo parte-parte-todo]

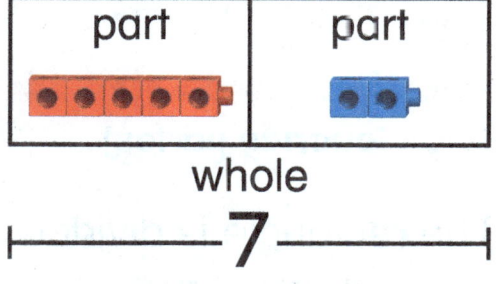

whole
7

---

picture graph [gráfico de imagen]

Favorite Class						
➕ Math	😊	😊	😊	😊	😊	😊
🔬 Science	😊	😊	😊	😊	😊	

Each 😊 = 1 student.

plus [más]

$$2 + 1$$

2 **plus** 1

Q

quarter of [cuarta parte de]

A **quarter of** the rectangle is shaded.

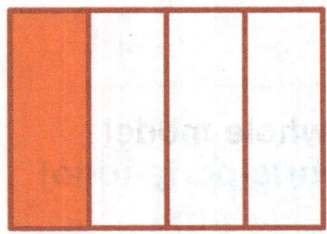

quarters [cuartas partes]

The rectangle is divided into **quarters**.

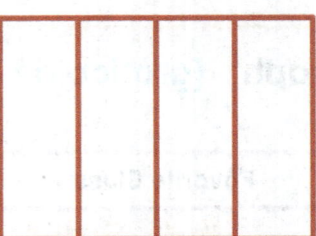

R

rectangular prism [prisma rectangular]

rhombus [rombo]

row [fila]

1	2	3	4	5	6	7	8	9	10
11	12	13	14	15	16	17	18	19	20
21	22	23	24	25	26	27	28	29	30
31	32	33	34	35	36	37	38	39	40
41	42	43	44	45	46	47	48	49	50
51	52	53	54	55	56	57	58	59	60
61	62	63	64	65	66	67	68	69	70
71	72	73	74	75	76	77	78	79	80
81	82	83	84	85	86	87	88	89	90
91	92	93	94	95	96	97	98	99	100
101	102	103	104	105	106	107	108	109	110
111	112	113	114	115	116	117	118	119	120

S

shortest [el más corto]

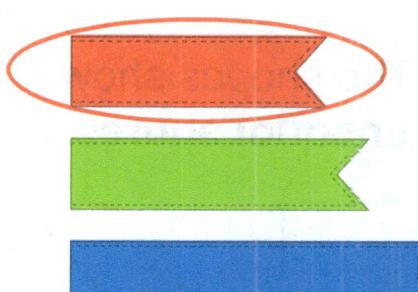

side [lado]

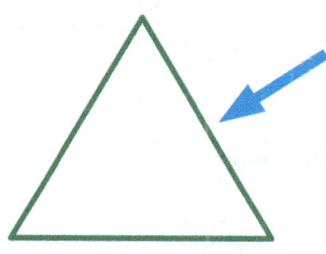

subtract [restar]

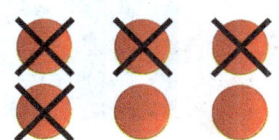

$6 - 4 = 2$

subtraction equation [ecuación de resta]

$9 - 5 = 4$

sum [suma]

$5 + 3 = 8$

T

tally chart [tabla de conteo]

tally mark [marca de conteo]

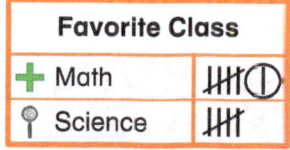

$| = 1, \cancel{||||} = 5$

tens [decenas]

23 has 2 tens.

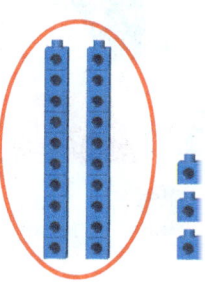

tens place [lugar de decenas]

23

---

three-dimensional shape
[forma tridimensional]

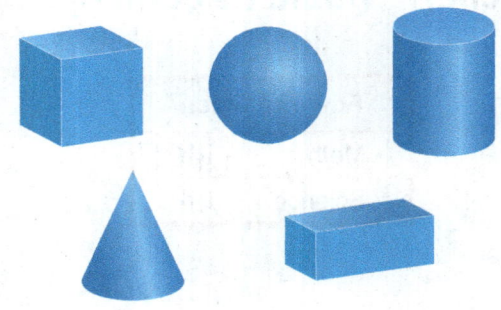

---

trapezoid [trapecio]

---

two-dimensional shape
[forma bidimensional]

---

unequal shares
[partes desiguales]

The shapes show **unequal shares**.

---

vertex [vértice]

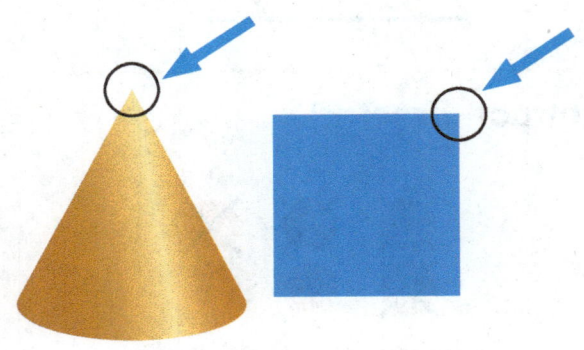

---

whole [todo]

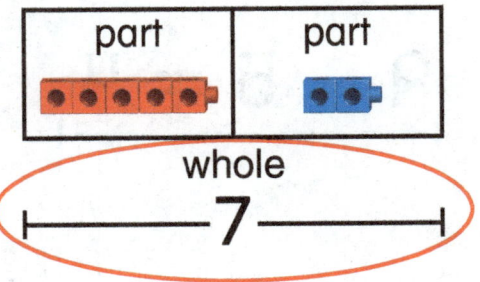

Index

Add to
    solving problems with, 3–14
        with change unknown, 45–50
        with missing addend, 45–50, 127–132
        with start unknown, 127–132
    writing equations for, 3–8

Addends, 10, *See also* Addition
    missing or unknown
        add to problems with, 45–50, 127–132
        making 10, 163–168
        part–part–whole model of, 94, 128–132
        put together problems with, 21–26, 51–56
        ten frame for finding, 100
    order of, 95–100
    same, in adding doubles, 83–88, 187–192

Addition
    of 0, 65–70
    of 1, 77–82
    in any order, 95–100
    using "count on" strategy, 101–106
        within 20, 199–204, 230
        of tens to number, 446, 449
    using doubles, 89–94
        from 1 to 5, 83–88
        from 6 to 10, 187–192
        within 20, 193–198
        with doubles minus 1 strategy, 89–94, 193–198
        with doubles plus 1 strategy, 89–94, 193–198
    using "make a 10" strategy
        adding 9 in, 217–222
        adding one-digit number to two-digit number in, 471–476
        adding three numbers in, 211–216
        adding two numbers in, 223–228
        adding two-digit numbers in, 482
        finding addends in, 163–168
    using part–part–whole model, 16–20
    using place value, 477–482
    practicing strategies of, 483–488
    solving problems using, 489–494
        within 20, 229–234
        add to, 3–14
        add to, with change unknown, 45–50
        add to, with missing addend, 45–50, 127–132
        add to, with start unknown, 127–132
        bigger unknown, 145–150
        put together, 15–20
        put together, connected with take apart, 51–56
        put together, missing both addends, 21–26
    of tens, 415–420
        using mental math, 403–408
        to number, 445–450
        on number line, 421–426, 446, 449
    of tens and ones, 459–464
        on number line, 465–470, 484, 490, 493
    of three numbers, 205–216

Addition equations, *See also* Addition
    add to, 3–14, 45–50
    completing fact families with, 169–174, 520
    definition of, 4
    put together, 15–26
    true or false, 157–162, 267–272, 372, 482
    writing, 3–8

Addition sentence, 4 (*See also* Addition equations)

Addition to subtract strategy, 113–118
    within 20, 249–254
    of tens, 439–444

All, subtracting, 71–76

Analog clock
 definition of, 584
 using hour and minute hand of, 595–600
 using hour hand of
  to tell time to half hour, 589–594
  to tell time to hour, 583–588
 using to tell time, 601–606

Another Way, 200, 446, 449, 466, 484, 487

Apply and Grow: Practice, *In every lesson. For example, see:* 5, 67, 129, 189, 245, 295, 357, 405, 461, 505

B

Bar graphs
 definition of, 554
 making, 559–564
 picture graphs compared to, 553
 reading and interpreting, 553–558
 solving problems with data from, 565–570

Bar model
 adding within 20 using, 231, 232, 234
 compare problems using
  with bigger unknown, 146–150
  with length measurement, 528–532
  with smaller unknown, 152–156
 definition of, 146
 subtraction using, within 20, 281, 282

Bigger unknown, compare problems with, 145–150

C

Challenge, *See* Dig Deeper

Change, unknown
 add to problems with, 45–50
 take from problems with, 133–138

Chapter Practice, *In every chapter. For example, see:* 59–62, 121–124, 177–180, 237–240, 287–290, 349–352, 393–396, 453–456, 497–500, 535–538

Charts
 120
  for counting by ones, 293–298
  for counting by tens, 299–304
  definition of, 694
 hundred
  for adding 10, 404, 406
  for adding tens and ones, 465–470
  for subtracting 10, 410, 413
 tally
  completing picture and bar graphs with, 559–564
  definition of, 542
  making, 541–546, 559
  picture graphs compared to, 547
  solving problems with data from, 565–570

Choose Tools, 627, 630

Circles
 combining shapes to make, 626, 632
 describing, 619, 621
 as flat surfaces, of shapes, 644–648
 identifying equal shares in, 676, 677, 679
  fourths, 688–692
  halves, 682–686
 taking apart, 639

Clock
 analog and digital, 601–606
 using hour and minute hands of, 595–600
 using hour hand of
  to tell time to half hour, 589–594
  to tell time to hour, 583–588

Closed shapes
 definition of, 614
 sorting, 614–618

Color tiles
 comparing length using, 528–532
 measuring length using, 516–526
 representing data with, 559–564

Columns, in 120 chart, 300

Combining shapes
 three-dimensional, 655–660
 two-dimensional, 625–636

Common Errors, *Throughout. For example, see:* T-22, 199

Common Misconceptions, *Throughout. For example, see:* T-22, T-40, T-102, T-128, T-148

Compare, definition of, 356

Compare problems, solving
    bigger unknown, 145–150
    how many fewer, 39–44, 151–156
    how many more, 33–38, 145–150
    length, 527–532
    smaller unknown, 151–156

Comparing length
    indirectly, using third object, 509–514
    ordering objects by length, 503–508
    solving compare problems, 527–532

Comparing numbers
    1 more, 1 less, 385–390
    10 more, 10 less, 385–390
    11 to 19, 355–360
    within 100, 361–366
        using number line, 379–384
        using place value, 367–372
        using symbols, 373–378
    quick sketches for, 357, 359, 365, 373–375, 444

Composing numbers
    11 to 19, 305–310
    to 120, 341–346
    counting by tens and ones for, 317–322
    decade numbers (tens), 311–316
    in different ways, 335–340
    quick sketches for, 323–328, 360
    understanding place value in, 329–334

Cones
    combining with other shapes, 655–657, 659
    definition of, 650
    describing, 649–654
    taking apart shapes containing, 661–666

"Count back" strategy
    definition of, 108
    subtraction using, 107–112, 434, 437
    within 20, 243–248, 280

"Count on" strategy
    addition using, 101–106
        within 20, 199–204, 230
        of tens to number, 446, 449
    definition of, 102
    subtraction using, 250–254, 440, 443

Counting
    to 120 by ones, 293–298
    to 120 by tens, 299–304
    to add 1, 78
    tens and ones, to write numbers, 317–322

Cross-Curricular Connections, *In every lesson. For example, see:* T-13, T-161, T-197, T-365, T-419, T-487, T-525, T-563, T-605, T-685

Cubes
    combining, to make new shapes, 655–660
    definition of, 650
    describing, 649–654
    taking apart shapes containing, 661–666

Cumulative Practice, 181–184, 397–400, 577–580, 697–700

Curved surfaces
    definition of, 644
    sorting shapes by, 644–648

Cylinders
    combining with other shapes, 655–657, 659
    definition of, 650
    describing, 649–654
    taking apart shapes containing, 661–666

D

Data
    bar graphs of
        definition of, 554
        making, 559–564
        picture graphs compared to, 553
        reading and interpreting, 553–558

solving problems with data from, 565–570
definition of, 542
picture graphs of
bar graphs compared to, 553
definition of, 543
making, 559–564
reading and interpreting, 547–552
solving problems with data from, 565–570
tally charts compared to, 547
representing, 559–564
solving problems involving, 565–570
tally charts of, 541–546
completing picture and bar graphs with, 559–564
definition of, 542
making, 541–546, 559
picture graphs compared to, 547
solving problems with data from, 565–570

Decade numbers, 300, 311–316 (See also Tens (10))

Decomposing
take apart problems, 52–56
taking apart shapes
three-dimensional, 661–666
two-dimensional, 637–642

Define It, *In every chapter. For example, see:* 2, 64, 126, 186, 242, 292, 354, 402, 458, 502

Differences, 28 (See also Subtraction)

Differentiation, See Scaffolding Instruction

Dig Deeper, *Throughout. For example, see:* 5, 67, 195, 245, 304, 357, 405, 482, 508, 555

Digit(s)
comparing in two-digit numbers, 367–372
definition of, 330
value in two-digit number, 329–334

Digital clock
definition of, 602

telling time on, 601–606

Doubles
using
within 20, 193–198
to find sum, 89–94, 193–198
adding
from 1 to 5, 83–88
from 6 to 10, 187–192
within 20, 193–198
with doubles minus 1 strategy, 89–94, 193–198
with doubles plus 1 strategy, 89–94, 193–198
definition of, 84

Doubles minus 1, 89–94, 193–198

Doubles plus 1, 89–94, 193–198

E

Edges, of three-dimensional shapes, 650–654

ELL Support, *In every lesson. For example, see:* T-2, T-127, T-235, T-282, T-312, T-385, T-430, T-465, T-586, T-682

Equal shares
definition of, 676
identifying, 675–680
shapes showing fourths, 687–692
shapes showing halves, 681–686

Equals (equal to), 10, 373–378

Equations
addition
add to, 3–14
completing fact families with, 169–174, 520
definition of, 4
put together, 15–26
true or false, 157–162, 267–272, 372, 482
writing, 3–8
subtraction
completing fact families with, 169–174, 520

how many fewer, 40–44
how many more, 34–38
take apart, 52–56
take from, 27–32
true or false, 157–162, 267–272, 372, 482
writing, 28–32
true, finding number making, 273–278
Error Analysis, *See* You Be the Teacher
Explain, *Throughout. For example, see:* 411, 450, 485, 505, 523, 541, 570, 600, 613, 686
Explore and Grow, *In every lesson. For example, see:* 3, 65, 127, 187, 243, 293, 355, 403, 459, 541

F

Fact families
completing, 169–174, 520
definition of, 170
Fewer
1 or 10, identifying numbers with, 385–390
definition of, 40
how many, compare problems solving for, 39–44, 151–156
Flat surfaces
definition of, 644
describing shapes by, 649–654
sorting shapes by, 644–648
Formative Assessment, *Throughout. For example, see:* T-6, T-74, T-202, T-276, T-344, T-406, T-556, T-604, T-646, T-678
Fourth of, 688
Fourths
definition of, 688
identifying shapes showing, 687–692

G

Games, *In every chapter. For example, see:* 58, 120, 176, 236, 286, 348, 392, 452, 496, 534
"Get to 10" strategy, subtraction using, 261–266, 426
subtracting nine in, 255–260
Graphs
bar
definition of, 554
making, 559–564
picture graphs compared to, 553
reading and interpreting, 553–558
solving problems with data from, 565–570
picture
bar graphs compared to, 553
definition of, 543
making, 559–564
reading and interpreting, 547–552
solving problems with data from, 565–570
tally charts compared to, 547
Greater than (>), 356, 373–378 (*See also* Comparing numbers)
Groups of objects, *See also specific operations and problems*
adding to, 3–14
compare problems
how many fewer, 39–44
how many more, 33–38
putting together, 15–26
taking apart, 51–56
taking from, 27–32

H

Half of, 682, 685
Half hour
on analog and digital clocks, 601–606
definition of, 590

telling time to
  hour and minute hands for, 595–600
  hour hand for, 589–594

Half past
  on analog and digital clocks, 601–606
  definition of, 590
  hour and minute hands showing, 595–600
  hour hand showing, 589–594

Halves
  definition of, 682
  identifying shapes showing, 681–686

Hexagons
  combining, to make new shapes, 628, 631
  combining shapes to make, 626–629
  definition of, 620
  describing, 619–624
  equal shares in, identifying, 677, 681
  halves of, 681
  taking apart, 639, 642

Higher Order Thinking, See Dig Deeper

Hour
  on analog and digital clocks, 601–606
  definition of, 584
  telling time to
    hour and minute hands for, 595–600
    hour hand for, 583–588

Hour hand
  definition of, 584
  using to tell time to half hour, 589–594
  using to tell time to hour, 583–588
  using to tell time to hour and half hour, 595–600

Hundred chart
  for adding 10, 404, 406
  for adding tens and ones, 465–470
  for subtracting 10, 410, 413

L

Learning Target, In every lesson. For example, see: 3, 65, 127, 187, 243, 293, 355, 459, 503, 541

Length
  comparing indirectly, 509–514
  measuring
    using color tiles, 516–526
    using like objects, 515–520
    using paper clips, 521–526
  ordering objects by, 503–508
  solving compare problems involving, 527–532

Length unit
  color tiles of, 516–520
  definition of, 516

Less than (<), 356, 373–378 (See also Comparing numbers)

Linking cubes
  for add to problems, 3, 9, 10, 13
  for adding 0, 65
  for adding 1, 77
  for adding doubles, 84–88, 90, 188, 189, 191
  for adding in any order, 96, 97, 99
  for adding three numbers, 205
  for adding within 20, 233
  for completing fact families, 169
  for composing numbers
    11 to 19, 306, 309
    decade numbers (tens), 312–316
  for doubles minus 1 strategy, 90, 91, 93, 194, 195, 197
  for doubles plus 1 strategy, 90, 91, 93, 194, 195, 197
  for grouping by 10, 312–316
  for put together problems, 21
  for take from problems, 27, 28, 31

Logic, 67, 70, 473, 476

Longest
  definition of, 504
  ordering objects by, 503–508

L-shaped vertices, 615, 616, 619, 622

"Make a 10" strategy, addition using
    adding 9 in, 217–222
    adding one-digit number to two-digit number in, 471–476
    adding three numbers in, 211–216
    adding two numbers in, 223–228
    adding two-digit numbers in, 482
    finding addends in, 163–168

Mathematical Practices
    Make sense of problems and persevere in solving them, *Throughout. For example, see:* 40, 119, 144, 226, 272, 388, 406, 565, 684
    Reason abstractly and quantitatively, *Throughout. For example, see:* 17, 122, 174, 225, 310, 461, 606, 639, 692
    Construct viable arguments and critique the reasoning of others, *Throughout. For example, see:* 21, 118, 231, 335, 355, 414, 476, 613, 675
    Model with mathematics, *Throughout. For example, see:* 112, 168, 192, 234, 264, 334, 518, 571, 622
    Use appropriate tools strategically, *Throughout. For example, see:* 4, 109, 163, 190, 270, 334, 438, 509, 563
    Attend to precision, *Throughout. For example, see:* 12, 114, 150, 204, 295, 372, 414, 503, 689
    Look for and make use of structure, *Throughout. For example, see:* 50, 178, 201, 301, 385, 441, 527, 583, 683
    Look for and express regularity in repeated reasoning, *Throughout. For example, see:* 34, 78, 135, 219, 249, 311, 379, 433, 681

Mental math
    adding 10 using, 403–408
    subtracting 10 using, 409–414

Minus (−), 28

Minute
    on analog and digital clocks, 601–606
    definition of, 596
    telling time to, 595–600

Minute hand
    definition of, 596
    using to tell time to hour and half hour, 595–600

Missing addends
    add to problems with, 45–50, 127–132
    making 10, 163–168
    part–part–whole model of, 94, 128–132
    put together problems with, 21–26, 51–56
    ten frame for finding, 100

Modeling, of numbers, *See also* Bar model; Part–part–whole model
    in different ways, 335–340
    as tens and ones, 323–328, 360
    two-digit, 329–334

Modeling Real Life, *In every lesson. For example, see:* 8, 70, 132, 192, 248, 304, 360, 408, 464, 508

More
    1 or 10, identifying numbers with, 385–390
    definition of, 34
    how many, compare problems solving for, 33–38, 145–150

Multiple Representations, *Throughout. For example, see:* 4, 103, 170, 218, 260, 306, 351, 446, 547, 692

Nine (9)
    adding, using "make a 10" strategy, 217–222
    subtracting, in "get to 10" strategy, 255–260

A17

Number line
    adding on
        within 20, 199–204
        using "count on" strategy, 101–106, 199–204, 230, 446, 449
        solving word problems with, 230, 234
        of tens, 421–426, 446, 449
        of tens and ones, 465–470, 484, 490, 493
    comparing numbers on, 379–384
    definition of, 102
    finding number making true equation on, 273
    open, definition of, 422
    subtracting on
        within 20, 243–254, 280
        using addition to subtract strategy, 249–254
        using "count back" strategy, 107–112, 243–248, 280
        using "count on" strategy, 250–254, 440, 443
        of tens, 433–438

Number Sense, *Throughout. For example, see:* 17, 20, 91, 94, 97, 100, 123, 159, 225, 263, 307, 366, 387, 390

O

120
    counting to, 341–346
        by ones, 293–298
        by tens, 299–304
    writing numbers to, 341–346

120 chart
    for counting by ones, 293–298
    for counting by tens, 299–304
    definition of, 294

Objects, groups of, *See also specific operations and problems*
    adding to, 3–14
    compare problems
        how many fewer, 39–44
        how many more, 33–38
    putting together, 15–26
    taking apart, 51–56
    taking from, 27–32

O'clock
    on analog and digital clocks, 601–606
    to half hour, 589–594
    to hour, 583–588
    to hour and half hour, 595–600

Ones (1)
    adding, 77–82
        in adding tens to number, 445–450
        in adding two numbers, with tens, 459–470
        in adding two-digit numbers, 477–482
        on number line, 465–470, 484, 490, 493
        one-digit numbers to two-digit number, 471–476
    in comparing numbers
        1 more, 1 less, 385–390
        11 to 19, 355–360
        within 100, 361–372, 374
    in composing or writing numbers
        11 to 19, 305–310
        to 120, 341–346
        counting for, 317–322
        in different ways, 335–340
        quick sketches for, 323–328, 360
        in two-digit number, 329–334
    counting to 120 by, 293–298
    definition of, 306
    subtracting, 77–82

Ones place, 306, 329–334

Open number line, *See also* Number line
    definition of, 422

Open shapes
    definition of, 614
    sorting, 614–618

Organize It, *In every chapter. For example, see:* 2, 64, 126, 186, 242, 292, 354, 402, 612, 674

Paper clips
    comparing length using, 528–532
    measuring length using, 521–526
Part, definition of, 16
Partitioning shapes
    into equal shares, 675–680
    into fourths, 687–692
    into halves, 681–686
Part–part–whole model
    add to using, 46–50, 128–132
    adding within 20 using, 233
    addition to subtract strategy using, 114–118
    completing fact families using, 170, 171, 173
    definition of, 16
    finding missing addend in, 94, 128–132
    put together using, 16–20
    put together/take apart using, 52–56
    subtracting within 20 using, 281, 283, 284
    take from problems using
        with change unknown, 134–138
        with start unknown, 140–144
Performance Task, *In every chapter. For example, see:* 57, 119, 175, 235, 285, 347, 391, 451, 495, 533, 571, 607, 667, 693
Picture graphs
    bar graphs compared to, 553
    definition of, 543
    making, 559–564
    reading and interpreting, 547–552
    solving problems with data from, 565–570
    tally charts compared to, 547
Place value
    in addition of two-digit numbers, 477–482
    in comparing numbers
        11 to 19, 355–360
        within 100, 367–372
    in composing or writing numbers
        11 to 19, 305–310
        to 120, 341–346
        counting tens and ones for, 317–322
        decade numbers (tens), 311–316
        in different ways, 335–340
        quick sketches for, 323–328, 360
        in two-digit numbers, 329–334
    understanding, 329–334
Plus sign (+), 10
Practice, *In every lesson. For example, see:* 7–8, 69–70, 131–132, 191–192, 247–248, 297–298, 359–360, 407–408, 463–464, 507–508
Precision, *Throughout. For example, see:* 29, 147, 369, 372, 517, 585, 588, 621, 624, 680
Prisms, rectangular
    combining, to make new shapes, 655–657, 659
    definition of, 650
    describing, 649–654
    taking apart shapes containing, 661–666
Problem solving, *See* Word problems
Problem Solving Strategy, *Throughout. For example, see:* 230, 233, 282, 490, 492
Problem Types, *Throughout. For example, see:*
add to
    change unknown, 45, 106, 168, 233, 400, 491
    result unknown, 4, 65, 162, 199, 228, 272, 408, 426, 450, 564
    start unknown, 130, 132, 233
compare
    bigger unknown, 146, 178, 204, 232, 240, 470, 486, 500
    difference unknown, 34, 119, 180, 246, 285, 451, 528, 576, 658, 697
    smaller unknown, 152, 179, 196, 264, 283, 432, 493, 530, 594
put together
    addend unknown, 98, 100, 175, 183, 562

both addends unknown, 22, 57, 60, 86, 192
total unknown, 16, 52, 119, 187, 205, 235, 418, 462, 480, 579
take apart
addend unknown, 116, 175, 183, 562
both addends unknown, 57, 397
total unknown, 52, 55, 62, 119, 258
take from
change unknown, 136, 138, 252, 279, 290
result unknown, 28, 71, 112, 243, 412, 436, 451, 526, 567, 578
start unknown, 142, 281, 290, 398, 700
Put together problems, solving, 15–20
connected with take apart, 51–56
missing both addends, 21–26

Q

Quarters
definition of, 688
identifying, 687–692
Quick sketches
for adding tens to number, 446, 449
for comparing numbers, 357, 359, 365, 373–375, 444
for modeling numbers as tens and ones, 323–328, 360
for modeling two-digit numbers, 329–334

R

Reading, *Throughout. For example, see:* T-7, T-87, T-155, T-247, T-297, T-425, T-513, T-551, T-587, T-679
Real World, *See* Modeling Real Life
Reasoning, *Throughout. For example, see:* 122, 153, 189, 461, 520, 543, 624, 639, 642, 692
Rectangles
combining, to make squares, 632
combining shapes to make, 626, 627, 633

definition of, 620
describing, 619–624
equal shares in, identifying, 676, 677, 679, 680
fourths, 688–692
halves, 682–686
as flat surfaces, of shapes, 644–648
taking apart shapes containing, 637–642
Rectangular prisms
combining, to make new shapes, 655–657, 659
definition of, 650
describing, 649–654
taking apart shapes containing, 661–666
Repeated Reasoning, 135
Response to Intervention, *Throughout. For example, see:* T-1B, T-115, T-137, T-201, T-241B, T-333, T-443, T-539B, T-587, T-615
Review & Refresh, *In every lesson. For example, see:* 8, 76, 210, 278, 372, 444, 514, 588, 624, 692
Rhombus
combining shapes to make, 627, 628, 633, 635
definition of, 620
describing, 619–624
Rows
in 120 chart, 293–294
in hundred chart, 404, 406, 410, 413

S

Scaffolding Instruction, *In every lesson. For example, see:* T-5, T-147, T-231, T-337, T-369, T-411, T-505, T-555, T-645, T-689
Shapes, *See also specific shapes*
three-dimensional
combining to make new shapes, 655–660
curved surfaces of, 644–648
describing, 649–654

edges of, 650–654
flat surfaces of, 644–654
sorting, 643–648
taking apart, 661–666
vertices of, 649–654
two-dimensional
closed or open, 614–618
combining to make new shapes, 625–636
definition of, 614
describing, 619–624
equal shares in, fourths, 687–692
equal shares in, halves, 681–686
equal shares in, identifying, 675–680
number of sides, 614–624
number of vertices, 614–624
sorting, 613–618
taking apart, 637–642
Shortest
definition of, 504
ordering objects by, 503–508
Show and Grow, *In every lesson. For example, see:* 4, 66, 128, 188, 244, 294, 356, 404, 460, 504
Show how you know, *Throughout. For example, see:* 24, 295, 208, 235, 278, 301, 349, 588
Sides, of two-dimensional shapes
definition of, 614
describing, 619–624
sorting by number of, 614–618
Smaller unknown, compare problems with, 151–156
Spheres
combining with other shapes, 655
definition of, 650
describing, 649–654
taking apart shapes containing, 661
Squares
combining, to make new shapes, 627, 635
combining shapes to make, 632
definition of, 620
describing, 619–624

equal shares in, identifying, 676, 677, 679, 680
fourths, 688, 689, 691, 692
halves, 682, 683, 685, 686
as flat surfaces, of shapes, 644–648
taking apart shapes containing, 637–642
Start, unknown
add to problems with, 127–132
take from problems with, 139–144
Straight sides, of two-dimensional shapes
describing, 619–624
number of, 614–618
Structure, *Throughout. For example, see:* 47, 50, 53, 73, 109, 129, 141, 171, 201, 260, 295, 384, 423, 467, 683
Subtraction
of 0 or all, 71–76
of 1, 77–82
using addition to subtract strategy, 113–118
within 20, 249–254
of tens, 439–444
using bar model, within 20, 281, 282
using "count back" strategy, 107–112, 434, 437
within 20, 243–248, 280
using "count on" strategy, 250–254, 440, 443
definition of, 28
using "get to 10" strategy, 261–266, 426
subtracting 9 in, 255–260
solving problems using
within 20, 279–284
how many fewer, 39–44, 151–156
how many more, 34–38
smaller unknown, 151–156
take apart, connected with put together, 51–56
take from, 27–32
take from, with change unknown, 133–138
take from, with start unknown, 139–144

of tens, 427–432
    using addition to subtract strategy, 439–444
    using mental math, 409–414
    on number line, 433–438
Subtraction equations, *See also* Subtraction
    completing fact families with, 169–174, 520
    how many fewer, 40–44
    how many more, 34–38
    take apart, 52–56
    take from, 27–32
    true or false, 157–162, 267–272, 372, 482
    writing, 28–32
Success Criteria, *In every lesson. For example, see:* T-3, T-71, T-139, T-267, T-323, T-445, T-521, T-583, T-661, T-687
Sums, 10 (*See also* Addition)
    adding zero (0) and, 66
    given, finding unknown addends for, 21–26
Surfaces, 644–648
    describing shapes by, 649–654
    sorting shapes by, 643–648
Symbols
    equal to (=), 10, 373–378
    greater than (>), 356, 373–378
    less than (<), 356, 373–378
    minus sign (−), 28
    plus sign (+), 10

T

Take apart problems, 52–56
Take from problems, solving, 27–32
    with change unknown, 133–138
    with start unknown, 139–144
Taking apart shapes
    three-dimensional, 661–666
    two-dimensional, 637–642
Tally charts
    completing picture and bar graphs with, 559–564
    definition of, 542
    making, 541–546, 559
    picture graphs compared to, 547
    solving problems with data from, 565–570
Tally mark, 542 (*See also* Tally charts)
Ten frames
    for composing numbers, 305, 307, 310
    for finding missing addend, 100
    for "get to 10" strategy, 261–266, 426
        in subtracting 9, 255–260
    for identifying true or false equations, 268, 271
    for "make a 10" strategy, 163–168
        in adding 9, 217–222
        in adding two numbers, 223–228
    for making true equation, 274
Tens (10)
    adding, 415–420
        in adding two numbers, with ones, 459–470
        in adding two-digit numbers, 477–482
        using mental math, 403–408
    to number, 445–450
    on number line, 421–426, 446, 449, 465–470, 484, 490, 493
    in comparing numbers
        10 more, ten less, 385–390
        11 to 19, 355–360
        within 100, 361–372, 374
    in composing or writing numbers, 311–316
        11 to 19, 305–310
        to 120, 341–346
        counting for, 317–322
        in different ways, 335–340
        quick sketches for, 323–328, 360
        in two-digit number, 329–334
    counting to 120 by, 299–304
    definition of, 306
    in "get to 10" strategy, 261–266, 426
        subtracting 9 in, 255–260

in "make a 10" strategy
    adding 9 in, 217–222
    adding one-digit number to two-digit number in, 471–476
    adding three numbers in, 211–216
    adding two numbers in, 223–228
    finding addends in, 163–168
subtracting, 427–432
    using addition to subtract strategy, 439–444
    using mental math, 409–414
    on number line, 433–438

Tens place, 306, 329–334

Think and Grow, *In every lesson. For example, see:* 4, 66, 128, 188, 244, 294, 356, 404, 460, 504

Think and Grow: Modeling Real Life, *In every lesson. For example, see:* 6, 68, 130, 190, 246, 296, 358, 406, 462, 506

Three-dimensional shapes
    combining to make new shapes, 655–660
    curved surfaces of, 644–648
    describing, 649–654
    edges of, 650–654
    flat surfaces of, 644–654
    sorting, 643–648
    taking apart, 661–666
    vertices of, 649–654

Time, telling
    on analog clock, 583–606
    on digital clock, 601–606
    to half hour, 589–594
    to hour, 583–588
    to hour and half hour, 595–600

Trapezoids
    combining, to make new shapes, 626, 628, 630, 633
    combining shapes to make, 627, 630
    definition of, 620
    describing, 619–624
    equal shares in, identifying, 676, 679
    taking apart shapes containing, 638, 639, 641

Triangles
    combining, to make new shapes, 625–630, 632, 633, 635
    definition of, 620
    describing, 619–624
    equal shares in, identifying, 677
    taking apart shapes containing, 637–642

True equations, finding number making, 273–278

True or false equations
    definition of, 158
    identifying, 157–162, 267–272, 372, 482

Two-digit numbers
    adding one-digit number to, 471–476
    adding using place value, 477–482
    comparing
        1 more, 1 less, 385–390
        10 more, 10 less, 385–390
        11 to 19, 355–360
    comparing, within 100, 361–366
        using number line, 379–384
        using place value, 367–372
        using symbols, 373–378
    understanding place value in, 329–334

Two-dimensional shapes
    closed or open, 614–618
    combining to make new shapes, 625–636
    definition of, 614
    describing, 619–624
    equal shares in
        fourths, 687–692
        halves, 681–686
        identifying, 675–680
    number of sides, 614–624
    number of vertices, 614–624
    sorting, 613–618
    taking apart, 637–642

U

Unequal shares
    definition of, 676
    identifying equal shares *vs.*, 675–680

Unknown(s)
   bigger, compare problems with, 145–150
   smaller, compare problems with, 151–156

Unknown (missing) addends
   add to problems with, 45–50, 127–132
   missing or unknown, making 10, 163–168
   part–part–whole model of, 94, 128–132
   put together problems with, 21–26, 51–56
   ten frame for finding, 100

Unknown change
   add to problems with, 45–50
   take from problems with, 133–138

Unknown start
   add to problems with, 127–132
   take from problems with, 139–144

Vertex (vertices)
   definition of, 614
   of three-dimensional shapes, 649–654
   of two-dimensional shapes
      describing, 619–624
      L-shaped, 615, 616, 619, 622
      sorting by number of, 614–618

Which One Doesn't Belong?, 603, 606
Whole, *See also* Part–part–whole model
   definition of, 16
   equal shares in
      fourths, 687–692
      halves, 681–686
      identifying, 675–680
   put together problems for finding, 15–20
   subtraction equation for finding, 139–144

Word problems, solving
   with addition, 489–494
      within 20, 229–234

   add to, 3–14
   add to, with missing addend, 45–50
   bigger unknown, 145–150
   put together, 15–20
   put together, connected with take apart, 51–56
   put together, missing both addends, 21–26
   with subtraction
      within 20, 279–284
      how many fewer, 39–44
      how many more, 33–38
      smaller unknown, 151–156
      take apart, connected with put together, 51–56
      take from, 27–32

Writing, 549, 552

Writing equations
   addition, 3–8
   subtraction, 28–32

Writing numbers
   11 to 19, 305–310
   to 120, 341–346
   counting by tens and ones for, 317–322
   decade numbers (tens), 311–316
   in different ways, 335–340
   quick sketches for, 323–328, 360
   understanding place value in, 329–334

You Be the Teacher, *Throughout. For example, see:* 79, 115, 231, 275, 301, 411, 479, 505, 597, 677

Zero (0)
   adding, 65–70
   subtracting, 71–76

Reference Sheet

Symbols

+ plus
− minus
= equals
\> greater than
< less than

Doubles

1 + 1 = 2	6 + 6 = 12
2 + 2 = 4	7 + 7 = 14
3 + 3 = 6	8 + 8 = 16
4 + 4 = 8	9 + 9 = 18
5 + 5 = 10	10 + 10 = 20

Equal Shares

 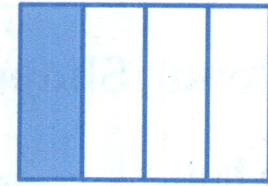 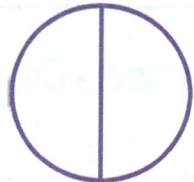 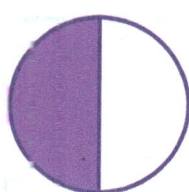

fourths / quarters   fourth of / quarter of   halves   half of

Time

analog clock   digital clock   An hour is 60 minutes.   A half hour is 30 minutes.

minute hand
hour hand

4 o'clock

half past 4

Two-Dimensional Shapes

3 straight sides
3 vertices
triangle

4 straight sides
4 vertices
rectangle

4 straight sides
4 vertices
square

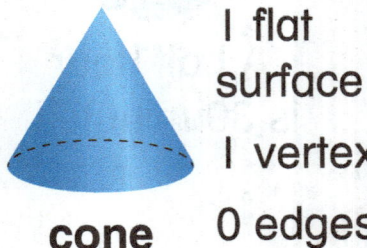
6 straight sides
6 vertices
hexagon

4 straight sides
4 vertices
trapezoid

4 straight sides
4 vertices
rhombus

Three-Dimensional Shapes

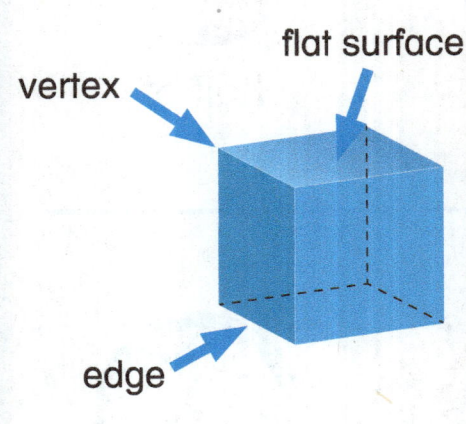
vertex
flat surface
edge

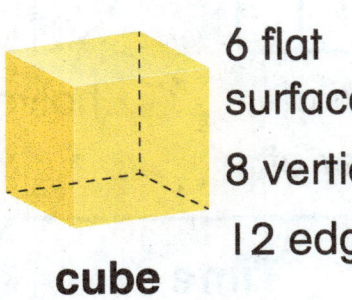
6 flat surfaces
8 vertices
12 edges
cube

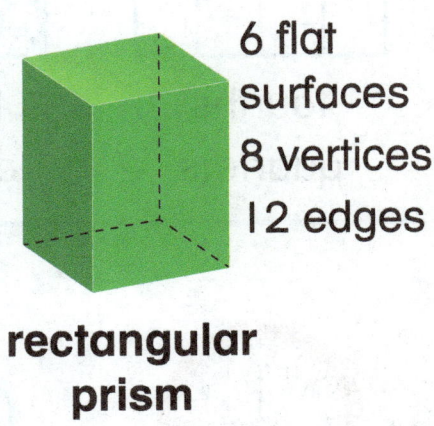
6 flat surfaces
8 vertices
12 edges
rectangular prism

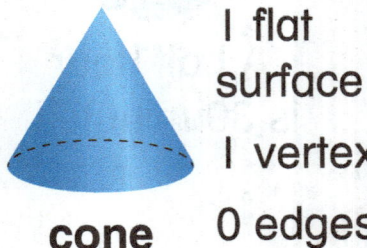
1 flat surface
1 vertex
0 edges
cone

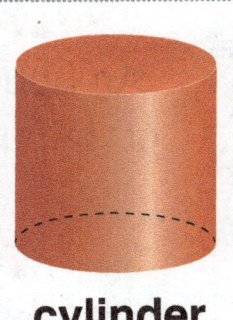
2 flat surfaces
0 vertices
0 edges
cylinder

0 flat surfaces
0 vertices
0 edges
sphere

Credits

Chapter 1
1 Rike_/iStock/Getty Images Plus

Chapter 2
63 Liliboas/E+/Getty Images; 80 Aratehortua/Shutterstock.com

Chapter 3
125 Nastco/iStock/Getty Images Plus, taratata/iStock/Getty Images Plus

Chapter 4
185 macrovector/iStock/Getty Images Plus

Chapter 5
241 DiyanaDimitrova/iStock/Getty Images Plus

Chapter 6
291 shutter_m/iStock/Getty Images Plus

Chapter 7
353 keita/iStock/Getty Images Plus

Chapter 8
401 PaulMichaelHughes/iStock/Getty Images Plus

Chapter 9
457 FatCamera/E+/Getty Images

Chapter 10
501 muchomor/iStock/Getty Images Plus

Chapter 11
539 PeopleImages/iStock/Getty Images Plus

Chapter 12
581 kali9/iStock/Getty Images Plus

Chapter 13
611 Jon (https://commons.wikimedia.org/wiki/File:Ultimate_Sand_Castle.jpg), „Ultimate Sand Castle", https://creativecommons.org/licenses/by/2.0/legalcode

Chapter 14
673 mediaphotos/iStock/Getty Images Plus

Cartoon Illustrations: MoreFrames Animation
Design Elements: oksanika/Shutterstock.com; icolourful/Shutterstock.com; Valdis Torms